GOLDEN GIRL

HOW NATALIE COUGHLIN FOUGHT BACK,
CHALLENGED CONVENTIONAL WISDOM, AND
BECAME AMERICA'S OLYMPIC CHAMPION

GOLDEN GIRL

MICHAEL SILVER
WITH NATALIE COUGHLIN

RODALE

© 2006 by Michael Silver

Printed in the United States of America

Rodale Inc. makes every effort to use acid-free ♾, recycled paper ♻.

Song lyrics on page 95 printed with permission of G2G Management

Photographs courtesy of Natalie Coughlin

Book design by Patricia Field

Library of Congress Cataloging-in-Publication Data

Silver, Michael.
Golden girl : how Natalie Coughlin fought back, challenged conventional wisdom, and became America's olympic champion / Michael Silver with Natalie Coughlin.
p. cm.
ISBN-13 978–1–59486–254–0 hardcover
ISBN-10 1–59486–254–0 hardcover
1. Coughlin, Natalie, date. 2. Surfers—United States—Biography. 3. Women surfers—United States—Biography. I. Coughlin, Natalie, date. II. Title.
GV838.C67S55 2006
797.3'2092--dc22   2005035306

Distributed to the book trade by Holtzbrinck Publishers

2   4   6   8   10   9   7   5   3   1   hardcover
2   4   6   8   10   9   7   5   3   1   paperback

FOR NATALIE SILVER,
MY OWN GOLDEN GIRL—
I'M AWED BY YOUR DIGNITY,
SWEETNESS, BRILLIANCE,
AND FIGHTING SPIRIT,
IN STILL WATERS
OR GNARLY SURF.

CONTENTS

ACKNOWLEDGMENTS

Spending hours soaking up the sunshine on an outdoor pool deck while watching bikini-clad coeds tone their athletic physiques is treacherous duty, so I should start by thanking my fantastic wife, Leslie, for greenlighting this project, and Teri McKeever for giving me access, trust, time, and insight into an incredible sport.

When I wasn't learning from Teri or her swimmers, I was soaking up knowledge from Whitney Hite, Jen Strasburger, Carol Capitani, Dave Salo, Adam Crossen, Tom McCook, and Milt Nelms. Thanks especially to Whitney and Milt for making me aware of such diverse philosophical approaches and explaining them in terms that even a football writer can grasp. And a big shout-out to McCall Dorr for her incisive portrayal of the aquatic experience.

Now that I understand at least a little about the sport's demands, I have mad respect for the many student-athletes with whom I got to hang. Thanks to all of the Golden Bear swimmers, especially: Gina Merlone, whose brilliant books I will someday enjoy; Helen and Emily Silver, my faux nieces and future world rulers; Marcelle Miller, for her principle and passion; Lauren Medina, for bringing salsa picante to the pool and beyond; Amy Ng, the ultimate high achiever; Erin Reilly, grinding in the water and grinning outside of it; Emma Palsson, everyone's favorite Swede, and for good reason; Lisa Morelli, for her kindness and enthusiasm; Ashley Chandler, high-energy rock and roll; Kate

Tiedeman, chopping down the Tree with a smile; Erin Calder, nobody yells louder; Kelly Sanders, Micha Burden, Keiko Amano, Rachel Ridgeway, and the rest of you water warriors. Thanks also to Haley Clark, Leah Monroe, and honorary Bear Keiko Price for the generous contributions to Natalie's story.

The Cal athletic department is blessed with some profoundly dedicated and dynamic people, beginning with my friend and former study partner Mohammed Muqtar, the de facto mayor of Berkeley and a huge reason that this project got started in the first place. Thanks also to Steve Gladstone, Mark Stephens, Teresa Kuehn, Sandy Barbour, Foti Mellis, Karen Moe Humphreys, Beth Nitzberg, Dayna Sannazzaro, Herb Benenson, Bob Rose, Josh Flushman, and so many of you others (you know who you are) at God's University. A big high-five to unofficial Cal sports minister Adam Duritz for hangin' around, and to all of the littlegamers and other athletic supporters who do our school so proud.

Even before she presented me with the most beautifully ridiculous hat ever conceieved, Kathie Wickstrand-Gahen enlightened me about the sport of swimming in general, and her very special friend in particular.

I am eternally indebted to the Coughlin family (Jim, Zennie, Megan, Chuck, and Zennie Bohn) for their kindness and generosity during an intensely charged time. They and the rest of our Athens entourage—Ethan Hall, Tom Griffin, and of course the iconic Dan (The Man) Pedone—were ambassadors of good will.

In addition to keeping a watchful eye over Natalie's affairs, the genuine and outstanding Janey Miller—with help from Michael (Keep Silver Away From My Gold Shoes) Johnson—had my back in Greece when I was flat on it.

I am thrilled to be represented by the unparalleled David Black, whose awesome agency (with the help of his colleagues Gary Morris, Jason Sacher, and David Larabell) is a writer's dream, and whose vision and determination made this book a reality.

Similarly, I owe a huge debt of gratitude to the good people of

Rodale (Steve Murphy, Heidi Rodale, Emily Williams, Jeremy Katz, Jessica Roth, and so many others) for believing in this project and getting it in fighting shape.

When I'm not hanging out on pool decks, I'm *Sports Illin'* like a villain, and I'm grateful to the Powers That Be (Terry McDonell, Norm Pearlstine, John Huey, et al) for their support. Thanks also to my football homies (Mark Godich, Mark Mravic, Peter King, Paul Zimmerman, Jeff Chadiha, Nunyo Demasio) for making life on the NFL beat grand, and to colleagues like George Dohrmann, Seth Davis, and Austin Murphy for helping me to stay somewhat sane.

Mike Fleiss, Rick Telander, Richard Weiner, Josh Elliott, Jarrett Bell, Karen Tongson, Mychael Urban, Groz, Gas, and Kate Troescher are among the highly creative friends whose work inspires me on those late-night caffeine binges. And Julie Foudy, Brandi Chastain, Mia Hamm, and Kristina Thorson are among the women from whose athletic brilliance I derive so much enduring pleasure.

Those closest to me made major sacrifices in the course of this endeavor, and everything I do or am starts with my boundless love for Leslie, Natalie, Greg, Robbie, and Dr. J. Mom, Dad, Elizabeth, Mark, Sofia, Ava, Barbara, Larry, the overflowing and outstanding Goyette clan; my awesome aunts, uncles, and cousins; and all the friends who haven't yet fled—thanks so much for being there. And our family would especially like to thank all the awesome healers in our lives, including Dr. Suruchi Bhatia, Dr. Nicole Glaser, Dr. Lenny Dragone, and Dr. Mary Jones.

Finally, in addition to being a fascinating interview subject, Natalie Coughlin is a great person whose faith, intelligence, and openness were the most important elements of this project. She has the dignity, grace, and self-awareness of a grandmother and the appetite of a teenager; some of the meals we shared were as memorable as the swims. Working with her could not have been more fun, and watching her fulfill her dreams was one of the coolest things I've ever witnessed.

I eagerly await the encore in Beijing.

INTRODUCTION

Sue came shooting off the wall like a human torpedo, gliding through the water with cold, relentless precision. Unleashing her incomparable, undulating dolphin kicks, Natalie Coughlin began to pull away from the field in the 100-meter backstroke, popping to the surface nearly a body length ahead of her closest pursuer. From that prime vantage point—with a picturesque view of the Athens sunset, a mere 35 meters between her and redemption—Coughlin was as good as gold.

The most talented female swimmer of her generation took a deep breath and closed in on the prize she'd been chasing for more than a decade. Six days shy of her 22nd birthday, Coughlin propelled herself backward through Lane 4, seven competitors and untold degrees of doubt, pain, and disappointment in her wake. Get to the wall, and she would forever be an Olympic champion, the haters and the traditionalists be damned. Just a dozen or so more strokes and she'd finish a 4-year struggle for self-determination that summoned every ounce of will in her being.

Just 25 meters to go, then 20, and the only question seemed to be whether Coughlin would break her own world record. Six thousand fans at the Athens Aquatic Center were cheering her home; tens of millions more would experience the suspense on television. And then... *Oh, no. This cannot be happening.* Coughlin felt an energy crash coming on—that insidious, instant loss of zip that every swimmer dreads. She grimaced as the lactic acid ripped through her leg muscles; instinctively, she bit down on her lower lip to combat the pain.

The last time this happened, in the final individual race of Coughlin's unmatched collegiate career, she had appeared so dead in the water that her father, Jim, a police sergeant in her working-class northern California hometown of Vallejo, had barely fought back the urge to race from the stands to rescue his little girl. On that March 2004 night in College Station, Texas, site of the NCAA Championships, Coughlin had been passed by two swimmers down the stretch of the 200-meter backstroke—the only time in 4 years the University of California, Berkeley, superstar had lost a meaningful race. Now, 5 months later, the nightmare was happening again.

Nooo! the voice inside Coughlin's head shrieked. *Not this! Not now!* Her arms felt like redwood stumps, her legs like jelly. She veered close to the lane line, her normally perfect technique beginning to give way to panicked thrashing. She was holding on, but for how long? No one in her line of vision was making a charge—certainly not Haley Cope, once her close friend and Cal teammate, now just another obstacle between Coughlin and her rightful gold. It *had* to be hers, after all she'd been through; after all she'd sacrificed to swim this race on this warm Monday night.

The threat, Coughlin knew, was unseen. Over in Lane 1, blissfully shielded from the wind-induced currents rippling through the pool, was Zimbabwe's Kirsty Coventry, the very same Auburn University swimmer who had caught Coughlin on that awful night in College Station. Coventry was coming, hard, as Coughlin figured she would be.

The previous night, in her semifinal heat, Coughlin had eased up to win in 1:00.17, setting an Olympic record. She was the only woman ever to have gone under a minute in the event, had held the world record (59.58) the past 2 years, and owned the four fastest times in history. Now, however, it wasn't about the clock. It was about finding a way to get to that wall before her worst fear was realized.

Fifteen meters to go, and Coughlin perceptibly slowed. She was sinking like the *Titanic*, and no lifeboat loomed. Her parents, Jim and Zennie, gripped each other's hands tightly, their stomachs in knots. Coughlin's sister, grandparents, and boyfriend watched beside them in agony; there was nothing they could do but pray. Coventry was edging closer, and Coughlin seemed to be coming back to the field as if hindered by an underwater rope.

This isn't happening, she thought. *Please, don't let this be real.* Were the gods of swimming this cruel? Were they taunting her once more? They'd given her talent, drive, and intelligence, along with an uncanny ability to feel the water that most sharks would have envied. Her "physical IQ," in the words of one stroke guru, was astoundingly high, meaning she was able to comprehend and effect specific technique alterations in a manner of seconds. Yet at so many key moments— before the 2000 Olympic Trials, when her shoulder gave out, and at the 2003 World Championships, when her fever spiked and her body collapsed—fate had conspired against her.

Now, once again, everything was falling apart—and oh, how this would hurt. She could see the headlines ("Coughlin Comes Up Short") and anticipate the disparaging words that would be whispered in Athens and on pool decks across America. She could picture the tears running down the face of her coach, Teri McKeever, who was crouching in the stands behind the finish line, too nervous to watch with the rest of the US delegation. She could imagine the legions of traditionalists weighing in on McKeever's methods and how they had doomed Coughlin to failure. And, clear as day, she could envision her former youth-club coach, Ray Mitchell, and hear him bellowing, "I told you so."

It was all unthinkably devastating, and for a split second, Coughlin felt herself go numb. And then, in an instant, the fire returned. *Screw that. This is* my *moment.* For the first time in her life, she had total, unequivocal clarity. *Ray's not in charge anymore. I am. I decide how this ends, and I choose victory. I'm in control now.*

Coughlin jerked her right arm up from the water, rotated backward, and slapped it back to the surface. Her kicks became steady and vigorous. She no longer saw Mitchell's face—nor could she see McKeever's, or those of her Cal or US teammates, or her friends or sister or parents. In her head there was only darkness, the shade of the predawn sky in Concord, California, when, as a teenager, she'd arrive at the pool before Mitchell and her Terrapins Swim Club teammates and sit in her car for 10 minutes, staring into nothingness and getting her mind ready for the task at hand. Then Coughlin would get out of the car, unlock the gate, and unravel the pool cover, shattering the early-morning silence by diving into the water and beginning another grueling practice.

Alone in the dark, Coughlin had been in control of her destiny—before the shoulder had given out and the rumors cropped up and the thoughts of quitting had begun to fill her mind. Saved by McKeever's intuitive touch, Coughlin and her coach had created an alternative model for success; yet even now, after all her triumphs, there were doubters—including some of her trusted college teammates—who expected her to choke when it mattered most.

Well, she had a surprise for them, for Mitchell, and for everyone who'd ever questioned her mettle: That wasn't going to happen. After thousands of miles' worth of laborious laps to prepare for this moment, she could gut out these last 10 meters. Yes, she wanted to win for her country, her family, her school, and, most of all, McKeever. But the last 10 meters would be for her, and her alone.

Slap. Her left arm hit the water, then her right arm. *I will not lose.* One stroke to go, maybe, if she could time it right. Her left arm reached backward and extended, glided through the water, and touched the wall.

Coughlin's heart was racing. This was the moment that would define her as an athlete, and she'd never wanted anything so badly.

With her right hand, she pulled off the outer swim cap she'd worn over her Team USA model, then lifted her goggles and looked to the scoreboard. She squinted upward, her eyes disbelieving. *Fourth? I got* fourth? *That can't be right.*

She scanned to check her time: 1:00.37. It wasn't a great effort by her standards, but *fourth*? She closed her eyes and took another look. Five seconds passed—not an especially long time, except when you're thinking your dreams have been dashed. Then, finally, Coughlin saw it: a big number "1" on the right of the scoreboard. Now she understood: The "4" had been a trick of the light. Normally, the scoreboard at a swim meet instantly rearranges itself at the completion of a race to rank the finishers from top to bottom. In Athens, for whatever reason, there had been a delay, meaning Coughlin, who'd raced from the fourth lane, was still fourth on the board when she'd looked up.

Now, at long last, the board rearranged, and her name was on top. That "1" was the loveliest, most comforting numeral she'd ever seen.

All the muscles in Coughlin's body relaxed in unison. Eyes closed, she raised her fist to the sky, then lifted it again, and again, and again. Her face was a mixture of resuscitated relief and unfettered joy. She had become the first US woman in Athens to capture a gold medal, and she had done it her way. Six thousand fans were on their feet cheering while tens of millions of viewers across the globe sat on their couches, watching her pretty face beaming across their television sets.

None of them, not even the people closest to her, could see the scars. But that didn't matter. Not now. As the sun went down on Athens and Coughlin's star began to shine, the healing process officially began.

CHAPTER ONE

JUST THE TWO OF US

The foreign journalist took the microphone, stood up in a crowded press conference, and, in perfect English, asked Natalie Coughlin a pointed question.

How does it feel to dishonor your country?

This was a strange time to have a bad flashback, but given her state of delirium, Coughlin wasn't entirely surprised. Here she was, at the 2003 FINA World Championships in Barcelona—the last major international competition before the Athens Olympics—slogging through some warm-down laps after one of the more astonishing outcomes of her career. Coughlin, the world record holder in the 100-meter backstroke since the previous summer, had just done the unthinkable: She'd failed to advance past the preliminary rounds. As she completed her last, painful turn in the warm-down pool, her Speedo goggles were filled with tears.

Coughlin's head, meanwhile, was full of dreadful possibilities. Her mind jumped back to her most recent international disappointment, at the 2002 Pan-Pacific Championships in Yokohoma, Japan, the previous August. In the wake of the favored US team's defeat to Australia in the 400-meter medley relay, Coughlin, after a slew of reasonable questions, had been asked how it felt to dishonor her country by the Asian sports media's answer to Mike Wallace on speed. At the time, she'd nearly started laughing. Coughlin hated to lose in anything, but coming up short in a relay against the formidable Aussies certainly didn't qualify as a domestic disgrace.

Now, however, as she exited the warm-down pool and gathered her belongings, she was in no mood to field outlandish queries. Physically, she doubted she could make it up the steps to the podium. Her face pallid, her body shivering under a nylon sweat suit, Coughlin felt disoriented. She was reeling emotionally as well. This was supposed to be *her* meet, and it had gone so terribly wrong. Poised to showcase her amazing versatility and stamp herself as the swimmer to watch at the Athens Games, Coughlin had taken ill at an inopportune time. Just as the weeklong competition was about to begin, she'd been felled by a virus that caused a headache, sore throat, and 103° fever.

La polivalencia, the locals called it.

The worst feeling in the world, Coughlin called it.

The previous evening she had sucked it up and, in her third race of the meet's opening day, propelled the United States to victory in the 4 × 100–meter freestyle relay with a blazing leadoff leg. Now, however, the woman who had hoped to win as many as seven gold medals at the Worlds had hit the wall. On this warm August morning, Coughlin, the only woman in history to have broken the 1-minute barrier in the 100 back, had finished her heat in 1:03.18, more than 3.5 seconds shy of her world record. By morning's end she was in 22nd place, not good enough to advance, an outcome that did not bode well for the rest of the meet.

It was the biggest story of the day, if not the entire meet, and Coughlin wasn't eager to be grilled by the press, even though she had a legitimate explanation. Following her warm-down swim, she shared her feelings with coach Teri McKeever, who urged her to meet with the media. "You're going to be competing in this sport for a long time,"

McKeever told her. "The classy thing to do is to go to the press conference, acknowledge that you don't feel well, and answer their questions."

So off Coughlin went, and McKeever braced herself for several days of poolside skepticism. Make that 12 *months*. Instead of validating 3 years of cutting-edge achievement, Coughlin was providing fuel for the cynics who'd doubted that she would ever come through on the big stage. That had begun before the 2000 Olympic Trials, when a torn cartilage in Coughlin's left shoulder derailed her designs on making the US team as a teenager. Skeptics wondered whether she was a china doll doomed to crack under pressure. With her body having failed her yet again at a critical juncture, the resolutely confident Coughlin was bound to be confronted with self-doubts, as well. It was, McKeever would later conclude, "the first time I've seen a chink in her armor."

Protective by nature, McKeever, 42, was like a surrogate mother to Coughlin, who'd come to her as an emotionally and physically scarred teenager on the verge of quitting the sport. The oldest of 10 children, McKeever had been a caretaker her entire life. In her march toward improbable success in her field, she had given so much focus to her career that she felt it had impacted her personal life—an issue, given that she harbored dreams of becoming a wife and mother. Instead, it was as if she had 25 de facto children, and Coughlin was the one with whom she was the closest.

McKeever had known something was wrong the day before the meet, when she realized Coughlin was literally hotter than the Spanish summer sun. As was her custom before a big meet, McKeever bought a small gift and a card for both of her swimmers in Barcelona—Coughlin and former Cal star Haley Cope, a backstroker/sprint freestyler—and scrawled personal messages that she presented separately to each woman. When Coughlin read McKeever's card, which spoke of their journey and the exciting opportunities ahead, she hugged her coach as a thank-you gesture. McKeever instinctively recoiled: "You're burning up." Coughlin conceded that she felt a little flushed but assured McKeever she could swim through it.

That night, a worried McKeever tossed and turned in her hotel bed.

Natalie never *gets sick*, she thought to herself. In 3 years together, the coach couldn't remember a single practice in which Coughlin had been too ill to participate. The girl was tough, mentally and physically, as if her intensely competitive nature wouldn't allow an infection to mess with her body.

Empathetic to the core, McKeever also had some selfish reasons for considering the impact of Coughlin's physical breakdown. A coach's prominence is often tied to the success of his or her elite swimmers, and with breaststroker Staciana Stitts, a recent Cal grad and a 2000 Olympian, having relocated to Southern California to swim for Dave Salo of the prominent Novaquatics club, Coughlin and Cope represented McKeever's best chance for career enhancement. Cope, perhaps the most unlikely world-class swimmer in recent American history, was regarded as somewhat of a miracle, having emerged from a broken home to become a world champion—and one who had continued to improve even after her collegiate career. But Cope at her best still wasn't as formidable as Coughlin on a bad day. McKeever knew that Coughlin, when it came down to it, was her ticket to Athens.

No woman had ever served on the coaching staff of a US Olympic swim team, and McKeever, one of the few prominent females in her profession, aimed to be the first. The process of naming assistant coaches was political and inextricably tied to the makeup of the team itself. Were Coughlin, as expected, to emerge as the centerpiece of the US women's squad, selecting McKeever as one of the assistants would be a natural means of keeping the swimmer in her comfort zone. McKeever had a good relationship with the University of Southern California's Mark Schubert, already appointed as the coach of the women's team, though their philosophies were strikingly different. The bottom line was this: With Coughlin at the peak of her powers, McKeever was a slam dunk to be selected.

Though this was hardly her primary goal, McKeever desired the distinction as a means of uplifting her program, which was struggling to break into the national top five, and because it might pave the way for other women in her field to achieve similar success. Most of all, though, she wanted to prove something to herself: that the sacrifices she had made over the past 2 decades—really, since she was 4 years old—had paid off in a blatant and tangible way.

Teri McKeever, by all rights, was ordained for athletic excellence. Her father, Mike, a USC football star, had an identical-twin brother, Marlin, who had also been a gridiron hero for the Trojans. The McKeever twins were famous across the land and seemed destined to be professional football players. A series of injuries derailed Mike's NFL hopes, but in 1961, the Los Angeles Rams would make Marlin the fourth overall pick in the draft, and he would enjoy a productive, 13-year career for four teams as a linebacker and tight end, making the Pro Bowl after the 1966 season. The popular twins also acted in several movies, including *The Three Stooges Meet Hercules* and *The Absent-Minded Professor,* and appeared on the covers of numerous national magazines.

Teri's mother, whose maiden name was Judy Primrose, had been a youth swimming champion who had once finished second in the mile at US Nationals. Had the Olympics featured an event longer than 400 meters for women back then—"long enough so that I could wear everyone else down," in Judy's words—she likely would have qualified to represent her country.

Like classic characters from an old movie, football hero Mike and homecoming queen Judy hooked up as college kids, got married, and started making babies. Teri was the first, and she was not an especially easy child. "From what I was told," Teri says, "I was sort of an awful little kid."

After Teri came Mac, and then Judy got pregnant again. The McKeevers had an idyllic life that seemed emblematic of the American dream. And then, in an instant, their picture-perfect existence was shattered. On December 4, 1965, Mike McKeever was broadsided by a drunk driver while driving in Long Beach. He fell into a coma. Ten days later, his second son, Barry, was born.

Teri barely remembers her father, but she distinctly recalls her mom telling her in the aftermath of the accident, "All right, I need your help now."

It was a heavy burden for a 4-year-old. From that point on, little Teri became a caretaker. She was especially protective of Mac: When he would rile his mother by, say, dropping his jacket on the ground, Teri would jump in and plead, "Mommy, don't yell at him. I'll pick it up for him."

On August 25, 1967, some 20 months after the accident, Mike McKeever died in a Los Angeles hospital. Teri remembers "sitting at the funeral and seeing people walking by and looking at us, and every one of them was crying." From then on, whenever she saw her uncle Marlin, Teri would chillingly be confronted with a vision of what her father would have looked like at that age.

Judy met a man named Gary Gannon and married him in 1969. The two ended up having seven kids together—for a total of 10 in the household. In reality, though, there were nine kids and a de facto third parent—Teri. She changed diapers and got her younger siblings dressed, fed, and bathed. When she turned 16 and got her driver's license, Teri also received a credit card from her mother, so she could do the grocery shopping and run other errands.

The family lived in Escondido, a town north of San Diego, in a nice house that had 25-yard and 50-meter pools in the backyard. Many of the kids gravitated toward sports—Mac played football for Long Beach State and San Diego State, while Barry played for Stanford. Years later, younger sisters Kelli and Kristi Gannon would earn spots on the US national field hockey squad.

Shy by nature, a trait she shared with her late father, Teri felt most comfortable in the water, an environment in which she could escape the hectic pace of a life spent caring for her brothers and sisters. Swimming also offered the best chance for individual attention from her mother, who imparted the lessons she had learned while training for legendary coach Peter Daland at the Los Angeles Athletic Club.

While many youth swimming standouts built their endurance bases through rigorous, monotonous workouts, that wasn't an option in Teri's world. Time was always of the essence. She typically swam in the back-yard while supervised loosely by her mother, who had one eye on her eldest daughter's technique and the other on the younger kids. "Sometimes

Mac and Barry would swim relays against me," McKeever recalls. "Sometimes the younger kids would be riding their bikes around the pool while my mom tried to coach me. I remember at least one time when one of them fell in, and my mom had to reach in and fish her out in the middle of my set. I never knew when my workouts were going to be, because it depended on everyone's nap schedule."

When mother and daughter did have uninterrupted time together, it was inevitably rushed, so it was essential that every minute count. The result was that Judy emphasized technique and form over mind-numbing repetition and often instructed her daughter to practice at race speed, rather than stressing the value of going long distances at slower speeds. Judy also felt that Teri's tall, slender build was not particularly suited toward the overtraining that most coaches favored. Instead, she focused on the mental aspects of preparation, painstakingly explaining the rationale for each element of the workout and imploring her daughter to participate mentally in the process.

Judy might not have realized it then, but she was creating the basis for a philosophy that would guide her daughter to an impressive stint as a competitive swimmer and a revolutionary career as a coach. At the very least, growing up in an environment that necessitated quality over quantity would later compel Coach McKeever to ask the questions that most of her peers dared not broach: Why do we make them swim so much more than their race distances, over and over again, in practice? If you're more efficient in the water, doesn't that also enable you to retain more energy for when you need it most?

Before becoming an all-American at USC, McKeever, a butterfly and middle-distance freestyle specialist, excelled as a youth swimmer and competed in numerous meets across the country. Those trips had special meaning for her, not because she was going head up against the best in the United States but because of the quality time she got to spend with her coach and traveling companion. While many of the competitors behaved like social butterflies, McKeever kept to herself, sitting with her mother and beholding the spectacle. "The only time I remember being alone with my mother," she remembers, "was at those national meets."

As an adult, McKeever essentially had more than two dozen children—and the big meets represented an opportunity to bond with the highest achievers. Coughlin, who arrived at Cal as a confused, burned-out teenager, had trusted McKeever like a child trusts her mother. In many ways McKeever was the one person—besides herself—in whom Coughlin had complete faith. Though Coughlin's parents were in Barcelona to watch her swim, it was McKeever to whom she turned for support when she fell ill.

Given Coughlin's symptoms, it was no surprise that her teammates weren't especially eager to be in her company during the competition. For 5 days, Coughlin spent the bulk of her mornings, afternoons, and nights lying in bed at the team hotel, alternately sweating and clutching her blankets, barely able to eat or sleep. "No one wanted to be around me, of course," Coughlin says. "Other than the doctors, Teri was the only one who'd deal with me."

McKeever would knock on the door of Coughlin's hotel room every hour or so to check on her, and the two would go down to team meals and sit alone at a table in the far corner of the room. None of this was visible to the rest of the swimming world, which saw only stunning failure, confirming some people's suspicions that Coughlin, as she had been before the 2000 Olympic Trials, was physically—or, as some erroneously speculated, mentally—vulnerable when the stakes were highest.

Having qualified for the 100-meter butterfly final on the first day of the meet, Coughlin, even after her illness worsened, and even after her plodding effort in the 100 back the next morning, decided to give it a go in the evening session of day 2. Her only chance, she and McKeever reasoned, would be to employ a "fly and die" strategy: Go out hard and see if her body could hang on for 58 seconds.

Coughlin flew at the start…and quickly died, finishing last in the field. She skipped the warm-down session, the series of slow laps all competitive swimmers rely upon to rid their body of lactic acid and thus spare themselves the aches and pains that result when the acid remains in the system. Coughlin didn't care—her body already ached miserably from the virus, and she didn't plan on reentering the pool anytime soon. Hunched over in pain, barely able to move her legs as she slowly hobbled to a car waiting to take her back to the hotel, Coughlin stopped and balanced herself on McKeever's arm. "Whoa," she said, cracking a tiny smile. "I haven't gotten *eighth* in a race in a long time."

But as the meet proceeded, Coughlin knew she was losing more than just a couple of races. On the men's side, 18-year-old Baltimore phenom Michael Phelps was doing what Coughlin had been projected to do—win race after race and position himself as the greatest American medal hope for Athens. Meanwhile, Coughlin's brilliance of the past 3 years was suddenly fading from memory, and the predictions of multiple individual golds were being downscaled.

Was she versatile and talented enough to approach the Olympics like Phelps and challenge Mark Spitz's record haul of seven golds (four individual) from the 1972 Olympics in Munich? Undoubtedly. Was her body capable of holding up? Even Coughlin began to wonder.

Cooped up in her hotel room, she had a lot of time to think. A major decision loomed—would Coughlin renounce her collegiate eligibility and cash in on endorsement offers that could exceed $1 million? The smart money said yes.

Or would she thumb her nose at conventional wisdom and return for her senior season at Cal? Few college athletes, let alone athletes who compete in nonrevenue sports, would think twice about leaving for such a bounty. But Coughlin, especially in the wake of her sudden fallibility, wasn't so sure.

Going into Worlds, Coughlin had all but decided to bolt. She could still attend classes at Cal and train with McKeever and the rest of the team, but she wouldn't be able to compete in collegiate competitions. Considering that college meets are contested in short-course (25-yard or, during an Olympic year, 25-meter) venues, while the Olympics are held in long-course (50-meter) pools, that wasn't a huge loss. It would be like skipping half-court, three-on-three hoops competitions while preparing for full-court, five-on-five action. Coughlin, who excelled at turns, had already proven to be the best short-course swimmer in the world; the key for her was pushing her long-course capabilities to the highest possible level.

Yet turning pro wasn't the no-brainer that everyone assumed it was. For one thing, Coughlin was true to her school like few other collegiate athletes, with a fervor that would have made the Beach Boys proud. As a high school senior, she had fought fiercely with her parents for the right to attend Cal, which she correctly sensed would be a better fit for her than Bay Area rival Stanford, her parents' preference. Not only was Coughlin excited by the idea of swimming for McKeever—and, though she respected him greatly, somewhat certain that Stanford's hyperintense coach, Richard Quick, would not be the best fit for her—but she also loved everything about Berkeley: the liberal legacy, the diversity, the probing encouragement of progressive and contrarian thought, the vibrant campus in a lush yet urban setting.

With Coughlin back for a fourth season, McKeever had a chance to push her program to the next level. Not insignificantly, Cal would also have an opportunity to defeat Stanford in a dual meet for the first time in 28 years, something both women craved the way Golden Bears seek honey. Coughlin would also have a chance to make history; already the only swimmer to sweep three individual events at three consecutive NCAA Championships, she'd be favored to make it four for four.

Besides, Coughlin thoroughly enjoyed being part of a team, getting lost in the fabric of collective goals, and, on occasion, getting to pretend she was one of the girls. As much as she stood out in the water and embraced her role as a star, she worried about being cast as an ordained Olympic hero before her time. Were she to turn pro and start showing up in commercials a full year before the games, she might suffer from the same type of overexposure that made some viewers regard Marion Jones's performance at the 2000 Sydney Games as a disappointment, rather than an exceptional accomplishment.

In one sense, her body's breakdown in Barcelona could have spooked her into taking the money while it was still on the table. But in another sense, Coughlin felt a greater need to cling to McKeever and remain in the protective cocoon that had revitalized her as an athlete.

It was not a stretch to say that McKeever saved Coughlin's career, both technically and emotionally. When Coughlin arrived at Cal, McKeever changed her stroke, giving it a more cyclical efficiency that reduced the stress on her injured shoulder and helped her reach a new level of excellence. She also altered Coughlin's outlook, making life in the pool fun and exciting and unpredictable. Coughlin, who'd taken to the pool because she enjoyed the sensation of frolicking in the water, redis-covered her love for the sport at Cal. By the end of their first year together, Coughlin had been voted the NCAA Swimmer of the Year and was on her way to becoming the greatest collegiate swimmer of all time. She was getting good grades; making appearances on behalf of the uni-versity; and projecting an image of beauty, grace, and well-rounded achievement.

What Coughlin didn't realize was that in the process, she was helping to save McKeever. Before landing Coughlin, the coach had been, quite literally, a woman on the verge of a nervous breakdown. Overworked and overstressed, McKeever suffered from depression, panic attacks, and a severely impaired self-image. She had reached a breaking point with her closest coaching confidant, Cal cocoach Mike Walker, and feared that severing ties with him would expose her shortcomings as a leader. Whenever McKeever felt like giving in and walking away, she would remember her commitment to Coughlin and the unique opportunity this special swimmer's presence afforded.

It was as if Coughlin's fragility superseded McKeever's, pushing the coach to challenge the limits of her own potential. "I was at the lowest point of my life," McKeever recalls. "And one of the things that pulled me through—though even Natalie may not know this—was her being here, that I'd made a commitment to someone that special. I'm a better coach than I was 4 years ago, and not just because of what I've learned from her in the pool. In many ways, she's the kind of person who makes everyone around her better, and I've probably been the biggest beneficiary."

One of the tenets of McKeever's philosophy is that the journey is as important as—or, in most cases, more important than—the outcome. Even as she felt Coughlin's disappointment in Barcelona, the coach viewed it as another chapter in her swimmer's odyssey toward growth and fulfillment, a trying time whose value might not be understood until after the fact. For the previous 3 years, things had been going so well, so consistently, in Coughlin's career, it was almost eerie.

Perhaps there was value in Coughlin's being forced to confront her frailty a year before the Olympics; surely she could learn another lesson in perseverance and handling adversity by fighting through the discomfort.

If a hope for redemption, however minor, were to present itself, McKeever was all for it. Jack Bauerle, the vaunted University of Georgia coach in charge of the US women's staff in Barcelona, kept asking McKeever if there was a chance Coughlin might be available for the meet-ending 400-meter medley relay. Because Couglin was the fastest US swimmer in three of the four strokes—all but the breaststroke—at 100 meters, leaving her off the medley relay was almost inconceivable. Yet the coaches knew that even if she began to feel better, Coughlin would be weak and out of sorts in such a competition. Swimming is a sport in which "feel for the water" is everything; skip a few days of training, and a swimmer is liable to behave like she hasn't been in a pool for months.

Bauerle asked McKeever about the possibility of Coughlin's swimming the backstroke leg in the prelims. That way, even if she performed poorly, the team's other swimmers would probably be strong enough to qualify for the final. It would also allow her to shed some of the rust, potentially clearing the way for a faster swim in the evening.

"Jack, the girl is spent," McKeever said. "The way I see it, she's got one swim in her, period."

Saving her for the finals would be a gamble, but McKeever and Bauerle agreed that it was a risk worth taking. Cope, the second-best US backstroker, could go only so fast; Coughlin at least offered the possibility of greatness. She led off the medley with a time of 1:02.26—nearly 3 seconds off her world record, but a respectable effort under the circumstances. The United States finished second to China, edging the powerful Australians, and Coughlin views the performance as a triumphant one. "I was really proud of myself for sucking it up and swimming through my sickness," she reasons. "Everyone thought the meet was a disaster for me and that I should be devastated, but it actually ended on a redeeming note."

After the meet, Coughlin joined McKeever, Cope, and a small US delegation on a side trip to Athens. They got the lay of the land, visited the Olympic swimming venue, and had a fancy dinner that featured local delicacies. For a couple of days she forgot about the disappointment of Barcelona, stopped worrying about whether or not to turn pro, and looked forward to her next big international test.

Next summer, she told herself, *I'll be healthy. Then all these people doubting me now will be the ones who feel like crap.*

CHAPTER TWO

WHERE THE HEART IS;
WHERE THE ACTION IS

She is staring at me—her bespectacled eyes cutting through my Quicksilver shirt and Billabong cargo shorts like scissors through notebook paper, her scowl a mixture of contempt and disgust. This frumpy, middle-aged woman clad in loose, earth-toned linens and clutching a copy of *The Nation* seems to regard me as the embodiment of all that is wrong with my gender, my age bracket, and Western civilization as a whole.

They're all staring, in fact, as, on a warm afternoon in late August 2003, I take a seat at Barney's, a casual burger joint in North Berkeley in the shadow of Alice Watters's chichi Chez Panisse. Across the table is a smiling, radiant Natalie Coughlin.

I'd like to believe that our lunch date is attracting attention because, even after her recent misfortune in Barcelona, Coughlin is the best female swimmer in the world, and I am a mildly visible sportswriter who whores it up on the airwaves on a semifrequent basis. But human nature being what it is, I know better. Much better.

What the people at Barney's see is what I see: a tall, muscular but certainly not substantial college student just turned 21, tanned and golden haired and blessed with gorgeous aqua eyes and perfect teeth and silky skin and an incredibly evolved sense of fashion (not that it hurts when you can bring traffic to a halt in ripped jeans, Pumas, and a sleeveless black top); preternaturally poised and prone to unleashing a wholesome yet slightly dangerous smile at precisely the right moment.

Then, when they've finished gaping at her, they notice me: a 38-year-old dude with expensive glasses and day-old stubble, dressed a little too young and casually; tall and curly haired and sporting a touch of gray, not to mention a disturbing abundance of ear hair; *very* happy to be there and, despite his valiant efforts to the contrary, giving off that creepy professor vibe, talking with his hands and in the process revealing—gasp—a wedding ring.

Any second now, I am sure, the frumpy lady or someone else like her is going to take a ketchup-drenched knife off her plate, sneak up from behind, and stab me through the jugular. Given our location—the PC capital of the universe—she just might get away with it. *Your Honor, what we have here is a classic case of justifiable homicide.*

It is a sensation I will experience many times over the next year, as I break bread (and pad Thai, and huevos rancheros, and greasy barbecue) with this young woman, who, when I was in her position—entering my senior year at UC Berkeley, contemplating some big decisions—was running around the backyard of her modest home in working-class Vallejo, spared the socialization of preschool because, her parents explained, she was "too smart" for such an endeavor. After a while, I came to accept the discomfort: Wherever we go, whatever we do, we're gonna get stared at together.

Most times, the gawkers don't see my reporter's notebook in my back pocket or the wallet photos of my lovely and age-appropriate wife (herself a frequent recipient of reproachful glares for the crime of being too naturally blond, too fit, and too fashion-conscious for the Frumpy

Police's tastes) and our three kids, the eldest of whom is, in fact, named Natalie. Such details tend to kill your game with the young, hot gold-medalists-to-be, just as the inevitable wink-wink/nod-nods and worse from your jealous friends (you're having lunch with *who*?) don't enhance your popularity on the home front. Because no matter how hard I may try to keep the interaction strictly professional, it nonetheless reeks of awkwardness. Were I a character in a movie whose attributes were some-what embellished—or, let's just say, a sportswriter who got paid as much as most of the NFL players he covers—Coughlin could pass as my cliché coed squeeze, a tragically naive second wife in waiting.

It could all be so heavy and self-conscious, except that Coughlin, bless her impossibly mature soul, doesn't allow it to be. Composed, asser-tive, and respectfully direct, she keeps our conversations frank and intense without their being charged or multilayered. I'm not sure whether this is an intrinsic gift or a skill derived from years of navigating her way through choppy waters both figurative and literal; all I know is that I'm grateful. It's not as though being a sportswriter for a national magazine is heavy lifting, but it does present its challenges, not the least of which is a need to bond with and cultivate the trust of intensely driven souls from all over the geographical and social spectrums. Thus I've rolled into a rented union hall in North Baltimore on an early spring Saturday night with Green Bay Packers receiver Antonio Freeman and a bunch of his boys, which was a good thing, given that of the 600 folks in attendance, I was the only one who happened to be white—and because of my obvious bond with "Free," I was as fawned over. I've done books with a mania-cally competitive, physically obsessive football star (Jerry Rice); a freak-ishly body-painted, exhilarating exhibitionist party animal and rebounding savant (Dennis Rodman); and an unfailingly sweet evangelical Christian quarterback (Kurt Warner) who believes, as I understand him, that Mother Teresa does not currently reside in heaven, because she died without having been saved, whereas if Charles Manson were to be saved tomorrow, then go on another killing spree, he would nonetheless be guaranteed admission to the pearly gates.

Of the three, by the way, Coughlin is the most like Rice, only with a much greater aptitude for disguising her rough edges.

The point is that in a quest to grow close with subjects such as these in a short period of time, I'm sometimes compelled to accelerate the process by any means necessary, meaning I will scream "Hallelujah!" or quote Pac or Biggie or flirt like a madman, as the situation warrants. For instance, when I had an audience with 16-year-old Russian tennis vixen Anna Kournikova—who I knew was about to split for a 2-hour drive across Southern California on an adventure that wouldn't end until morning—I managed to overcome the protective presence of both her mother (we ended up delving into my Ukrainian heritage) and her agent (whom Anna would order to "get us a stretch lee-mo") by shamelessly cashing in on that enduring fantasy, "If I could go back to high school knowing what I know now…" Come to think of it, there were occasions on which I shamelessly flirted with Rodman, too, though I probably didn't realize it at the time, what with the Jägermeister and the Goldschläger and the kamikazes and all.

With Coughlin, flirting was unnecessary, from the day we first talked business at Barney's to that emotional moment 11 months later in the cavernous Long Beach Arena when, as she exited a press conference after having qualified for the Olympic team, we saw each other and silently hugged, neither of us caring in the least who stared, because we both understood how elated and relieved and vindicated she felt and, indeed, would continue to feel, from that night forward.

≈

Would she turn pro? What events would she try to swim in the Olympics? Did she want someone tagging along and taking notes in the year leading up to the Games?

These were the questions Coughlin and I pondered during that meeting at Barney's—we had actually met once before, when I had hammed it up for the team on the deck of Spieker Pool more than a year earlier as one of McKeever's weekly guest speakers (I'd been recommended by my old college buddy Mohamed Muqtar, now Cal's director of student services)—and over the next couple of weeks as her senior year began. I quickly came to understand that there were two, and only two, people involved in these decisions: Coughlin and McKeever, who essentially served as her manager, agent, and public relations director.

The first question was the most pressing: Take the cash and renounce her collegiate eligibility, or wait until March, after the NCAA Championships, to sign with Speedo or Nike and whoever else came calling? Before Barcelona, it didn't seem to be much of a mystery. Coughlin was as good as gone, with McKeever's blessing. She had done so much for the university and for the program that the coach didn't even allow her own obvious interests to cloud her judgment. McKeever truly wanted what was best for her greatest swimmer, and the combination of reducing Coughlin's competitive load and ensuring her financial security while padding her bank account seemed too good to pass up.

Now, though, as she rejoined her Cal teammates at Spieker and began grinding her way back into shape, Coughlin wasn't so certain. For one thing, the vibe seemed so much better than it had the previous spring, when a team already decimated by mass defections had grown increasingly fractured, with drama over stolen boyfriends and intercepted instant messages to boot. Then there were the feuding stars—Coughlin and breaststroker Staciana Stitts, a 2000 Olympic gold medalist (as a relay swimmer, thanks to a leg in the preliminaries, but *still*) who had completed her final season of eligibility in 2003. Stitts, who suffers from alopecia, was a popular performer whose bald head was a recognizable symbol of Cal's resurgence under McKeever.

McKeever and Stitts were close, but Coughlin's arrival coincided with a dip in Stitts's performances, and the two ultracompetitive swimmers, who'd been good friends during Coughlin's freshman year, soon grew estranged. Stitts seemed to resent Coughlin's presence, sometimes complaining to McKeever that special treatment was being afforded the team's new star. "Stace, I understand how you could feel that way," McKeever told her, "but I care about both of you. Does a mother love one child more than the other?"

Alas, any chance at friendship between Stitts and Coughlin was officially extinguished at the NCAA Championships in March 2002. The Bears were preparing for the 200-yard medley relay, with Coughlin swimming the lead-off backstroke leg, and Stitts following with the breaststroke leg. As the whistle blew to signal the backstrokers to enter the water in preparation for the start, Coughlin, as was her custom, waited to be the last one into the pool.

There was just one problem: Texas's swimmer Kelley Robins remained on the deck as well. McKeever instantly figured out what was happening: Mike Walker, the longtime coaching associate she had gotten rid of shortly before Coughlin's arrival at Cal, was now the Longhorns' co–head coach. Walker, who'd been active in the recruiting of Coughlin, clearly knew about her superstition and had instructed his swimmer not to jump in before her.

On deck, a game of chicken was playing out. The wait was getting uncomfortable—technically, both swimmers risked disqualification if they failed to enter promptly. Finally, Coughlin bit her lip and got in first. However, she did not bite her tongue, unleashing a stream of expletives at Robins in the seconds before the race began. Further fueling Coughlin's anger was the reaction of the other Texas swimmers when she jumped into the pool: They started cheering, as if getting her to jump in first had been some sort of psychological victory.

At that point a meet official approached McKeever and said, "If this happens again, there's going to be a DQ." McKeever answered in response to the threat of disqualification, "Fine, but tell *them*," pointing at Walker and his fellow coaches. "This wasn't about two athletes jockeying. This was a personal attack against me and my program."

McKeever knew what was coming next. "Watch," she said to the people near her. "Nat's going to *destroy* her." When the starting signal sounded, Coughlin burst underwater with fury and never let up. As she touched the wall at 50 yards, the Bears had an unfathomable 1½-second lead over the next-fastest team. Her split was so swift, it met the NCAA-meet qualifying standard for the 50-yard *freestyle*.

The Bears ultimately finished second, just .09 behind Stanford, which set an American record in the process, but Stitts was hardly in a triumphant mood. The next morning she and several other teammates, including Coughlin, were replaying the incident in a van headed from their hotel to the pool. "That was great," Coughlin's teammates told her. "You took her down." Stitts, however, voiced a different opinion: "That was selfish. You could've gotten us DQed." Stunned, Coughlin replied, "We weren't going to get DQed. I wasn't even the last one in the water." Stitts rounded on her, screaming, "You're not a team player!" As Coughlin began to yell back, McKeever, who was driving, intervened and ended the conversation. But the damage was done. The next season, Stitts's final year of eligibility, was so miserable for Coughlin at times that she began to dread coming to practice.

But in the summer of 2003, Stitts moved to Orange County to train with McKeever's closest coaching confidant, Dave Salo of Irvine Novaquatics, in an effort to qualify for the 2004 Olympics. With Stitts gone, Coughlin suddenly felt as though a weight had been lifted. She felt something else, too—a tangible sense of optimism that the Bears might be ready to do something they'd often talked about but had always seemed far-fetched: Take the program to the next level.

The key, from Coughlin's perspective, was Whitney Hite, the new assistant McKeever had hired that May. Though close with Hite's predecessor, Adam Crossen (who ended up coaching Stitts as one of Salo's Novaquatics assistants), Coughlin felt that Hite's presence had injected the team with a spark that had been lacking. Whereas Crossen had been confused by McKeever's semifrequent exasperation with certain swimmers during periods of intense stress, Hite seemed unfazed. He exuded an attitude of "We're the coaches; you're the swimmers, so get to work, damn it." Judging by the intensity of his sets, it was best not to test that premise.

Before filling the opening, McKeever had asked Hite, as well as the other candidates she considered, to take a behavioral test administered by her close friend and "life coach," Kathie Wickstrand-Gahen. A former swimmer who became a successful collegiate coach at Northwestern and other schools, Wickstrand-Gahen had convinced McKeever that she needed someone whose personality strengths would complement her own, and Hite hadn't hesitated to submit to the exam. He figured, *I am who I am. If she likes me, great. If not, it's not the right place for me anyway.*

The test in question is known as the DISC, with each letter representing a different element of one's behavioral style. The *D* stands for *dominance*, the *I* for *influence*, the *S* for *steadiness*, and the *C* for *compliance*. McKeever's scores on the *S* and *C* scales were especially high, while her *D* and *I* were low. In Wickstrand-Gahen's estimation, McKeever needed someone with a high *I* score to augment her coaching style and relieve some of the burden of recruiting. Sure enough, Hite's *I* was especially elevated, indicating he is a people person.

Hite was used to winning, having been part of an NCAA championship team while swimming for the University of Texas, then capturing three more team titles while serving as an assistant coach for the University of Georgia's women's team from 1999 to 2001. The Bulldogs finished second to Auburn each of the next 2 years, which did not sit well with Hite. Upon arriving at Cal, he instantly set his sights on the top, despite the fact that the team was not fully funded, meaning it had fewer scholarships to disperse than the NCAA-allowed limit.

Yet, a few days after moving to Berkeley, Hite had buyer's remorse. *I think I just made the worst mistake of my life,* he thought to himself. Nobody on the team seemed happy about swimming. Athletes were grumbling about their workouts (nothing new), about each other, and about McKeever, and everyone seemed to be going through the motions. Even Coughlin, despite her obvious dedication, appeared to have one foot out the door.

Slowly, that started to change. In the coming months, even Hite was taken aback at how his arrival seemed to coincide with a transformation in the team's attitude. The most tangible difference to the swimmers was Hite's effect on McKeever. She seemed calmer, happier, and less prone to voicing frustration with them during practice. She clearly trusted Hite's leadership skills and technical knowledge, and his firmness and conviction had a soothing effect on her.

The bizarre thing was that philosophically, Hite and McKeever were hardly clones. Hite's orientation was more traditional. He believed that for the team to improve, mental and physical toughness had to be instilled in the form of long, grueling workouts—in the pool, on dry land, and in the weight room. "In my heart I believe that if you get a swimmer in shape, get her a little bit stronger than she's been, and then rest her, she'll swim fast," Hite explains.

At Georgia, working under the exacting Jack Bauerle, Hite had helped develop stars like sprinter Maritza Correia by pushing them past their preconceived physical limits. Yet he also understood the benefits of technical excellence, something he had picked up while swimming for Texas's Eddie Reese, whose style was a blend of high-volume training and precision, especially on starts and turns. It was Hite's ability to impart that kind of attention to detail to swimmers like Correia, who would capture a school-record 11 individual and relay NCAA titles during her collegiate career, that allowed him to work his way up from volunteer assistant to one making $9,000 a year to serving as a full-fledged member of Bauerle's staff.

Though his new team wasn't on Georgia's level, Hite saw similar potential at Cal, particularly in swimmers like Ashley Chandler, a former US national champion coming off a disappointing freshman season; fellow distance swimmer Erin Reilly, a skinny freshman with loads of untapped talent; and Lauren Medina, an ultracompetitive junior freestyler who had already surpassed her unspectacular swimming pedigree.

Early on, "Whitney's Group" became a dreaded term at Spieker Pool. Swimming for Hite meant you were in for a punishing workout and could expect no sympathy from the architect. Hite, with a gleam in his eye, seemed to revel in his role as torturer. At the same time, the swimmers inherently trusted his plan to uplift the team's standing. "We're a top-10 program, and this year we can become a top-5 program," Hite told me before the season. "But they're going to have to work for it like they've never worked for anything before."

No one was less eager to experience Hite's workouts than Coughlin, who avoided his lanes—or, some of her teammates felt, was shielded from them by McKeever—as though they were full of sewer water. Hite's sustained, high-speed sets triggered bad memories from her teenage years, when Ray Mitchell, Coughlin felt, pushed her to exhaustion (and, ultimately, to serious injury) as a point of pride. She also correctly surmised that her combination of body awareness and ability to shift into the highest gear on cue made her less suited to Hite's workouts than her teammates were. "I understand what it means to sprint," she explains, "and when a coach says sprint, I really go for it. A lot of other girls aren't at that point, so they don't get nearly as tired."

Yet Coughlin, paradoxically, became a Hite devotee almost from the start. She loved his intensity, confidence, candor, and passion. "He tells you exactly how he feels," she says, "and doesn't sugarcoat it at all. If he doesn't like something, he'll let you know." Most of all, Coughlin sensed that Hite had stirred a sincerity in her teammates that they had lacked before. This year, she felt, when the team mapped out its goals for the season—going undefeated in dual meets, beating Stanford for the first time in 28 years (after three consecutive narrow defeats), finishing in the top five at the NCAA Championships—her teammates actually believed these ambitions were attainable.

To Coughlin, Hite's presence gave the team the best of both worlds— an innovative, new-age strategist in McKeever and a traditionalist in Hite, each open to exploring the other's ideas. On a campus known for fostering creativity and outside-the-box thinking, she felt this was a fitting setup: The Bears weren't being ordered to prepare a certain way or employ a specific approach. Rather, they were being given a multitude of ideas and techniques that could help them succeed, the overriding message being "There are many different ways to be good in this sport. Here are some that might work for you."

Above all, Hite exuded a toughness that he seemed to pass down to his swimmers. During his first few months on the job, the tall, lanky 30-year-old trained for the Chicago Marathon, fighting through chronic pain in his lower right leg while putting in the necessary distance work. In October, he flew to the Windy City and ran the race in a personal-best time of 3 hours, 22 minutes, grimacing through much of the back end as his leg throbbed. He finally saw a doctor upon his return to Berkeley—and X-rays revealed a stress fracture of the tibia. (As if to top that, Hite would run the '04 Chicago Marathon in far more pain as, from the 2nd-mile mark, each step he took with his left leg sent a shooting sensation throughout his body. He finally started walking after 14 miles but later resumed running and, after a furious sprint, finished 13 seconds shy of 4 hours, out of principle. This time, X-rays would reveal a significant break in his left fibula, with a nerve coiled around the bone.)

When the Cal swimmers heard about Hite's Marathon of Masochism, their fear factor intensified. "See," they joked to one another, "he *is* crazy." What they didn't know was that on the spectrum of fighting through pain, running 26.2 miles on a broken leg wasn't the gnarliest test he'd endured.

In fact, it wasn't even close.

∼

"Most people become swimmers because they enjoy the water," McKeever tells me on a late-August afternoon as she paces the Spieker deck. "It's quiet and calm and soothing, and they like the way it flows over their body. A lot of times, as swim coaches, we beat that out of them. What I'm trying to do is find a way to tap into that feeling and celebrate it."

I would soon learn that those three words—*feel the water*—are central to McKeever's coaching philosophy. If the typical swimming practice is as monotonous as a statistics lecture, McKeever's workouts are more like extension-course seminars, with an emphasis on communication and experimentation. McKeever, unlike most other coaches, makes a point of giving her swimmers the rationale behind the drills and sets she chooses, many of which are highly unique. For example, whereas the traditional approach to interval training calls for short breaks between intense sprints, McKeever sometimes asks her swimmers to take five "underwater bobs" before resuming their sets. By inhaling deeply, sinking to the bottom of the pool, and then floating to the surface, the swimmers, McKeever feels, are able to reset their systems and achieve a purer form of rest before continuing the workout.

So much of McKeever's coaching approach centers on getting her swimmers to become attuned to the mechanics of their bodies. Some, like junior breaststroker Marcelle Miller, didn't respond to such teachings, instead preferring to grow stronger through hard, sustained sets. Others, like junior freestyler Keiko Amano, seemed immune to such instruction for extended periods before it finally began to kick in. Then there was Coughlin, whose ability to process and implement specific information regarding her physical movements borders on the freakish. In Hite's words, "She has such great mind and body control, such an amazing ability to connect the dots. She's always trying something new, always tinkering, and watching her and Teri work together is truly illuminating. Teri will say something about her technique or body positioning, and Natalie will say, 'Oh, I felt that' or 'I'll try that,' and then immediately incorporate it into her stroke. It's like telling (Oakland A's pitching star) Barry Zito, 'I want you to move your finger a half millimeter to the left when you throw your curveball from now on, and tell me how it feels,' and then he's instantly able to alter his grip and pitch even more effectively."

However, McKeever was smart enough to understand that what worked for Coughlin might not prove as effective for an athlete less in tune with her own thresholds and without the same propensity for summoning high-intensity performances. As Hite says, "Natalie has a much different mental capacity than anyone else. She can stay sharp and be 'in the zone' for a lot longer than the other girls, and so those technique-specific practices are lost on a lot of them. They simply won't get a good workout."

To their credit, rather than wage a philosophical tug-of-war, McKeever and Hite opted for a logical division of labor. Despite his background with swimmers such as Correia, Hite focused mostly on distance specialists like Chandler and Reilly, as well as workout warriors like Miller. McKeever, who had a long history of milking the most out of sprinters—and, by extension, of fielding relay teams more potent than the projected sum of their parts—devoted more of her energies to those who swam shorter distances. Given collegiate swimming's short-course layout, McKeever's ability to drill home lessons in technique, as well as her focus on starts and turns, gave her sprinters a huge edge in a sport typically decided by hundredths of a second.

For example, on any other top-10 college team, the sight of a 5-foot-2 sprinter would provoke poolside laughter. But Amano, such an afterthought as a recruit that McKeever was stunned to learn she was coming to Cal—she and a group of team members, after all, had actually lost Amano for nearly half an hour during a recruiting trip to San Francisco's Pier 39—had become a viable contributor to the Golden Bears' sprint relays. In another 7 months, she would unleash one of the most stirring anchor legs in school history.

Somehow, as they splashed through the water at the start of the fall semester, the Bears were starting to resemble a team. They certainly weren't one big, happy family, but they'd been infused with a common quest for improvement. That, ultimately, was all Coughlin needed to see. She pictured herself closing out a fulfilling career by helping to launch a new era of excellence—and, she hoped, by rewarding McKeever with one hell of a parting gift. *Before I leave this place*, Coughlin said to herself, *we are going to beat Stanford.*

Oddly enough, it was the coach of one of Cal's other rivals, USC's Mark Schubert, who helped Coughlin finalize her decision to stay. Schubert was talking about Coughlin's decision with McKeever on the phone one day when the Cal coach asked, "You've been on seven Olympic staffs, and you've seen people go through situations like this. How do I help this person?"

Schubert offered to fly up and meet with McKeever and Coughlin to discuss the decision. McKeever was flattered and floored. A few days later, the three of them went to lunch at a Mexican restaurant on University Avenue, and Schubert shared his experiences with backstroker Lenny Krayzelburg, who'd won three gold medals at the 2000 Olympics and faced a similar decision in the years leading up to those games.

Schubert said he'd advised Krayzelburg not to make any dramatic changes. "You've found something that's working for you," the coach had told him. "Is now the best time to change it?" He then explored the various scenarios with Coughlin, wondering, "If you decide to turn pro and go outside your familiar mix, what will that look like?"

Coughlin took it all to heart and, one morning in September, walked into McKeever's office and said, "I've made my decision. I'm staying." McKeever smiled. They hugged. Perhaps Barcelona, in an odd way, had been a blessing, the coach thought. *Instead of feeling too good about ourselves, we'll dig in and work that much harder.*

Coughlin's illness at the World Championships had affected another important decision: how many events to swim in Athens, and which ones. Before Barcelona, Coughlin had been tempted to push her physical limits and shoot for a record medal haul. Now that she'd been confronted with her body's fragility, her ambition was somewhat muted. Twice now, at crucial junctures—before the 2000 Olympics and at the '03 Worlds—her body had failed her. She feared that if she pushed herself too hard, her entire dream could disappear.

In the wake of his impressive effort in Barcelona, Michael Phelps was already talking about attempting to match or exceed Mark Spitz's record. Phelps, however, had two distinct advantages over Coughlin: He believed he was bulletproof, having never experienced any adversity in his swimming career; and the Olympic swimming schedule made such a bold attempt plausible.

The schedule at the Olympics—and at the US Olympic Trials, which mirrored the Athens itinerary—could not have been less kind to Coughlin. In theory, she was the best US swimmer in five events—the 100 back, 200 back, 100 free, 200 free, and 100 fly. She held the world record in the 100 back and American records in the 100 free and 200 back; in the 100 fly and 200 free, only two Americans had ever swum faster, and she'd be a legitimate medal threat in each. Coughlin also figured to be the centerpiece of the US efforts in all three relays—the 400 free, 800 free, and 400 medley (in which she'd likely swim the backstroke but could also swim free or fly).

Yet the schedule didn't allow her to showcase that versatility. On the second night of swimming at the Games, for example, the 100-meter backstroke semifinal would be followed by the 100-meter butterfly final, with only a pair of men's 200-meter freestyle semifinal races in between. "I checked," McKeever said in late August, "and they're talking about a gap of like 18 minutes."

So the 100 fly was out. The 200 free, an event in which Coughlin was growing increasingly comfortable, was intriguing, but the schedule killed her there as well. The 200 free semis on the third night of competition were before the 100 back finals, meaning Coughlin, at the very least, would be winded for her featured event. Before Barcelona, she might have been willing to risk it, but now her attitude was "Take care of the 100 back, and everything else will fall into place." Had the two races been reversed, with the 100 back final shortly before the 200 free semis, it might have been worth a shot; unfortunately, the schedulers clearly hadn't had Coughlin's best interests in mind.

That left the 200 back and the 100 free, two events that (surprise) also conflicted. To swim both would require another vicious turnaround: On the sixth night of the competition, Coughlin would have to swim a rigorous 200 back semi just before the 100 free final, with only the men's 200-meter individual medley final between them. This time, the gap would be as little as 12 minutes. "Nat's good," McKeever said, laughing, "but she's not *that* good."

Most likely, then, Coughlin would attempt to swim all three relays, the 100 back, and either the 200 back or the 100 free. On paper, it didn't seem like a subject much worth debating. The 200 back was an event considered to be so weak internationally that Coughlin, even if she wasn't at her best, would be a prohibitive favorite to win the gold.

Yet the 200 back had one distinct disadvantage: Coughlin hated it. "It's a lousy event to swim, and it's boring," she explained one September morning as she rested on the Spieker Pool wall between sets. "It's just not exciting at all."

"Well," McKeever interrupted, "it might be somewhat exciting if you break a 12-year-old world record while winning it at the Olympics."

The coach let the thought sit, then continued down the deck to go over a set with some of her other swimmers. It was true that the 200 back was the smart play; the 100 free would be a much tougher event, one likely to feature 2000 Olympic gold medalist Inge de Bruijn of the Netherlands, budding Australian stars Jodie Henry and Libby Lenton, and, quite possibly, US legend Jenny Thompson. It was also a race in which someone could come out of nowhere—whether chemically enhanced or clean—and become a surprise contender. It was clear that McKeever preferred that Coughlin not subject herself to a scenario so rife with potential disappointments.

"Yeah," Coughlin said with her coach out of earshot, "but the 100 free is where the action is."

CHAPTER THREE

JIGGLE, JIGGLE, JIGGLE

All the guys out of the pool!" Ray Mitchell intoned, interrupting a typically rigorous early-morning workout at northern California's hottest youth swim club. Recoiling with trepidation, 16-year-old Natalie Coughlin and the other girls on the Terrapins, the Concord-based team Mitchell cofounded and ran with an iron whistle, congregated on one side of the pool as their coach hovered menacingly above.

The team had just finished its summer break following US Nationals, the longest stretch away from the pool that any of the Terrapins would enjoy for another year. Some of the swimmers had even taken 3 weeks off, an eternity in a sport that beats up its young like few others. If gymnastics and figure skating were the gravest examples of sports whose coaches habitually inflicted physical, mental, and emotional distress on elite-level youth standouts—a comprehensive tragedy documented so masterfully in Joan Ryan's *Little Girls in Pretty Boxes*, a landmark book published in 1995—swimming was quite possibly the next worst. It had many of the same pitfalls: an overarching obsession with physique; training philosophies that bordered on the sadistic; talented girls peaking before they were old enough to vote in some cases; and an alarmingly high rate of burnout, injury, and eating disorders.

Coaches like Mitchell, of course, didn't seem concerned with those types of big-picture issues. They wanted their kids to swim fast, especially the most talented ones—and Coughlin was the kind of once-in-a-lifetime swimmer whose success could add to Mitchell's already significant position in the sport. For more than 3 years, Coughlin had been a reasonably happy member of one of the nation's most successful clubs. But now, as she struggled with the first serious injury of her career, Coughlin was feeling Mitchell's wrath.

Because Coughlin's swimming fortunes were so inextricably intertwined with his own success, it was natural that Mitchell had become particularly hard on her—not that he was soft on anyone. As Coughlin and the other girls sat shivering in the pool that September morning in 1998, they braced themselves for another upbraiding from their impossible-to-please coach.

"You girls are fat," Mitchell yelled. "Look at you—I can see it in your asses and your thighs when you walk on deck, and it's unacceptable. You need to watch what you're eating and get in shape if you want to have a prayer of succeeding."

Coughlin boiled with rage. It was hard enough to be a teenage girl; being a teenage girl in a swimsuit, with nowhere to hide any pubescent chubbiness, was out-and-out torture. It didn't help that unlike runners, cyclists, or other athletes who engaged in cardiovascular exercise on an intense basis, female swimmers didn't seem to shed their weight, perhaps because the cool water kept their bodies from sweating out calories. Also, according to Kathie Wickstrand-Gahen, "studies show that the more efficient you are, the fewer calories you burn. It's like a whale or a dolphin—if you can figure out a way to glide through the water and cut down on resistance, it requires less energy."

At the same time, as anyone who has ever hosted a kids' pool party can attest, few activities provoke such voracious spells of hunger; swimmers *love* and need to eat. Yet whereas young male swimmers tend to have faster metabolisms that allow them to stay trim, their female counterparts aren't so fortunate. Already self-conscious about their muscular physiques, female swimmers learn from a young age that they have something to hide. "Swimmers are notorious for eating full meals before dates," says Cal's Amy Ng, herself an exceptionally fit athlete. "That way, we can eat light on the date. Guys tend not to like it when you eat more than they do; it freaks them out."

It's also true that body fat can be a positive in swimming—it increases buoyancy, allowing a swimmer to ride higher in the water. Over the years, however, most coaches have viewed it primarily as a sign of laziness. "The obsession with female swimmers and their weight used to be out in the open," says Georgia assistant coach Carol Capitani, who, as Carol Felton, was an all-American swimmer at Cal from 1988 to 1991. "Women used to have to get on scales and weigh in, and (male) coaches would tell them, 'You're fat.' They'd have those hydrostatic scales out there on the deck, and the men would yell 'moo' as the women got up there."

So it's not as if what was going on at Mitchell's club was unique or new. In fact, he might have sincerely believed that he was helping his swimmers to stay fit. Like Vince Lombardi and so many successful coaches in so many sports, he was attempting to motivate through fear—and this was yet another form of exerting control over impressionable young minds. When he employed similar tactics with his male swimmers, they were more able to shrug off the message and understand the intention behind it. But young girls in bathing suits and with surging hormones were a different matter.

At swim meets, when his athletes would dine together at restaurants, Mitchell inevitably took note of everyone's culinary choices. Girls who ordered cheese on a burger or mayonnaise on a sandwich risked being subjected to Mitchell's taunts. As Coughlin recalls, he'd issue warnings like, "jiggle, jiggle, jiggle," as the rest of the table fell either silent—or into giggles.

Coughlin was uncomfortable with those comments at the time, and as she grew older and saw that many of her fellow Terrapins struggled with eating disorders, she became increasingly disturbed. At one point during her senior year at Cal, Coughlin told me how hurtful and inappropriate she felt Mitchell had been and that disordered eating was widespread among her former teammates. I assumed she'd been exaggerating, but about a year later I ran it by Leah Monroe, a former Terrapins swimmer who followed Coughlin to Cal but quit the swim team during her sophomore year. Monroe, who described herself as "less disgruntled than any of the other girls" who swam for Mitchell—she spoke highly of him as a coach and motivator—agreed with Coughlin's assessment. Both she and Coughlin told me specific stories about teammates who'd battled bulimia and anorexia; one had been hospitalized in college after her weight dropped to 70 pounds.

According to Monroe, a relatively petite breaststroke specialist, Mitchell never hassled her about her weight, partly because her proclivity for junk food became an inside joke between them. "The first time I really interacted with Ray was when I was 14, and I was trying to make my Senior Nationals cut for the 200 breast," Monroe recalled. "About an hour before my race, I had a hot dog and a Drumstick (ice cream cone), and then I went out and made the cut. It became a joke between us: He'd say, 'Leah's about to swim, so she'd better go eat some junk food.'"

Ultimately, of course, this was no laughing matter. Swimming, partly because of the obvious degree to which young girls' bodies are exposed, has been shown to have a higher incidence of eating disorders among competitive females than numerous other sports. The official website of USA Swimming posts an article on the subject, condensed from the National Youth Sports Safety Foundation, Inc., fact sheet, which notes, "Athletes participating in all sports are susceptible to eating disorders, but it is found in some sports more often than others. Athletes more at risk of having eating disorders are ballet dancers, gymnasts, cheerleaders, figure skaters, divers, wrestlers, and swimmers."

While the article asserts that "coaches alone have very little control in helping cure an athlete with an eating disorder," it also insists that "coaches and parents need to be sensitive to the role they play in focusing undue attention on weight and body image." According to the article, "Sometimes eating disorders can be triggered by a single comment from someone very important to the athlete. An off-handed remark that refers to an athlete as 'pudgy' or 'thunder thighs' can become deeply imbedded in the mind of a potential anorexic or bulimic."

A 2001 article in *The Sport Journal*, published by the United States Sports Academy, revealed the findings of a study in which 62 female swimmers from seven college teams participated. The study, by West Chester University PhD Justine J. Reel and University of North Carolina at Greensboro PhD Diane L. Gill, found that more than half (51.6 percent) of the swimmers agreed with the statement, "There are weight pressures in swimming." The most frequently reported weight stressors were the revealing team uniform/swimsuit (45.2 percent), the perception that lower weight helps swim performance (42 percent), teammates noticing weight (16.1 percent); crowd scrutinizing body (12.9 percent), and the feeling that the lightest swimmers have a performance advantage (9.7 percent). Reel and Gill cited prior research, such as a 1993 study by Benson and Taub which reported that "swimmers may be especially vulnerable to disordered eating due to the display of their bodies in a tight and revealing team uniform." The authors also quoted a 1993 study by Thompson and Sherman which hypothesized that swimmers face unique pressures to lose weight in their sport. A 1990 study by Thornton, the article notes, demonstrated that Olympic female (swimmers) were told to lose weight and body fat to cut times."

The article by Reel and Gill concluded that "coaches may benefit from an awareness of weight-related pressures for competitive swimmers. It is important to understand that while swimmers may become more comfortable than the general public about wearing swim suits, they may experience the stress associated with wearing very small and competitive suits for competitive purposes. More importantly, swim coaches need to be aware that while many swimmers may have healthy body image, there may be some swimmers that have highly negative feelings toward their body." Among the 12 coaching strategies offered in an appendix are, "Discourage team members from making weight-related comments to other swimmers," and, "Watch comments that suggest swimmers shold drop weight to cut times."

It's unclear how cognizant Mitchell was that numerous girls under his tutelage were struggling with eating disorders, but he might have been aware that many of the swimmers he sends to collegiate programs felt they had already maxed out their potential. This isn't unusual for female swimmers; few youth standouts continue to improve during college and beyond. Swimmers train so intensely from such young ages that a major crash is always right around the corner. Once a swimmer falls off the horse—due to injury, burnout, or just plain leveling off—she is rarely able to get back on, or at least not at the same speed as before.

In that regard, Coughlin was a true anomaly. By the time she defied that pattern and revived her career under McKeever, she was convinced that virtually everything about her final year with the Terrapins—from Mitchell's rigorous training sessions to his controlling personality to his stubbornness in dealing with the injury that nearly drove her from the sport—had been detrimental to her overall development. Mitchell, of course, would see it far differently, claiming that he was as responsible as anyone for Coughlin's ultimate success. In an interview with the *San Jose Mercury News* shortly before the 2004 Olympics, Mitchell said, "We feel we developed her from nothing to a national level. It would have been nice to get a little more respect for our contributions to her success. She fixates on that last year. We get the credit for the injury, but not for the rehabilitation."

Specifically Mitchell, like many youth coaches, believes that repeated high-volume workouts at an early age establish an "aerobic base" that a swimmer can draw upon throughout his or her career. While some, including Coughlin, question the scientific basis of this theory, it inevitably is used to justify the punishing workouts teams like the Terrapins routinely endured. Pummel them early, the thinking goes, and you'll reap the dividends for years to come.

Of course, when a swimmer becomes *slower* upon reaching physical maturity, this theory is never cited.

The mere notion that Mitchell had "developed" her as an athlete irked Coughlin. *If a coach were capable of creating such a successful athlete,* she wondered, *why wouldn't there have been 10 or 15 swimmers just like me on that team? And why do these coaches take so much credit for their successes but never for their failures? When a swimmer fails, it's always his or her fault.*

In Coughlin's view, "It's always a symbiotic relationship. Obviously, athletes need their coaches for structure, support, and expertise. But it is ultimately up to the swimmer to make the right choices and put in the hard work. It's like that saying, 'You can lead a horse to water, but you can't make him drink.'"

Certainly Mitchell, like a majority of his peers, believed in intense, high-volume workouts as the most effective means of improving a swimmer's performance. Like many youth swim coaches—and, to be fair, like many coaches in all competitive sports—he favored an approach that leaned on strict discipline and aimed to control his athletes' behavior both in and out of the pool. While some members of the swimming community were opposed to such a coaching style, few could argue that many of the men and women who employed it were often achieving desirable results.

During the years Coughlin trained with Terrapins, Mitchell was in the process of making a name for himself as a coach who successfully pushed talented teenagers into the ranks of the nation's elite. His bio on the Terrapins' website proudly notes that Mitchell, who cofounded the club in 1989, was the USA Swimming developmental coach of the year in 1998, 1999, and 2003, and the Pacific coach of the year in 1998. "As the Terrapin Head Coach," his bio continues, "Ray's teams have racked up over 30 top-10 team finishes at junior and senior nationals since 1990, including national championships in 1997 and 2000. His swimmers have qualified for USA National Teams, including the Pan Pacific Games, Pan AM Games, World University Games, Short Course World Champs, National Jr. teams, Goodwill Games, World Championships, and USA National "A" and "B" teams.

Coughlin concedes that for the most part, she enjoyed swimming for Mitchell during her first 3 years with his club. She had joined at 13 and, until the end of her junior year of high school, was willing to put up with his autocratic style because of her success in the pool and, more important, the fun she was having with the other swimmers. In fact, Mitchell's authoritarian approach served as a bonding mechanism, as Coughlin and her friends would close ranks as common sufferers. They privately called their coach "Stalin" and made fun of his mannerisms and platitudes. Meanwhile, when they were able to get away from swimming, they enjoyed being *kids*. "We'd go surfing practically every Sunday, down at Linda Mar Beach in Pacifica," Coughlin recalls. "We were terrible, but we loved it."

Though Coughlin joined her friends in lampooning Mitchell as a pitiless taskmaster, her heart wasn't really in it until her senior year of high school. Early on, she'd noticed that there always seemed to be a scapegoat in his group, a swimmer he would ride extra hard, as though making an example out of him or her. *I'd hate to be that person*, Coughlin often thought to herself. As it became clear that her shoulder injury would not easily heal, and Mitchell grew more and more frustrated, it began to dawn on her: *Damn. I* am *the scapegoat.*

"In his mind," Coughlin says, looking back, "he believed that he was challenging you through a 'tough love' relationship. But I felt that it was emotionally abusive."

Coughlin's introduction to swimming had been far more frivolous, as it is for most kids. When she was 10 months old, Coughlin received her first exposure to her parents' tiny backyard pool in Vallejo, California, a working-class town 35 miles northeast of San Francisco. Her father, Jim, a Vallejo police sergeant, and mother, Zennie, a paralegal, weren't frustrated ex-athletes, and neither was especially interested in cultivating a future Olympic champion.

Coughlin took to the water like a baby seal. After Natalie thrived in summertime lessons, her parents decided that signing her up for a swim team would be less expensive. She joined the nearby Benicia Blue Dolphins and began racing in local competitions at the age of 6. Both

Coughlin girls were suitably determined—Megan hiked to the top of Oahu's Diamond Head at age 3—but Natalie's focus and drive stood out. "Natalie was always goal oriented," Jim Couglin recalls. "No matter what she did, she had to know everything about it. And when it came to swimming, whatever level she was on, she'd pick out the fastest person around and make a point of saying, 'That's the one I'm going to beat.'"

Natalie was so intense that in backstroke races, she often powered into the finish and hit her head on the wall. On a questionnaire the nationally ranked swimmer filled out for the Blue Dolphins, at age 9, one of the queries was "What are the reasons you swim on a US team?"

"The reason," Coughlin wrote, "is because I live in the United States."

Says Natalie: "I think I always had this incredibly inflated sense of self, even when it wasn't merited. There's a video of me doing this dance routine when I was a little kid, and it was awful, but watching it, you can tell I thought I was great."

Young Natalie wasn't particularly fond of swim practice but found the meets—and the culture at large—alluring. She'd get so excited about upcoming competitions that she'd insist on wearing her oversize, baggy racing suit around the house the entire day before a meet. Before leaving for the pool the next morning, Zennie would carefully French-braid her daughter's hair. Natalie would then place a cap on top, put goggles over her eyes, and strut around the house in full battle regalia.

By all measures, Jim and Zennie were exemplary parents in a sport in which perspective often vanishes. The Coughlins spent most weekends at swim meets across northern California, hanging out under pop-up tents, serving sandwiches to their daughters and other team members as endless games of hearts and go fish played out and the girls kept up with their homework. They'd do embroidery and macramé, make necklaces and bracelets out of beads—anything to pass the time between races. As Natalie recalls, "We'd be playing tag, playing cards, goofing around. You'd get so caught up in what you were doing that occasionally you'd miss your event. It was just so great being with your friends and being outside burning off energy, instead of being inside, playing video games or watching TV. I loved being active, and swimming was the only thing I was good at. I did gymnastics, ballet, tap dance; in junior high I played volleyball. I was very uncoordinated, fat, and clumsy, except when I was in the water."

As much as they enjoyed an environment they considered reasonably wholesome, Jim and Zennie recoiled at the sight of obsessive parents in their midst. "Some kids leave the sport because their parents drive them nuts," Zennie says. "I guess we were really bad 'swim parents,' because we never knew the times, and really, we still don't." Jim remembers seeing "parents running around with two or three stopwatches. We never knew anything about times. We just wanted the girls to have fun, do their best, and, if possible, win races. Other parents were always talking about this standard or that standard—and timing everything. There'd be an official clock at the meet, but parents would still be out there with their stop-watches, timing the races, talking about splits."

One day, when Natalie was older, the Coughlins hosted a party at which the guests watched her compete in a televised international meet. "She's standing on the starting blocks," Jim recalls, "and one of the dads pulls out a watch and starts timing her *off the TV.* That's when I knew things had officially gotten out of control."

Long before that, Jim and Zennie, without getting caught up in splits or rankings, had come to understand that swimming was not merely a casual activity for their firstborn. Jim remembers watching Natalie swim at a pool on Vallejo's Mare Island alongside Marines who were antiter-rorist training instructors. "Here was this 10-year-old girl, beating them," he recalls. "They were like, 'Who *is* this kid?'"

Around that time, Mitchell noticed Natalie at a local meet and began assessing her potential. He regarded her as a thrasher, a natural talent with choppy form and loads of technical problems, as well as a kid who didn't understand the first thing about racing. In that sense, she was perfect: He could refine this rough-edged jewel and turn her into a champion. Named after the Grateful Dead song "Terrapin Station," his club was hardly counterculture: Mitchell, like so many other youth coaches across the United States, wanted to produce the fastest swimmers at the youngest possible age. He was good at it, too—even before Coughlin arrived, the Terrapins had developed a reputation as one of the region's top producers of standout swimmers.

The Terrapins were based in Concord, an East Bay suburb half an hour from the Coughlins' home in Benicia (they'd relocated from nearby Vallejo)—or longer, when there was traffic. Nonetheless, in an effort to indulge their daughters' competitive desires, Jim and Zennie tolerated the twice-daily commute. Then, on August 23, 1996, Jim was driving his daughters across the crowded Benicia Bridge when a chain-reaction accident occurred. His Nissan pickup slammed into the car ahead, the fifth car in a five-car accident, and he and his daughters were violently jolted forward. Jim broke a rib and lost oxygen, while Megan smacked her head against the seat in front of her. "An ambulance came," Jim recalls, "and the two of us were sitting on the bridge, wrapped up like mummies." Jim and Megan were taken to the hospital by ambulance; Natalie was left alone on the bridge. A firefighter ended up driving her home in her father's truck, which, remarkably, was still in working order.

With Natalie about to begin her freshman year at Carondolet High in Concord—the sister school of De La Salle, which had recently set a national record with 151 consecutive football victories—the Coughlins decided enough was enough. By moving to Concord, they could get closer to Zennie's job in Oakland and send their daughters to more desirable, Catholic schools. If someone had to commute, it would be Jim. "We loved our house in Benicia," Zennie recalls, "but after the accident, we couldn't allow her to commute in that traffic every day. It was a very big financial hardship for a while, but we made it work." (Natalie remembers things differently, noting that Megan had already been attending a private school in Concord at the time of the accident and that her neighbors, who went to De La Salle and swam for Terrapins, also drove her across the bridge at times. "It's not like the only reason they moved was because of my swimming!" Natalie says, laughing.)

In any event, Natalie repaid her parents with a ferocious dedication to her craft. Told that morning swim practice began at 5:15, she took the edict more literally than her peers, who would arrive in the locker room by that time. Coughlin figured she had to be *in the pool* by then and was often the first to show at the outdoor facility on Cowell Boulevard, usually by 5 a.m. "The water heater would always break, which was brutal, because in the winter it would be like 30 degrees in the mornings," she remembers. "There'd be tarps covering the pool, and I'd have to unroll them onto this big wheel. Then I'd run in and get into my suit and run into this little shed about 15 yards from the pool and sit under this heater." One by one, her teammates would join her until, en masse, they would bolt from the shed and jump into the water, screaming as they leaped, trying to swat the plastic flags high above the lane lines.

Coughlin stood out so much among the younger Terrapins that the summer before starting high school, she was moved up to Mitchell's "senior group," where she often outraced older boys in a variety of strokes and distances. At 15, she became the first US swimmer to qualify for all 14 events at US Nationals and the first-ever sophomore to be named national swimmer of the year. Mitchell had a full-fledged wunderkind on his hands, and he knew it. This was an opportunity to vault himself and his program to national prominence, and he was not about to blow it.

So Mitchell, already an overbearing autocrat—"Sometimes he'd put down another coach by saying, 'He doesn't have control of his swimmer,'" Jim Coughlin recalls—cracked down even harder on Natalie. "I'd say we all got it pretty bad, but it was different for Nat," Leah Monroe recalls. "She was at a new level Ray had never dealt with before. Ray's going to put more of himself into his fastest swimmers; he was going to invest as much as he could in her success."

To say Mitchell was demanding would be like calling the Pacific Ocean big. Jim Coughlin still laughs at the memory of a vacation to Kauai the family took when Natalie was 13—each morning they'd have to find a pool, then go to a hotel with a fax machine so that he could send copies of Natalie's workout sets and corresponding times to Mitchell. "He didn't want her to go on vacations, period," Jim says.

Natalie Coughlin and her fellow Terrapins did get to travel to competitions, where Mitchell and his assistants kept a watchful eye. "Most of us were closer with our swimming friends than with our high school friends," Monroe says. "We were all very social. Ray would say to us, 'You need to forget about your social life and your high school friends and not go to parties on weekends.' At away meets, he would give us curfews; otherwise, we'd hang out and talk all night and do the things teenagers do. He couldn't keep us from sneaking out of our rooms and hanging out together, but he'd try. He would stand outside the hallway forever and threaten us: 'If anyone comes out of your room, I'll send you home.'"

To Mitchell, everything came down to focus. He lived, ate, and breathed swimming, and he wanted his charges to do likewise. "Ray would tell stories of swimmers who would lie in bed at night and visualize their races," Jim Coughlin recalls. "Natalie was like, 'Uh, okay.' That just wasn't her; she was good at compartmentalizing." Mitchell wasn't. To him, having diverse interests meant swimming for your high school team in the spring, as well as for his team. Even then, Jim says, "after every race, a Terrapins swimmer would have to leave their (high school) teammates and go up into the stands and check with him. He'd sit up there in the stands receiving them, like the godfather of swimming." This wasn't especially unusual—swimmers such as Natalie Coughlin weren't instructed by their high school coaches on a daily basis—but to observers there was little doubt as to who was in charge.

The kids he coached had another nickname for Mitchell: the Devil. Incur his wrath, and risk public humiliation and physical exhaustion. Monroe says Mitchell once punished a pair of male swimmers, Quinn Fitzgerald and Ben Hanley, who, she recalls, "had missed a set during morning workout or something. The next workout after that, he put them in a different lane from the rest of the team and told them to swim freestyle as hard as they could until he told them to stop. This lasted 3½ hours—it was like 13,000 or 14,000 meters—until finally Ray left and had someone else stop them." While that might be the most extreme example, Monroe says the concept of extra swimming was an established one. "He'd make you swim a certain time—say, three 200 breaststrokes at 2:25 apiece—and if you didn't hit the time, you—and sometimes the whole group—would have to keep swimming. One time, he made me swim 20 of those."

That was hardly Monroe's worst memory of her time with the Terrapins. When she was 14, shortly after she'd been moved up to the senior group (inheriting Coughlin's status as its youngest member), she had a particularly slow practice, during which Mitchell abruptly told her to exit the water. She remembers being berated and starting to cry. "We had these motivational posters at the end of each lane, pressed up against the gutters, that we were supposed to read after our sets," she says. "He made me go from lane to lane, reading each one aloud." Monroe cried even harder as she moved from poster to poster, all the while interrupting her fellow swimmers, none of whom had any idea what she was doing in their lane.

Some of Mitchell's disciplinary measures took place in full view of parents, which led to some awkward situations. "One time my dad heard Ray yelling at me after a meet and went over and confronted him," Monroe says. "He told me later he wished he had thrown Ray into the pool; that's how mad he was. It was some throwaway meet, and Ray had put me in with a 10-year-old group because I'd been sick, and he didn't like the way I was swimming. My dad heard him cussing me out and went over and confronted him. It was weird: Ray completely backed down and told him, 'I didn't mean for it to sound that way.'"

Jim Coughlin had a similar reaction to one of Mitchell's tirades—but his daughter kept him from going off on the coach. "Natalie's the one who really put me in my place," Jim Coughlin recalls. "It was at the Santa Clara meet in '96 (when Natalie was 13); Natalie and another swimmer did not swim to Ray's satisfaction, and he pulled them aside and started yelling, 'You guys aren't taking this seriously; I can tell by your times.' I was about ready to rip him right out of his shoes—*You get them upset and I'll get you upset*—but Natalie said, 'Dad, this is my battle. Don't fight it for me.'"

For the most part, parents gave Mitchell the leeway to discipline their children because they were so pleased with the results. "Parents knew what was going on, but they were okay with it because of how fast we were swimming," Monroe says. "I was extremely happy swimming under Ray. He was a tough, authoritarian-style coach, but I was able to respond to that. I know I wouldn't have swum nearly as fast under a different coach."

Looking back, however, the Coughlins aren't so sure they should have subjected their daughters to such an environment. As Natalie blossomed into womanhood, Mitchell became increasingly scrutinizing of her behavior. "He had a hard time realizing that she was growing up," Zennie Coughlin says. "He never really treated her as an adult." Adds Jim: "As Natalie she progressed, he wanted to keep control of her. Even as she got older, he treated her like she was 13; he wanted to know where she went in her free time and what time she went to bed."

Around the time she turned 16, Coughlin began dating Ethan Hall, a tall, quiet Terrapins breaststroker who was 3 years older. Coughlin had developed a crush on Hall years earlier, and the two had become fast friends. For a while, he seemed like the surer bet to make an Olympic team—in 1995 he set a US national age-group (15 and 16) record in the 200-meter breaststroke. But a series of knee injuries kept Hall from achieving greater glory, though he never stopped fighting. Coughlin remembers marveling at Hall's competitive drive as he attempted to fight through the pain. "He would work so hard," she recalls, "that he would vomit during a lot of the practices."

By Coughlin's sophomore year, Hall had accepted a swimming scholarship to the University of North Carolina, but after his sophomore season he decided to return to the West Coast and made plans to transfer to University of California, Santa Barbara. During Coughlin's senior season of high school, he was back home in the Bay Area, training with the Terrapins, and he and Coughlin grew closer.

"He was really what got me through that horrible year," she says. "He was someone I could talk to about what I was going through. He'd been through injuries; he knew about the environment at Terrapins. Plus, he's such a mellow person. He's really goofy and funny and incredibly smart.

If he wasn't there, I definitely would've moved to another club, in Orinda or Walnut Creek. But because of him I stayed."

Mitchell, naturally, viewed the relationship as a threat to Coughlin's focus. Monroe remembers that about the time Coughlin and Hall started dating, Mitchell took a group of Terrapins on a swing through Europe that included several World Cup meets. "We were at a meet in Paris, and after one of my races I went up into the stands and had my 'personal talk' with Ray," Monroe says. "He was angry about the race, and he said, 'You aren't swimming well right now because of the mental problems you're having.' When I got back over to the team, Natalie asked me how the talk had gone, and when I told her, she started cheering and said, 'Me, too! That's exactly what he said to me—that I have mental problems.' We both thought it was complete b.s."

Once, during a meet in Washington, Mitchell and an assistant called Coughlin and Hall into a room inside the pool complex and dressed them down. "You two are in your own little bubble," Mitchell charged, "and it's making you uncoachable."

The struggle to control a young swimmer's private life—especially a young, female swimmer's—was by no means a unique one. In the eyes of Milt Nelms, the Australia-based stroke consultant who worked extensively with Coughlin during the months before the 2004 Olympics, "A lot of (youth-club) coaches are kind of in a state of arrested adolescence, so they're basically dealing with their own peer group." (I would encounter this phenomenon during the 2004 Olympic Trials in Long Beach, California. One night after the competition, I found myself at a crowded restaurant table, discussing Coughlin's career with a group that included a veteran youth-club coach from Southern California. The coach, with a tone of utmost certainty, declared, "It's impossible for a young woman to be an elite swimmer and have a romantic relationship at that age—she's just not capable of balancing the two." When I noted that Coughlin, who had just qualified for the Olympic team by winning the 100 back, was still together with Hall, the conversation took an irrevocable turn for the worse.)

~

The boyfriend was one thing. But when Coughlin suffered a serious shoulder injury in March 1999, suddenly imperiling her seemingly preordained path to the 2000 Olympics, it seemed Mitchell really became concerned.

Injuries, in general, are frowned upon in elite swimming circles. Coaches encourage their ailing athletes to "swim through it" whenever possible, and those who can't either end up quitting the sport or being labeled as malingerers. Monroe remembers a frequently injured Terrapins breaststroker, Maggie Konstantinova, getting berated by Mitchell whenever she couldn't swim. "Ray would accuse her of being a hypochondriac," Monroe says. "He'd say, 'Oh, Maggie, you're always injured, always sick. There's something always wrong.' In her defense, she really did get hurt a lot."

At first, there was no disputing the severity of Coughlin's injury. After completing a typically intense butterfly set toward the end of an afternoon workout, Coughlin went home assuming everything was fine. That night she was awakened by a throbbing pain in her left shoulder that brought her to tears. The next morning she tried to suck it up and swim, but as she tried to remove the pool cover, she realized she couldn't move her arm. She had torn the labrum, a cartilage rim around the shoulder joint, and was told she needed surgery.

Coughlin was hesitant to have the operation, especially after having spoken to some older, high-profile swimmers who'd had similar injuries. They told her she would be facing an extended rehab, her range of motion would suffer, and there was no guarantee it would prove a permanent solution to the problem. The other option was physical therapy, and Coughlin was referred to one of the best therapists in the business: Lisa Giannone of ActiveCare, a San Francisco clinic that had extensive experience with prominent athletes. While playing for the 49ers, future Hall of Fame receiver Jerry Rice had, with Giannone's help, returned to the football field a mere 3 months after surgery to repair a torn anterior cruciate ligament. He was just one of Giannone's well-known success stories, and Coughlin began a program that emphasized resistance exercises to strengthen her back and other surrounding muscles.

Mitchell, to his credit, accompanied Coughlin to all of her doctor's appointments. But, she recalls, "the doctor would say one thing—'You need to rest the shoulder for a month' or 'You're risking future damage'—and Ray would walk out of the room and say I could swim through it. I'd be like, '*What?* You were *there*.'" Mostly, Coughlin tried to swim through the injury—and attend high school classes and make 1½-hour round-trip drives to San Francisco for physical therapy three times a week. Often, in an effort to rest the shoulder, she'd grab a kickboard and do nothing but leg work in the slow lane for the duration of practice. That would later prove to be a blessing, as she further developed the already tremendous dolphin kick that made her an underwater dynamo in the backstroke. But at the time, her failure to overcome the pain—and, when timed, to approach her old form—tormented her impatient coach.

"You worked harder when you were 13!" Mitchell would bark from the deck. He began to view her injury and her relationship with Hall as one and the same—both symptomatic of Coughlin's lack of focus, a theory he'd broadcast to her and anyone in listening range. As 1999 bled into 2000 and that summer's Olympic Trials neared, Mitchell became convinced that Hall stood between Coughlin and a spot on the US team. "For Ray it came to a point around the Trials where he felt, 'Ethan is your boyfriend, but he's getting in the way,'" Monroe says. "He wanted to get her boyfriend out of the way because he felt it was a distraction."

Finally, Mitchell flat out urged Coughlin to end the relationship. "Just until Trials," he implored her. "Take a 6-month break so you can focus on making the Olympics, and then if you want to get back together, fine."

By then, however, Hall was about the only person Coughlin trusted. She was still steamed at her parents in the wake of the protracted battle they'd waged over where she'd attend college the next fall. Jim and Zennie had insisted she sign with Stanford, but Natalie prevailed and accepted a scholarship to swim for McKeever at Cal. Even then, she viewed college swimming merely as a vehicle to get a free ride to the school of her choice. She began to detest the sport she'd once loved. She feared, with legitimate reason, that she had become yet another promising talent who'd reached a premature plateau and, after suffering a setback, could never come near that level again.

Mentally and emotionally, she was a mess. As Trials approached, Coughlin, like most of Mitchell's swimmers, was being monitored constantly—lactose readings, blood tests, heart rates, and the like. At one point, she recalls, she was tested for cortisol, a hormone released in the body during stressed or agitated states. The range that USA Swimming considered normal was between 8 and 20; Coughlin's measured 60.

Just a few more months, Coughlin told herself. *After that, I will never swim again.*

By the time she flew to Indianapolis for the Olympic Trials, she either had let go of the pressure inside or, perhaps, simply couldn't feel it anymore. She felt indifferent about her prospects for making the Olympic team in the lone event she entered, the 200-meter individual medley. She qualified for the finals and, to her surprise, felt reasonably strong as the race played out. Swimming from an outside line by virtue of her slower time in the preliminaries, Coughlin touched the wall believing she'd snuck onto the team as the second-place finisher. When she looked up and realized she'd finished fourth, she felt a surge of disappointment. *Whoa, I did care.*

About an hour later, that feeling was gone. She was okay with not having made the Olympic team; given what she'd been through the past 15 months, she could take pride in how close she'd come. In a matter of days, she would move to Berkeley, live in a dorm like any other student, and, for the first time in a long time, swim for someone other than a coach who seemed to resent her for her failure. "When she didn't make the Olympics, I think Ray took that very badly," Monroe says. "It was almost as if she'd let him down. I think he had such high expectations, and when it didn't happen, he was hurt more than anything. I can see how he took a lot of it out on her."

Looking back, Coughlin deeply resents the way she was treated by

Mitchell and understands why she wanted so desperately to replace him with McKeever. "I was ready to get away from my coach, who I believe was emotionally abusive and manipulative—a man who wanted to control every aspect of my life," she says. "Teri was the most easygoing and honest college coach I encountered, and she seemed to care more about her swimmers as people than other coaches did."

Certainly, Coughlin treasures her better moments and positive memories of the Terrapins. But once she hurt her shoulder and stopped shining in the pool, she experienced the dark side of competitive swimming on the youth-club level. "Ray has been quoted as saying that I have a tendency to fixate on that last year," she says, "and that's absolutely true. That last year was such a betrayal to me—and to all the work, time, and emotional effort that I had put in over 5 years."

CHAPTER FOUR

THE HARD SELL

J im Coughlin could smell a brown-noser from a mile away, no matter how prevalent the whiff of chlorine. As a Vallejo police detective, his job was to interview suspects and determine whether they were dangerous criminals, innocent incidentals, or something in between. In doing so, he had come to learn the cues, body language, and instinctual stench of disingenuousness. Now, he suspected, a man purporting to have his daughter's best interests at heart was feeding him a load of crap, and nothing could have irked him more.

Mike Walker, Jim decided, was full of it, and there was no way he'd consent to entrusting a guy like that with something as important as Natalie's future.

Walker might have been able to charm most people he encountered, but Jim Coughlin wasn't one of them. As McKeever's co–head coach—and Cal's self-described recruiting specialist—Walker had been the dominant presence during the coaches' interactions with the family, and Jim understandably wondered whether McKeever was a mere figurehead. On a Saturday afternoon in the fall of 1999, during lunch at a Berkeley café called Julie's, Jim made a point of asking McKeever a direct question, and when she opened her mouth to answer, Walker cut her off and provided the response. This happened a second time, and upon hearing Walker's reply, Coughlin felt he was being conned. Every time Coughlin would make a point or express an opinion, Walker would enthusiastically agree.

An hour later, as the group sat together in Memorial Stadium during a Cal football game, Jim finally snapped, telling Walker, "Why don't you stop kissing my ass for a second and tell me what you really think, instead of what you think I want to hear?" It was an uncomfortable moment for everyone, especially McKeever, whose self-esteem was somewhere at the bottom of Spieker Pool.

McKeever was at a crisis point, personally and professionally, when she entered the recruiting derby for the young woman who would ultimately facilitate her dramatic coaching breakthrough. Something about Coughlin—the degree to which she'd been wounded by her experience with the Terrapins, the mature manner in which she carried herself—told McKeever they belonged together. Similarly, Coughlin had an almost intuitive feeling that this socially awkward yet well-meaning woman was exactly the person she needed to rekindle her enthusiasm for swimming. Had the two of them been left to their own devices, they would have sealed the deal and commenced the mutual healing process. But the presence of a slick co–head coach, a distrusting father, and a worried mother made this a tricky proposition.

"When we dealt with Cal, Mike Walker did most of the talking," Jim Coughlin recalls. "We didn't really get to know Teri at all. He was the reason I didn't feel comfortable about Berkeley. My attitude was 'I am *not* turning our daughter over to him.'"

McKeever knew none of this at the time. By her estimation, she was more anxious talking to Natalie than the teenage recruit was talking to her. But even before Coughlin told her later that fall that she wanted to come to Cal—and before having to sweat out the next 6 weeks as Natalie and her parents clashed over whether she would actually sign a letter of intent—McKeever had gained something from the process.

That day at Julie's, as Walker cut her off and talked right over her before she could answer Jim Coughlin, McKeever finally made a decision that had been more than a year in the works: to stand up to Walker and have the courage to become the coach she'd always wanted to be. Watching the entitled look on her cocoach's face as he stepped on her yet again, McKeever very nearly lost control. She almost started screaming at him, then thought better of it. Instead, she glared at Walker with a look that said, *You will never do this to me again.*

Parting ways with Walker wasn't so simple, however. His big personality, dripping with charisma and bravado, activated McKeever's fears about everything she wasn't. She was introverted and awkward around crowds; Walker was popular and funny. Yet she also regarded him as passive-aggressive, a man who knew exactly how to push her buttons, usually when she felt the most vulnerable. In McKeever's words, "As Mike got bigger, I got smaller."

McKeever had come to Cal in 1992, during a down period for a program that had finished as high as fourth nationally—a total of seven times in 14 years—under Karen Moe Thornton. McKeever's first Cal team finished 15th at the '93 NCAAs, then sank as low as 28th 2 years later. Walker, at the time he came aboard as an assistant in 1995, had been an ambitious 26-year-old who, like McKeever, had set his sights much higher than reentering the top 20. McKeever was aware that her coaching ability was viewed as suspect by some—"A lot of people thought I only got hired because I was a woman, that I'd never get it done at Cal," she says—and made it her mission to prove them wrong. "When I get us into the top 10," McKeever used to say to Walker, "I'm gonna tell everyone to (screw) off, and then I'm gonna leave."

But the Bears finished ninth in 1997 and fifth in '99, the first time any program had gone from being unranked to finishing in the top five in 6 short years—and McKeever stuck around. Walker grew frustrated, and in an effort to placate him, McKeever agreed to make him the co-head coach (a nominal designation of equality, if not an entirely accurate one) in May 1997. That confirmed the suspicions of many outsiders who believed Walker was the true architect behind the Bears' revival. In her more vulnerable moments, McKeever wondered, too: Despite her prior success at Fresno State, she would occasionally question whether her unconventional coaching philosophy could succeed at an upper-echelon program without Walker's more traditional techniques to augment it. That was what stopped her from initiating a breakup on the spot as he kept her from answering Jim Coughlin's questions.

"I was personally afraid that without him, it would all fall apart," McKeever says. "My self-esteem was so low, I believed that I couldn't be me and be successful. Mike wanted to control every piece of the operation, and what had once been a good situation evolved into something dark and ugly."

Low self-esteem wasn't McKeever's only issue. She was suffering from panic and anxiety attacks, as well as depression. She was, in her words, "pretty much of a mess."

A few months earlier, McKeever had turned to Kathie Wickstrand. The two had been friends since early in McKeever's tenure at Cal, when one day she picked up her office phone and, out of the blue, dialed Wickstrand's number. Though the two had been acquainted only casually to that point, what followed was, in Wickstrand's words, "a really powerful conversation" that ended with a proposition. "I'm part of this international organization that does these experimental workshops for women, designed to empower us," Wickstrand told McKeever. "We're having one a few weekends from now in Lake Delevan, Wisconsin. Why don't you come out?"

There was a short pause before McKeever answered, "Okay." She got on a plane, bonded with Wickstrand, and began a long journey toward self-realization.

Five years later, McKeever became the first person to hire Wickstrand, who later took the married name Wickstrand-Gahen, as a life coach. Her major professional issue was her strained relationship with Walker, but she learned a valuable lesson in the process. "If you have stress and anxiety in your life," McKeever says now, "don't blame other people—work on yourself. This is the message, after all, that I'm trying to give to my athletes."

Wickstrand-Gahen's initial strategy was to try to repair McKeever's relationship with Walker—she met with the two individually and together and tried to improve the dynamic before ultimately viewing it as irrevocably fractured. "I basically just loved her for like a year," Wickstrand-Gahen says. "It took her about 2 years to get the courage and strength to get rid of him. She had given him too much power."

McKeever's friend Dave Salo, whose Irvine Novaquatics club is one of the nation's most successful, concedes that "Teri was scared to hell at the prospect of getting Natalie. Her confidence wasn't there, and that's partly because of the way the situation was up there. Mike Walker had a way of manipulating Teri, of preying on her lack of confidence. He's the same way as a recruiter. He finds that weakness and uses it to get you to like him."

That was the idea, at least. Even after that uncomfortable exchange with Jim Coughlin at the stadium, even as Coughlin dug in with all his might to prevent his daughter from swimming at Cal, the co–head coach kept telling McKeever he had the family sold.

In October, Natalie called McKeever and told her, "I'm coming to Cal." But McKeever could hardly celebrate, as there were still 6 weeks until national signing day. Those would turn out to be the longest 6 weeks of McKeever's career. It got to the point where the coach was hesitant to call the Coughlin household; she instinctively sensed that Jim and Zennie were not on her side. Instead, she called Ray Mitchell to pick his brain. Sure enough, the Terrapins coach confirmed her suspicions that Coughlin's parents had serious reservations about Natalie's coming to Cal and were trying to change her mind. Then, referring to Walker, Mitchell told her, "The dad wants to know which one of you is calling the shots."

That's it, McKeever thought to herself. *Whether Natalie comes here or not, something has to change.*

≈

Nearly 4 years later, on a Saturday evening in late September, Coughlin is practically skipping up Berkeley's fantastic Telegraph Avenue with a group of teammates and several wide-eyed recruits in tow. "SC Sucks!" Coughlin jubilantly screams to each group of red-and-gold-clad visitors she encounters. The Golden Bears have just pulled off the biggest upset of the 2003 college football season, a 34–31 victory over the eventual national champion University of Southern California Trojans in triple overtime, and one of the greatest athletes in the university's esteemed history is, like thousands of other students in her midst, enjoying the hell out of being a rowdy college kid.

"It's gonna be a lo-o-o-ng trip home!" Coughlin informs any SC fan within earshot. "Hope you had a pleasant stay."

The high school swimmers tagging along can scarcely believe what they're hearing. Some recruits on official visits have been so timid around Coughlin that they were barely able to speak; others have asked for her autograph. These girls are grateful to see this superstar swimmer acting, well, *human*.

As meticulously planned as McKeever's recruiting weekends are, this kind of spontaneous revelry is totally off the script. It's a big weekend, too—one of the recruits, Southern California backstroker Diana MacManus, is a major talent who McKeever believes could help ease the pain of Coughlin's departure. The other five visitors, especially backstroker/sprint freestyler Brooke Bishop, have plenty of potential as well. Inevitably, when Coughlin is not around, each recruit puts the same question to the other Cal swimmers: Does Natalie get special treatment?

"No, not at all," they reply—although most of them believe that actually she does.

Yet there is no denying Coughlin's star power—and, as a bonus, most recruits leave Berkeley surprised by how down-to-earth she is. But the chance to rub elbows with a future Olympian isn't the only thing going for Cal. McKeever highlights the university's esteemed academic reputation, noting that UC Berkeley is the nation's top-ranked public school (in 2004, the *Times* (London) would rank it second in the *world*, behind only Harvard). She extols the virtues of a vibrant, diverse campus that's just across the bay from San Francisco. Most of all, she presents a team that is close-knit and united in its dual-edged purpose—to push the program to even greater heights while enjoying the journey.

If nothing else, recruits who visit Cal are sure to be blown away by the precisely planned weekends. Once sheepish about her natural inclination to organize and map out itineraries—these were traditionally thought to be skills better handled by an assistant coach—McKeever, in the years since Walker's departure, learned to embrace these strengths. Her attention to detail sets her apart from most of her peers.

Each Cal swimmer has a key responsibility toward ensuring that the recruiting weekend is a success. In an e-mail to the team that October, McKeever included a comprehensive schedule for the upcoming weekend's visitors, one of whom potentially was a huge prize: Seattle-area sprint freestyler Emily Silver, whose older sister, Helen, was a standout sophomore backstroker for the Bears. In theory, signing Emily should have been a slam dunk, but the situation was more complicated than it appeared. For one thing, though Helen had been a typical McKeever late bloomer, exceeding all projections with an impressive freshman campaign, she had also drawn her coach's ire at times. Plus, McKeever had to consider the possibility that her fervent wooing of Emily might rankle Helen. Emily, at least in theory, had a chance to be even more of a star than her older sister; would this cause tension in the family, or, more important, could it disrupt the team dynamic?

In any event, with Emily and four other swimmers—Anna Miller, Caitlyn Short, Emily Verdin, and Sherry Tsai—set to arrive the following Thursday afternoon, McKeever was determined to provide a weekend packed with activities and information. The itinerary was painstakingly meticulous, basically accounting for each recruit's whereabouts at all times. Some highlights:

Thursday, October 23, 2003

4:45 p.m. Whitney picks up 15-passenger van at Enterprise.

5:30 p.m. Teri w/Nat C. and Micha to check in and decorate at Doubletree Berkeley Marina.

9:40 p.m. Caitlyn arrives on Southwest #2336 from Portland—Teri picks up.

10:08 p.m. Anna arrives on United #481 from Knoxville (Chicago)—Teri picks up.

10:41 p.m. Emily Silver arrives on Southwest #476 from Seattle—Whitney picks up.

11:30 p.m. Emily Verdin arrives on JetBlue #319 from Washington/Dulles—Whitney picks up. Caitlyn Short with Anna Miller; Emily Silver with Emily Verdin.

Friday, October 24, 2003

7:00 a.m. Rise and shine, get ready for a great day.

7:45 a.m. Whitney picks up all four recruits at Doubletree for breakfast; will leave bags in van.

8:00 a.m. Breakfast at New Dining Commons with Teri, Whitney, freshmen, plus Lisa, Amy, Kate, Helen.

8:50 a.m. (Anna Miller/Emily Silver) Depart with Whitney and Kelly for meeting w/Professor Sanchez at Barrows.

8:50 a.m. (Emily Verdin) Walks back to office to meet with Teri.

8:50 a.m. (Caitlyn Short) Annie/Catherine meets at DC to walk to business class at Wheeler.

12:00 noon (Emily Silver) Annie walks from class at Mulford to lunch at Bear's Lair.

12:05 p.m. Lunch for everyone that does not have class at Bear's Lair. Amy and Lisa will buy sandwiches at Cheese 'n' Stuff (10 sandwiches/chips/drinks). Plan to stay until 1 p.m. or until Whitney arrives.

3:30 p.m. Time to return to hostess or they can go for a swim: Anna w/Lisa and Emma; Caitlyn w/Kelly; Em Silver w/Erin and Catherine; Em Verdin w/Lauren and Amy.

6:30 p.m. Pizza party and dinner at Teri's.

7:30 p.m. Trip to the City for ice cream, etc. (Gina, Ashley, Marcelle, Helen, Cheryl, Kelly).

And so it went, from the Cal football game against Arizona on Saturday afternoon through that night's plans, with seven swimmers designated as "social" hostesses and one in charge of any recruits who might prefer "quiet" time. Beginning at 5 a.m. Sunday, McKeever would make the first of three separate trips to the Oakland airport and accompany each recruit to the security line.

As far as Emily Silver and her parents could tell, McKeever seemed genuinely interested in offering her at least a partial scholarship. At the time, they had no idea how badly the coach wanted her to come to Cal. "This girl is good," McKeever said shortly after Emily's visit concluded. "But if we can get her here, she has a chance to become *really* good. I just hope she enjoyed herself, because I would love to coach her."

Coughlin remembers when she was the one being wooed. It felt strange to be so wanted, because her shoulder injury had sapped both her confidence and her love for the sport. Beaten down by her battles with Ray Mitchell, she saw swimming merely as a vehicle to get her to the college of her choice. Maybe she'd stay with the team for a year or two; perhaps, if things didn't improve, she'd take the money and run. At that point, she didn't trust many people, so she didn't know what to make of the excitement that her visits to Cal, Stanford, and UCLA were generating among the coaches in question.

Despite the fragility of her shoulder, Coughlin had been regarded as a prize recruit. Her uncanny versatility and short-course excellence made her highly desirable. "Even if she were to swim the same times she was swimming with the bad shoulder and not improve, she'd have been one of the nation's top three swimmers in everything," McKeever says. "Plus, getting a swimmer that talented would give credibility to the program."

Coughlin knew two things: She wanted to go to school in California, and she wanted to swim for someone as dissimilar to Mitchell as possible. She took a trip to UCLA and liked coach Cyndi Gallagher, but she didn't feel as though she fit in well with the team. That left Cal and Stanford, the two Bay Area rivals and academic giants. Whereas the Bears were in the process of reemerging as a legitimate national player, the Cardinal boasted the preeminent women's program in the country.

Stanford's coach, Richard Quick, was the biggest name in the business. In 1998 he had won his sixth NCAA title in 7 years, and seventh overall since he'd come to Palo Alto a decade earlier. He had taken the Stanford job immediately after having won five consecutive national championships at Texas. From the time he'd taken the Texas job in 1982, he would complete an incredible 2-decade stretch in which each of his teams would finish in the top three.

While recruiting Coughlin, Quick had already been selected as the US women's head coach for the 2000 Olympics, the third time he'd received that honor since the Seoul Games in 1988. He had also beem the men's head coach in Seoul and an assistant in '84 and '92. Recruiting wasn't difficult for this hyperintense 56-year-old—he simply went after the biggest names in swimming (Jenny Thompson, Janet Evans, Summer Sanders) and got most of them, filling out his roster with a stable of high school all-Americans and former national champions.

Quick wanted Coughlin and figured he'd get her. Unlike McKeever, he was a man who lived, ate, and breathed swimming and wasn't particularly concerned with the nooks and crannies of a successful recruiting weekend. When Natalie visited Stanford, Jim Coughlin recalls, "Richard's attitude was 'What you see is what you get. I am the best; this is the best place to swim; this is the best school.' Whereas Teri looked at the entire person and tried to give them an idea of what it would be like to be living at Cal and attending school there, Richard didn't bother with specifics. He'd say, 'This is a great campus. People make a lot of money who go here. We are the best.' But when it came to how she'd spend her time on the visit, Richard didn't have a plan."

Among the other reasons Coughlin blanched at signing with Stanford: She was tired of being told what to do, and she had a natural affinity for the underdog. Quick, she knew, would push her, and he would favor a more traditional approach to training. That's not to say that he was an old-school thinker; he was more like an old-world faith healer, constantly searching for the miracle potion or training technique.

Coughlin was fond of Quick and respected his coaching ability immensely. But his intensity made her uncomfortable, and it certainly worked to McKeever's advantage that she was a comparatively nonaggressive woman. "It's like the superstrict parents who won't let you go out—their kids turn out to be the most rebellious," Coughlin explains. "Teri is easygoing and honest and trusts her swimmers to prepare themselves, rather than having to micromanage their behavior. That's why I work so well for her."

"Natalie liked Richard," Jim Coughlin says. "But she had come from a male coach who acted like, 'Whatever I say is right, and whatever you have to say, keep it to yourself.' Teri is someone who, as she coaches you, wants to hear your opinion. She might try to get you to change it, but she still wants to hear your perspective."

That was the backdrop under which Coughlin evaluated her choices and, with conviction, decided to go to Cal. She called McKeever to give her the news, then told her parents—and that's when the fireworks began. During the 6 weeks between the phone call and the day she could officially sign her letter of intent, Coughlin's parents argued stridently that she was making the wrong choice. Part of Jim's opposition, to be sure, was his distaste for Mike Walker, but there were other forces at work.

"Both Jim and I got our 4-year degrees long after we had started working, so neither of us had experienced a classic college experience," Zennie says. "Natalie would tell us, 'You don't know what you're talking about,' and I guess in a sense we didn't. We did look at the financial aspects of it and think that Stanford was a better deal. At Cal, you're on your own after the first year in terms of housing, whereas at Stanford you can stay in the dorms. I was thinking, 'My poor daughter is going to have to cook for herself'—which is funny now, because she cooks gourmet meals all the time. But that whole college selection process was so stressful. She hated us."

Says Jim: "Oh, God, she hated us. That whole situation was really ugly, and it took about 2 years for us to live it down. As a parent, you always want the best for your daughter, and Cal's dorms certainly weren't the best—plus, you'd be on your own after your freshman year."

None of this resonated with Natalie, who became enraged when her parents took the financial argument to its next conclusion: Stanford, a top-of-the-line private school, cost far more to attend than Cal, a first-

rate public university that was a comparative bargain for California re
dents. Thus, the Coughlins reasoned, a full scholarship to Stanford was
worth far more than a full ride to Cal. "That's crazy!" Natalie shrieked.
"A full ride is a full ride, and Cal is a better school!"

McKeever was mostly oblivious to the conflict that was going on.
She had her own issues—the impending professional breakup with
Walker; coaching a senior-heavy team that 6 months later would produce
a fourth-place finish at the NCAAs, the school's best in 9 years; and
anxiety and depression that had reached a crisis point.

"It was, on paper, the high point of my coaching career," McKeever
says, "and it was one of the lowest points in my life. We had finished fifth
in '99 and came in fourth in 2000. We had Marylyn Chiang, who was the
Pac-10 Swimmer of the Year; we had Elli Overton, a three-time
Olympian, and a bunch of other swimmers (Joscelin Yeo, Waen
Minpraphal, Staciana Stitts) who ended up making the 2000 Olympic
team. Yet I made the mistake of letting somebody tell me I was a bad
coach—and then actually believing him.

"I really, honestly believe it was my turning point in life. Only in the
last couple of years have I finally been able to look in the mirror and
really like the person I see. So if you look at it that way, I'm glad I went
through it, because I would not be who I am today if I hadn't."

When McKeever told Walker she wanted to break up the partnership, they agreed that their public spin would be that he wanted to seek
a head-coaching opportunity. The irony was that Walker suggested to
McKeever that she delay an announcement because "I think I can get
Natalie. If she knows I'm leaving, you might lose her." Mistaken as
Walker's premise may have been, many coaches might have been tempted
to follow his recommendation with so much on the line. Not McKeever.
"If we lose her, we lose her," McKeever told him. "I'm not going to mis-
represent my program just to get her here; then, when she finds out you
were leaving the whole time, what's she gonna think?"

It was the right call for several reasons, and not at all a surprising one
to the people who know McKeever best. "Teri is someone who follows
the rules to a T," Kathie Wickstrand-Gahen says. "There's a right way to

do things and a wrong way, period. She's someone who's never going to jaywalk. Natalie, incidentally, is the same way."

When it comes to wooing athletes, McKeever makes a point of playing up her program's virtues without degrading the competition. "Teri simply won't engage in negative recruiting, and I think it hurts her," sophomore breaststroker Gina Merlone said in October 2003. "The thing is, every other coach is out there doing it to her, and we all wish she'd fight back, but she's just not that kind of person. So we probably end up losing out on a lot of talented athletes."

It's not as if McKeever doesn't know that some of her foes out there are bad-mouthing her: Even after Coughlin signed with Cal, McKeever assumed the skeptics were giving it an insidious spin: "I'm sure there were people who thought, 'She went there because it's not as serious as Stanford. She picked that because her swimming isn't as important to her anymore.'"

Of course, Coughlin knew exactly what she was doing. Many people close to her believe that had she gone to Stanford, the scarred swimmer would have quit by Christmas of her freshman year—not because Quick's program isn't exceptional but because it wouldn't have allowed her to rediscover her love for the sport. "The truth is, she didn't care that much about how good a coach I was," McKeever insists. "She wanted to be in an environment where she was going to be respected, where she could have a voice, and that was the most important piece for her. And I'll bet I turned out to be a better coach than she expected."

∾

It's just before midnight on a cloudy Sunday night in early October, 2003, and McKeever, the 2002 American Swimming Coaches Association Coach of the Year, is putting the final touches on the upcoming weekend's recruiting itinerary. "Who else is gonna do it?" McKeever asks rhetorically. While many of the nation's top swimming programs have a secretary or an administrator assigned to such tasks, McKeever serves as her own executive assistant.

"I can tell it's October," she muses, "because I've had four breakdowns in the last few days." She's referring not to her own emotional ebbs but those of four of her swimmers. "Two are breaking up with their boyfriends—and one has *two* boyfriends. And yesterday I kicked a girl out of practice, and now she's disappeared on me. She said, 'I'm not feeling well.' I'm like, 'Yeah, I don't feel good, either.' I didn't take enough psychology classes for this."

The next afternoon McKeever, a tall woman with curly dirty-blond hair, has bags under her eyes and looks like she could use about three espresso shots. She's sitting in the same chair in the same office in which she spent much of the previous night. "Are you okay?" asks Coughlin, who has been telling her coach about the condominium she's about to purchase in nearby Emeryville, a couple of blocks from the eastern edge of San Francisco Bay. "You look tired."

"I *am* tired," McKeever says. "I know you are, too."

As thrilled as she is to have Coughlin back for another season, McKeever has also paid a price for the swimmer's decision to remain an amateur. With Coughlin not allowed to hire an agent, McKeever dutifully fills the role, doing everything from setting up magazine photo shoots to handling travel plans for award-presentation dinners.

In the meantime, she's trying to get some big-time recruits in the fold to keep her program humming. And it seems one of them, Diana MacManus, has a little history with Haley Cope, the unlikely former Cal star who is still in Berkeley, training with McKeever in an attempt to make the 2004 Olympic team. MacManus, who as a 14-year-old in 2000 came scarily close to making the US Olympic team in the 100-meter backstroke, captured both the 100 and 200 back at the '02 US Nationals, the former race at the expense of the second-place Cope.

Coughlin, a good friend of Cope's, once laughed as she recounted the infamous incident: "So they're up there on the medal stand, and Diana reaches down and smiles and shakes Haley's hand. And Haley glares at her and says, as they're getting the medals, 'Let's see how tough you are when we're in a dark alley.' It was like, *Whoa.* But that's Haley—if you know her, you understand."

CHAPTER FIVE
GOLDEN BARE

Haley Cope had two goals in life: to set a world record and to pose nude in *Playboy*. Within a 6-month period that bracketed the turn of the millennium, she managed to accomplish both.

In October 1999, the 5-foot-11 blonde was featured in a "Girls of the Pac-10" pictorial under the alias Natasha Paris, the nom de plume employed as a means of satisfying NCAA rules. For a while, Cope toyed with the idea of appearing in the magazine as Teri McKeever before thinking better of it—not that prudence was one of Cope's strongest traits.

Six months later, Cope, swimming the leadoff leg for the Golden Bears in the 200-meter medley relay at the NCAA Championships, set a world standard of 27.25 seconds in the 50-meter backstroke. By relay's end, the team of Cope, Staciana Stitts, Waen Minpraphal, and Joscelin Yeo had also set a world record. Fifteen months after that, having just completed a stellar career at Cal, Cope became a world champion, winning a close 50-meter backstroke race in which Coughlin finished third at the 2001 Worlds in Fukuoka, Japan.

To people in the swimming community, Cope was considered one of the most improbable success stories in the history of their sport. Born in Crescent City, California, a coastal town near the Oregon border, to a 17-year-old mother and her 21-year-old boyfriend, Cope spent most of her childhood in rural Chico, 90 miles north of Sacramento. Cope lived with her single mother, and the family was poor enough that she received free lunches at public school throughout much of her upbringing. At 12 she began swimming for the Chico Aqua Jets, and her early success in local meets began to attract some attention. Two years later, Cope's mother, who had married, moved to Maine when her husband got a job with L.L.Bean. Noting that at the time Maine ranked last among states in terms of youth-swimming programs, Cope told her mom, "I'm not coming."

Her mother was upset, but Cope had a plan: She would live with her father, a man she now describes as "a nice guy, but he's never worked more than part-time; he drinks too much, parties too much, and doesn't know the slightest thing about discipline or setting rules. It's funny, because my dad has three daughters, from three different mothers, and we're all the same: We're the feistiest, orneriest, most stubborn girls, and he has no idea how to handle us. I don't blame my mom for being mad—to lose your kid when she was only 14?" The structure in her life would come from another source—Aqua Jets coach Brian Clark, to whom Cope had grown attached. Thus, over her mother's objections, Cope stayed in Chico, spending the next several summers with her mother in Maine.

Clark not only developed Cope as a swimmer but also became her closest confidant, and the two officially became a couple during her time at Cal. Nearly a decade later, a few months after Cope had married Clark in October 2002, she accompanied the Cal team to Maui on its annual winter training trip. Driving a rented minivan to the pool in Lahaina one afternoon, Cope was asked by one of her teammates in the back, "When did you know you wanted to marry Brian?"

"When I was 12 years old," Cope responded, giggling at the open-mouthed reactions of her passengers.

It is a statement Cope stands by, and there is a story to go with it: "I remember the exact moment. It was 2 weeks before my 13th birthday, and I was in a fight with one of my friends at school. She said, 'If you and Brian were any closer, you'd be sleeping with him.' I started thinking about it, and I said, 'You know, she's probably right.' I don't know if Alison realizes she helped me come to that conclusion, but here I am, married to Brian."

However unusual his relationship with Cope might have seemed to some of those on the outside, Clark handled his prize swimmer's athletic development with the utmost tenderness. Unlike the Ray Mitchells of the swimming world, Clark was not overly seduced by the notion of making a name for himself by pushing his athletes to great heights at young ages. Early-morning practices during the school year were unheard of, at least until Cope began initiating her own two-morning-a-week routine in high school. Clark's daily afternoon sessions, rather than focusing on yardage or on maintaining specific times for a series of repetitions, were long on variety and short on drudgery.

"Brian coaches because he likes kids," Cope says, "so his attitude is why make them miserable? And unlike most coaches, he's not into making them go fast so he looks good. People in his program might quit swimming because they have other interests, but no one leaves because they don't like Brian, or because they don't like the environment there, or because they're overtrained."

When Cope was getting ready to enter her senior year of high school, Clark met McKeever while sitting next to her at a coaching clinic, and he told the Cal coach about his relatively raw backstroke and freestyle-sprint specialist. "None of the big programs recruited me; it was mostly lower-level Division I schools," Cope recalls. "The only interest I got was based on what Brian could drum up. I begged for a recruiting trip to Texas, and I went on it, and they never called me back. I mean, I came from a team where I could shave my legs all year. When I went to Texas and Indiana, they said, 'We stop shaving until October' (in an effort to make their times drop dramatically at the start of the season). It was a total culture clash."

On her trip to Indiana, a team clinging to the outer edges of the top 25, Cope made a couple of her trademark flippant comments and also deviated from the script when she declined to wait for her host to return from a date, instead sleeping at another team member's apartment. When she returned from the trip, she remembers, "Indiana wrote me a letter saying, 'We think you'd fit in better somewhere else.' I think I had too much personality for that team to handle."

A self-described free spirit, Cope was understandably attracted to "Berzerkeley," with its quirky street people, funky shops, and overall whiff of unorthodoxy. Having trained in a less traditional program open to experimentation, Cope also recognized McKeever as a logical match. The question in the spring of 1997 was, would McKeever come after Cope? She didn't make an official visit to Cal, instead driving down on her own and checking out the campus and team for herself. Even after McKeever, sensing the potential of a swimmer so raw and unexposed to high-volume training, became more interested, the coach offered her only a partial scholarship. "Two thousand dollars a year," Cope recalls. "After my first year, they upped it to $4,000. Fortunately, my family was so dirt poor that I was able to get government grants and aid."

Cope jumped at the $2,000, then earned every penny—and then some—as a swimmer while taxing her coach's patience on a daily basis. From her seemingly unbreakable bad habits in the water to her blunt, tactless comments in the locker room, Cope continually provoked McKeever's ire. Yet the coach also rewarded the standout swimmer with loyalty and affection, simultaneously propping up Cope's self-image while holding her accountable for any destructive behavior.

If McKeever was like Cope's surrogate mother, Cope was the wild teenage daughter McKeever had never had. As Cope began making a splash on the collegiate level, then internationally, admiration for McKeever's leadership grew. "The more people get to know Haley," McKeever said in September 2003, "the better a coach I become in their eyes."

"That woman could become a serial killer for the next 20 years and still get into heaven for the way she handled Haley Cope," stroke guru Milt Nelms says of McKeever. "Nobody I've ever met in the United States could have done what she did for Haley. She was totally dysfunctional when she got to Cal, and Teri made her into a world record holder. It was a mixture of tolerance and holding Haley responsible for what she did and said. Teri just wouldn't let her go."

It wasn't just that some people found it difficult to cope with Cope and her penchant for ill-timed put-downs or melodramatic pouting. They also had trouble wrapping their heads around her increasingly impressive performances in the water. Unlike so many other swimmers, Cope began to blossom once she got to college. That, she believes, is a direct result of the way she was coached in Chico. Many Aqua Jets—Gina Panighetti, who graduated a year before Cope; Sarah Hernandez; Dale Rogers—have had success at Wisconsin, while others, including current Oregon State swimmer Kristin Huston, have done well at other schools.

"Most club coaches beat up their kids so much that by the time the athlete gets to college, she thinks, 'I can't possibly train any harder,'" Cope says. "They're physically worn down, and mentally they also don't see where they have to go to get better. At Chico, we talked about getting better, year by year, since I was a little kid. With a lot of club coaches, those kids don't ever get any faster than they are coming out of high school. With my husband's coaching, that's not the case at all. We all get better, and we almost all end up making NCAAs our freshman year. When I was being recruited, I saw that 55s were making NCAAs in the 100 back. I had gone 56.4 (seconds, short-course), and I told coaches, 'I think I can do 55 my freshman year.' They didn't believe me, of course. But I think I ended up going 54.85."

Then Cope continued to improve, even after her eligibility expired. By the spring of 2003, Cope, at 24, was swimming the fastest times of her life. That just doesn't happen in elite women's swimming circles, and people were forced to try to explain it. All they knew was that whatever McKeever was doing, it was pretty damn effective.

"Hey, Teri, guess what?" Dave Salo said while walking across the deck of McDonald's Swim Stadium near the University of Southern California campus on a warm spring afternoon in 1987. "I found your job."

Salo, a USC graduate student in exercise physiology who was moonlighting as an assistant for legendary Trojans coach Peter Daland, had been telling his fellow assistant McKeever for months that she needed to run a program of her own. McKeever, a two-time all-American swimmer for the Trojans who, during her senior year in 1983, was named the school's outstanding student athlete, was in the process of earning her master's degree in athletic administration. Salo, who was working toward his PhD, had bonded with McKeever based on a shared sense that the traditional wisdom in their sport was flawed. Each had alternative ideas for increasing swimmers' performance—Salo's drawn from a more scientific orientation, McKeever's from an instinctive awareness that technique and efficiency were more important than volume and brute force.

"You've got all these interesting notions, and you need a place where you can go and implement them," Salo had been insisting to McKeever. That day on the pool deck, he was sure he had found the ideal opportunity for his young friend. "The women's job at Fresno State opened up," Salo told McKeever. "That's *your* job."

McKeever went after it and, at 25, moved into the heart of California's Central Valley, a region that produces much of the nation's lettuce and precious few prominent swimmers. With a limited operating budget and a low-profile program, McKeever knew she couldn't compete with the upper-echelon schools in terms of attracting talent or generating buzz. Thus, she had to find a way to get less decorated swimmers to outperform their pedigrees. She needed to rely on team chemistry and intangibles like drive and focus. She had to find late bloomers and kids with obvious flaws, at least on paper.

She had to turn a group of low-level recruits into McKeever's Overachievers. And she did.

Monitoring McKeever's progress from 180 miles to the south, Salo swelled with pride. Like McKeever, he was sure the two of them were onto something new and different—they just hadn't been able to test it out on a large enough sample size. McKeever's now running her own show was, at least, a start.

A native of Rohnert Park, California, a Sonoma County town about an hour's drive north of San Francisco, Salo headed south to attend college at Long Beach State University and swam for John Urbanchek, the esteemed coach who later presided over Michigan's swimming and diving program for 22 years, winning the 1995 NCAA title. Though traditional in his approach, at least in terms of yardage, Urbanchek, Salo says, favored workouts that were "much more planned, sophisticated, systematic, and methodical. He didn't just slam you. He's not someone who coaches from an instinctive fear, who tries to motivate by calling you soft if you don't do what he says, like a lot of others do."

Searching for money to help pay for school, Salo was working the counter at Cookie Munchers Paradise, until he walked by the university job board one day and saw a listing for an assistant swim coach for the club team of the city of Downey. Salo got the job, and within 6 months he'd switched places with the head coach, a man whose son was on the team and who, Salo recalls, had a habit of smoking cigarettes on deck. Six years later he left to pursue his PhD at USC, where he was approached by Daland and asked to help out with the men's team. Meanwhile, women's coach Don LaMont hired McKeever, who had been teaching in the San Diego area and contemplating her career options.

"Teri was the arbiter between the women and Don," Salo recalls. "If they didn't swim well, he figured, it must be because they needed to work harder. They had weigh-ins every Monday on deck, and he just beat them up."

When he wasn't coaching or attending classes, Salo had a job in the neurobiology lab, where he ended up with an advisor who had a friend on the USC medical school's campus. From there Salo got hooked up with a pair of exercise physiologists who were studying the effects of aerobic activity on the heat-shock protein. When Salo would tell them about the popular methods of coaching in swimming, they and others in their field would look at him like he was speaking through a snorkel mask. "Exercise physiologists and academics think swim coaches are the goofiest people in the world," Salo says. "They'd say, 'If you're only doing an event that lasts 2 minutes, and you're essentially doing a marathon's worth of training every day—why would you do that?' I didn't have an answer."

So Salo started tinkering with the model, cutting back on some swimmers' yardage and instead emphasizing concentrated, intense bursts of training. It was, to put it in its most general terms, a race-pace model—and Salo found that the results it produced were better than those garnered by the tried-and-true method. In 1983 Salo began writing a column in *Swimming World* magazine espousing some of his theories, including a memorable piece to which editors attached the eye-catching headline "The Distance Myth." The column challenged coaches to look for the minimal model of preparation, rather than the maximal. "This," Salo explains, "is the philosophy of science."

As soon as the magazine hit the racks, swimming traditionalists began calling out "Doctor Dave" as a quack.

"In our sport, people's credentials are judged on the athletes you've coached," Salo says. "A few coaches wrote letters to the magazine that were highly critical, including Bud McAllister, who coached Janet Evans. He said, 'Who are you? You're a nobody.' And he was right."

That didn't mean, however, that Salo's insights were wrong, and he continued to refine them over time. At one point, in an effort to show that his ideas need not be confined to the pool, he decided to apply his race-pace principles to training for the Long Beach Marathon. Over a 12-week period, Salo spent 3 days a week running short distances at brisk paces. At first he would run no more than 30 minutes in a given day, later building up to 45. One day he felt so good that he ran about half of the 26.2-mile marathon distance; otherwise, he never ran more than 6 or 7 miles at a time.

On marathon day, Salo not only completed the race but also did so much faster than he'd anticipated. Though he started crying at 20 miles, having hit a physical and emotional wall, Salo's final time was a brisk 3 hours, 25 minutes, about a mile per minute faster than his desired speed. "It proved to me I could train on a minimal model," Salo says. "The thing I wasn't prepared for was the physical damage; it took me a long time to recover."

Salo eventually left USC to start his own swim club, the Irvine Novaquatics, where, in most people's eyes, he continued to operate on the fringe of the sport. Then, in 1995, Salo attracted notice because one of his swimmers, a 13-year-old breaststroker named Amanda Beard, was developing so rapidly at such a young age that her performances stunned the swimming world. "We hadn't seen a young kid like that since Donna de Varona in the '60s," Salo says. Far from the typically overtrained swimmer, Salo remembers Beard as "kind of a reluctant participant. If something else better had come along, she probably would have done it."

Most swimmers her age were working out nine times a week and swimming a minimum of 5,000 yards per training session. But 5,000 yards was the most Beard would ever swim, and she typically practiced no more than five times a week, as Salo applied his race-pace principles to her training.

A year later in Atlanta, Beard became the second-youngest Olympic medalist in US swimming history, winning a pair of silvers in the breast-stroke events and a gold as part of the 400-meter medley relay. Her youth was highlighted by her habit of bringing her teddy bear with her to the starting blocks, and though Beard, who posed provocatively in *FHM* magazine before the 2004 Olympics, has grown up in a big way—"She's past the teddy bear stage," Salo says, "and into the teddy stage"—she has improved with age (after a post-high-school lull), setting a world record in the 200 breast at the 2004 Trials and winning a gold and two silvers in Athens.

Some skeptics wrote off Beard's breakthrough as a fluke and continued to dog Salo, but his club kept producing talented performers—he boasts that no outfit has placed more swimmers on the past two Olympic teams. One thing the biggest names (Beard, backstroker Aaron Peirsol, sprint freestyler Jason Lezak) have had in common, Salo points out, "is that they keep getting better. We didn't ruin their long-term development."

Like McKeever, Salo was part of the 2004 US Olympic coaching staff. But it wasn't *that* long ago that many of his peers were scoffing at his coaching philosophies. At one point, says Milt Nelms, "the (US) national team director made public statements saying, 'Don't listen to him.' He was a pariah for a long time."

McKeever had her own obstacles to contend with—the dearth of women in her profession, an absence of outside-the-box thinking among her peers, and the challenge of making an impact at a school most people believed was located in the middle of nowhere. Yet at Fresno State, McKeever prodded her teams into producing better-than-expected results and even coaxed some of her swimmers into meeting qualifying standards for the NCAA Championships. After two seasons of coaching the women, she was offered the concurrent duty of overseeing the men's team as well. For the next three seasons, McKeever applied her alternative approach and technique-oriented workouts to swimmers of both genders, and most of them responded by exceeding their own expectations.

"The guys were a little apprehensive at first, but eventually they loved her," recalls Cass Dilfer, a captain on McKeever's last team at Fresno State. "They responded to her partly because she had such a strong athletic background, and she could relate to them as athletes. When they found out she was leaving to take the Cal job (in '92), they were pissed, because they loved her. And these were not wimps—they were big, tough guys."

McKeever became so popular at the school that athletes from other sports, even the troubled basketball program, would frequently find their way to her office to discuss their problems. They revered her for her compassion, her belief that athletes should be well-rounded, and her willingness to seek meaning in the process of training and competing, rather than obsessing solely on the outcome.

Saddled with substandard facilities and facing funding shortages, McKeever was industrious and proactive. On hot summer days she'd send her female swimmers, clad in shorts and bikini tops, to wash the bleachers at the school's football stadium for extra cash. It was during such a session that Dilfer, then named Cass Franzman, attracted the attention of her future husband: Fresno State's star quarterback Trent Dilfer, who would later quarterback the Baltimore Ravens to a Super Bowl championship.

A few months after joining the team, Franzman rolled her eyes when McKeever, on a training trip to San Diego, put the swimmers through several touchy-feely exercises designed to facilitate bonding. "First she broke us into 10-person groups, and you had to go around and say something you liked about each person," she recalls. "It seemed silly at first, but hearing all those nice words really helped. Then she had us jumping off bridges and tethering ourselves together and all those sorts of things. It was great, because swimming is a sport in which, even when you're on the same team, you're naturally competing against the person in the next lane every day at practice. But with Teri, it felt like it was always about the team."

The Bulldogs performed as a team, excelling in relays—partly because of McKeever's attention to detail in teaching the proper technique for starts and turns—and faring surprisingly well in dual meets. Fresno State's women went 12–3 in dual meets during McKeever's final season, which helped her to earn Big West Coach of the Year honors in '92. She might have been working her magic in the middle of nowhere, but people in the swimming community were starting to notice.

"Her kids were getting better every year, and that alone was unusual," Salo says. "The criticism of her was 'They're just Fresno State kids.' A lot of people assume elite athletes are so much different than the athletes who are at Fresno State, but the same principles apply. When Teri first got the Cal job, she needed to learn that as well."

Hired to replace Karen Moe Thornton (now Humphreys) in '92, McKeever, while socially conservative, fit in perfectly at Berkeley, becoming yet another unorthodox freethinker on a campus known for harboring such mavericks. Soon McKeever's Overachievers were clogging the lane lines at Spieker Pool, excelling in relays and dual meets, and transcending the sum of their parts. Not fully funded, and behind in terms of facilities, the program was overshadowed by Richard Quick's

Stanford juggernaut; it finally cracked the top 10 at NCAAs in the spring of 1997—the season before Cope arrived.

It began to dawn on McKeever that she had come up with a formula for getting less polished swimmers to overachieve, just as many of her peers struggled with the opposite problem—their onetime star recruits would lose motivation, level off, and then quit or slip precipitously. She was onto something big; the problem was, she lacked the confidence to implement her system as comprehensively as her instincts told her to. With Mike Walker doing his best to convince her she was little more than a glorified administrator, McKeever doubted her teaching ability even as she saw evidence to the contrary.

In 1999, senior Marylyn Chiang set an NCAA record in winning the 100-yard backstroke and was named the Pac-10 Swimmer of the Year. Cope earned the same honor in 2000, while Coughlin won it the following 3 years—giving McKeever's swimmers a 5-year stranglehold on the award. By now she was attracting higher-level recruits, many of whom, unlike Cope, came from more intensive, traditional training backgrounds. Whereas Cope was open to experimentation, McKeever shied away from imploring some of her other prominent swimmers to make radical changes. Coughlin, too, might have fit into this latter category had it not been for the severity of her shoulder injury. Because she was so scarred, physically and emotionally, Coughlin not only was open to a drastic overhaul when McKeever inherited her, but almost demanded it. Like McKeever, she operated largely on feel and instinct, and everything she saw about her new coach's philosophy intrigued her.

McKeever was one of the few coaches in the country who allowed their swimmers an entire afternoon off during the week. After their Wednesday morning swim, even during heavy training periods, the Bears were on their own until Thursday morning practice. Most of her peers frowned upon such an arrangement, partly because they viewed it as a break from valuable training (though McKeever's Wednesday morning workouts typically were the hardest of the week) and partly because they were uncomfortable with their swimmers having that much freedom.

"There's probably not an age-group program in the country that gives you an afternoon off, and maybe five college programs do," Georgia assistant coach Carol Capitani says. "Teri had the guts to say, 'This is what we're doing.'"

By mixing in yoga, Pilates, and spin classes, along with more typical weight training and dry-land work, McKeever spiced up the otherwise monotonous routine and got her athletes thinking about body positioning and balance. Then, when McKeever introduced them to numerous drills in the pool that touched on similar concepts, they were able to relate the two. Further, unlike most coaches, McKeever explained the purpose of every exercise and asked her swimmers for feedback. "Most coaches think they're being generous and allowing input by saying, 'You can swim butterfly or backstroke today,'" Cope says. "Teri and Mike Walker really did make us part of the process."

There was also an element of unpredictability—and excitement—to Cal's workouts. "As an athlete, it was fun to go to practice," Cope recalls. "They'd tie you to strings, stick a monofin on your feet, even have underwater wrestling contests as a form of hypoxic exercise. What they tried didn't always work, and sometimes it was just terrible, but it was still interesting. The thing was, as bad as things eventually got between Teri and Mike, they were by far the best coaching combination I've ever seen. The way they worked together and bounced ideas off each other was awesome; they were willing to try anything. We'd do IMs (individual medleys) in reverse order but then descend them or do different 25s underwater—anything to keep it fresh. The two of them competed with each other to be the athletes' favorite, to see who could have a more exciting practice and come up with the coolest thing."

Eventually, the strain between McKeever and Walker became so great that practices became far less fun—which was about the time Coughlin was getting ready to enroll at Cal. With Walker gone and the number-one recruit in America entering as a freshman, McKeever was forced to identify her coaching philosophy and chart the direction of her program. "Until you have the confidence, it's tough to define that philosophy,"

Dave Salo says. "She had to prove herself—not only to her peers but to herself."

Until Coughlin came, succeeded wildly, and severed ties with Ray Mitchell, McKeever was viewed mostly as a benign experimentalist by most of her peers. Before Coughlin, McKeever simply wasn't a threat to the more established figures in the sport. In the fall of 2000, Coughlin's freshman season, Mitchell told Terrapins swimmer Leah Monroe, who was being recruited by Cal, that McKeever would be great for her development as a swimmer. "He would tell me wonderful things about Teri," Monroe recalls. "He'd say, 'She's a really good coach. She's doing great things with Natalie. She has a new coaching style. It would be a good match for you.'" (Mitchell would sing a different tune the following May, when Coughlin decided not to go back to train with the Terrapins over the summer. McKeever insisted the two of them go to Concord to tell Mitchell the news in person. After asking Coughlin to leave the room, Mitchell proceeded to scream at McKeever for the next several minutes, accusing her of stealing his swimmer and vowing never again to send another Terrapins prospect to Cal.)

Coughlin enjoyed everything about McKeever, but there was one especially redeeming quality: "Teri doesn't try to run my life. She trusts us and gives us the freedom outside the pool to make our own decisions. If I'm working my ass off, I'm not going to ruin it by going out and partying or by not doing my shoulder exercises. Teri understands that if we take swimming seriously, we're not going to do things to screw up our chances for success." As McKeever—and Haley Cope—would soon learn, few people take competitive swimming as seriously as Coughlin.

Cope admits that she likes to talk trash, tracing it back to her days in Chico, when Clark, her coach, would encourage playful banter as a way to teach his swimmers to focus. "To so many girls it's annoying and offensive," Cope says. "I swear I never, ever—well, rarely—mean it to be a bad thing. I can be abrasive to people who don't know that I don't mean it, and I've been told I can be very scary to people who don't know me."

Toward the end of one of Coughlin's first practices at Cal, she found herself in a lane next to Cope, the reigning Pac-10 Swimmer of the Year.

The last drill was a series of 30 hard reps, and Coughlin beat her the first 27. Then, in the final three, Cope swam furiously to overtake the heralded freshman. Her competitive fires stoked, Coughlin touched the wall, glared at Cope, and asked, "What was *that*?"

"When we're in a race," Cope replied coldly, "you remember that I beat you."

Sitting at a popular breakfast spot in Kensington, an enclave in the hills north of Berkeley, on a mid-October morning, Coughlin laughs at the recollection. "At the time, I was like, *Whoa*," she says. "But the bottom line is that guys can be competitive like that, yet most women can't take it. There's a part of me that loves that about Haley. Even though we're totally different, we ended up becoming good friends. She'll just blurt things out sometimes, and if you know her, you'll say, 'That's just Haley.' When I hear her say some of those things, I know she's joking, so I can laugh. But most people don't pick up on that. If you don't know her well, like a lot of people on the national team, they'll react like, 'I can't believe she just said that.' Then they look at me and think, 'She's one of her best friends. She must be crazy, too.'"

Polishing off the rest of her chorizo-and-eggs special at 8 a.m., Coughlin raises her voice over the din of office-bound businesspeople and creative types who've just rolled out of bed and provides a recent example. It seems Cope, still training with the team as a postgraduate, not only is comfortable revealing her own body but also doesn't hesitate to critique the physiques of others. In the locker room shower earlier that week, Cope had told several young Cal swimmers, "The reason Teri's making us run so much is because you guys are so fat. There weren't nearly as many fat-asses when I was here."

The next day, in the weight room, a tall sophomore named Cheryl Anne Bingaman walked past Cope in a hunched-over manner. "Hey, Quasimodo," Cope said to the unassuming swimmer, "are you done with that machine?"

"You don't actually laugh, because it sounds so cruel," Coughlin said. "But you sort of want to."

CHAPTER SIX
THE HORSE WHISPERER

Milt Nelms vividly recalls the first time he got an up-close-and-personal look at Natalie Coughlin, and it is not a pleasant memory. On a warm afternoon in the summer of 2000, Nelms stopped by Spieker Pool during one of Teri McKeever's practices to check out the prize of Cal's incoming freshman class, and when he caught his first glimpse of Coughlin in a one-piece swimsuit, he instantly knew something was amiss. A former sculptor who became a swimming coach before morphing into his largely unofficial role as mysterious stroke guru, Nelms was struck by the asymmetrical appearance of the almost-18-year-old swimmer. As they stood there on deck, having a casual conversation about Coughlin's academic intentions, Nelms remembers, "I just got a spooky feeling."

Nowadays, when most people see Coughlin for the first time, they're overwhelmed by either her physical beauty or the mellifluous fluidity of her stroke—or both. Nelms had a far less pleasant reaction. The word he uses to describe his first impressions of Coughlin, in and out of the water, is *grotesque*.

"You know when you close one eye, you can see the edge of your nose and make a line with it?" Nelms asks rhetorically. "I closed one eye and looked at her, and half of her face was literally angular—the muscles in her trap, shoulder, and face were prominent. The other side looked like a normal girl's face would look. Her neck was off center by at least half an inch. It was almost like a comic book caricature. I asked her, 'Would you mind turning around?' And when she did, she was just this misshapen thing, with her spine curved around a shoulder blade, and one shoulder literally 2 inches lower than the other. Her pelvis was way out of whack—it looked like you were watching John Wayne in midstride. It was like someone had taken pictures of half of two people and pasted them side by side."

Nelms, who at the time was based in Oregon, had seen Coughlin swim as a youth standout and was vaguely aware of her shoulder injury. Earlier in the summer he had been at Berkeley, working with Haley Cope at McKeever's behest, employing principles of anatomy and physiology while analyzing her technique, and now he was back to meet with Nort Thornton, Cal's longtime men's coach. McKeever, with whom Nelms was only casually acquainted, had asked him to speak to her team about swimming technique and to spend some time with Coughlin—a rather bold move, considering the stakes involved. McKeever had just jettisoned Mike Walker while landing the most decorated recruit of her career.

Certainly, Coughlin's form left something to be desired. Cal assistant Adam Crossen, who had been hired by McKeever to replace Walker, says his first thought upon seeing Coughlin swim in Berkeley was *Eccch*.

Now, as he took the time to study Coughlin's musculature, Nelms drew attention to the severity of the problem. He looked at McKeever, and the two of them exchanged *Do you see what I see?* looks.

"Natalie, do you breathe on both sides when you swim freestyle in practice?" Nelms asked softly.

She shook her head no; only one. Nelms and McKeever exchanged another look. Coughlin was hardly the only swimmer not to engage in alternate breathing, but it would go a long way toward explaining the asymmetry—in Nelms's words, "It'd be like walking and having a lift in one shoe, and moving very aggressively, over and over again. Over time, you get this imbalance. Then, when you factor in the shoulder injury, what'll happen to someone who's growing is that the difference in strength will relocate the skeleton and create bone-mass changes. Her entire skeleton had changed."

Nelms asked Coughlin to get in the water and swim a few laps of freestyle. Again, he was overwhelmed by the imbalance of her body, almost to the point of nausea. "It was like splicing two different freestylers together," he recalls. "On one side she was really linear, aggressive, and forceful, and on the other side she was like a skateboard, just gliding into the next stroke. It was really arrhythmic, almost like watching a coyote run after it had chewed its leg off in a trap. On one side, she was practically dislocating her shoulder, hyperextending her arm as she reached forward, yanking her elbow up in the air and shoving the water back. I couldn't believe someone so small and feminine-looking was that aggressive in the water."

When Coughlin finished, she got out of the pool and related the history of her shoulder injury to Nelms. A bald, engaging, soft-spoken man, Nelms listened intently and replied, "I'd suggest that you breathe bilaterally 100 percent of the time and try to round your stroke off, instead of reaching way out and pushing way back in the water with your arms. In other words, try to get your body to do what it feels like it should do, rather than what people have told you to do."

When Nelms finished talking, Coughlin just stood there and stared. He didn't know whether she was skeptical, confused, or angry—or whether she was merely digesting his words and assessing their value. She just stood there, expressionless, looking back at a man to whom she'd been introduced minutes earlier and who had suggested she drastically change her stroke. And then, to Nelms's utter astonishment, Coughlin jumped back into the water, pushed off the wall, and proceeded to do exactly what he had just advised.

"She got in the water," Nelms recalls, "and it was, like, fixed. I mean, think about it: She took a verbal message from someone she had just met, translated it into a physical language, and got in the water and assimilated it completely and instantaneously. It was eerie. I looked at Teri and said, 'I don't believe that I just saw somebody do that.' Teri said, 'I don't either.'"

It wasn't as if that initial adjustment suddenly cured Coughlin's shoulder after nearly a year and a half of agony. There was still plenty of fine-tuning to be done, and Coughlin's times suffered as she began rounding off her strokes, shortening her entry point, and relying upon a more circular, cyclical motion, rather than one comprised of right angles. "All in all, it probably took 2 to 3 years to deprogram her prior habits, and really, it's an ongoing process," McKeever says. Yet that first meeting had established several abiding attributes among the parties involved: Nelms's acute ability to diagnose inefficient and unnatural physical processes, McKeever's intuitive understanding of such concepts, and Coughlin's sense of bodily awareness and willingness to tinker with her form.

∾

The fir tree tantalized him, like a hot fudge sundae being delivered across the table from a dieting diner, and the tired teenager found it too inviting to ignore. Exhausted after his third rigorous workout of the day, 15-year-old swimmer Milt Nelms was walking back to his home in suburban Portland on a summer afternoon in the mid-1960s when he saw a shady tree and decided to take a break. He took a seat on the grass underneath the massive fir, rested his head against it, and, 3½ hours later, woke up with a start. "When I finally got home," Nelms recalls, "I got my ass kicked for being late. The next day, when I walked to practice and saw the tree, I started crying."

It would be overly simplistic to claim that a tree was responsible for the end of Nelms's career as a competitive swimmer, but that ill-timed nap carried its share of symbolism. For most of his childhood, Nelms remembers, he "loved playing grab-ass with all the other guys on the swim team," typically swimming no more than 4,500 yards a day. Then, one weekend, his coach went to a clinic in Santa Clara conducted by the legendary George Haines—the man whose youth club had spawned the career of a kid named Mark Spitz. Haines advocated a far more rigorous approach to training: multiple workouts totaling 14,000 to 15,000 meters a day. Like a lot of other American youth swimming instructors, Nelms's coach bought it.

"The day after he got back, the shit hit the fan," Nelms says. "That was the last happy day of swimming."

Later, after scraping his leg while getting out of the pool, Nelms ended up with bone rot, further souring him on the sport. He turned down a chance to swim at the University of Oregon and, like so many other curious young people in the second half of the 1960s, drifted down to northern California. He worked in a warehouse south of San Francisco, loading trucks, and rode his motorcycle into the city, where he studied art under a man named Thomas Leighton. "I had always been very visual," he says, "and I started doing sculpture when I was pretty young." He also took a job coaching at a swim club and later landed a similar position at a club in eastern Oregon before deciding to leave the business. Eventually he gravitated back to the Park Rose Swim Club, near Portland—the very club for which he'd swum as a youth.

Nelms had been brought back to the sport after attending the wedding of one of his ex-swimmers. "There were 800 people there, including a whole lot of kids I'd coached who were now in their mid-twenties," he recalls. "A bunch of them got some booze in them and started telling me how important I'd been to them, and it really touched me. After that I figured, 'If I'm gonna do this again, I'm gonna do it right.' So I started at the bottom."

Nelms started coaching in lesson-type groups at Park Rose three nights a week while working a full-time job. After a year he moved to a club in nearby Vancouver, Washington—another cramped operation—quit his job, and began coaching full-time.

At Vancouver, Nelms remembers, conditions were hardly optimal: "We had 2 hours of pool time a day in 85° water. We had six lanes at 25 yards with an L-shaped dive." Still, after 4 years, Nelms produced a pair of world-ranked swimmers and three junior national record holders. Seeking a new challenge, he took a job at a club in rural Springfield, Oregon, figuring, "I'll just work the same magic." He didn't. "It was like coaching in Appalachia," he says. "After a couple of years, the aquatics director called me in and said, 'You've got to stop the parents of the swimmers from doing drugs in the parking lot.' I began to realize that maybe I'd had a little bit of luck before."

Nelms also began to refine his theories about swimming, most of which had very little in common with what his peers were teaching. To Nelms, moving in the water is a complicated activity—one influenced by lack of gravity, the need to propel oneself horizontally, and the effect of water resistance on a rapidly accelerating swimmer—yet an endeavor that can be mastered with blissful simplicity by those who feel comfortable doing so. To Nelms, that the dolphin and the shark and other water creatures move beautifully and efficiently through the water is not a mere by-product of the environment but an adaptive wonder whose principles should be emulated by competitive swimmers.

In other words, a swimmer should lean on his or her gift for *feeling the water*, and we should all revert to our inner animal whenever possible.

In Nelms's eyes, physiological lessons are best illustrated through animal analogies. He talks about cats and cheetahs and chimpanzees so regularly that those less receptive to his teachings find it comical. "He's telling them to move through the water like a monkey," one coach groused during the 2004 Olympic Trials. "Yeah, we're primates, but I'm sorry—I don't see any monkeys swimming."

As a kid, Nelms spent his summers with relatives on a ranch in eastern Oregon. "There were two things going on at the ranch," he says. "First, there were animals everywhere, and I always watched them move. Second, every day you've got to deal with work and with physics. If something doesn't work, you've got to figure out a way to make it work, and so I really got into the mind-set of understanding those processes. I also remember, even at 14, watching people go by in the water and thinking, 'Why does he look so smooth? And why does *he* look so strained?'"

In 1989, Nelms was introduced to Bill Boomer, who spent 30 years as the University of Rochester's swim coach before retiring to study and lecture on technique. Boomer, says Nelms, "was the first guy to talk about efficiency as a way to improve velocity." The two bonded instantly, and Nelms immersed himself in Boomer's teachings. As Boomer's profile increased, thanks largely to his appearances at coaching conferences, Stanford coach Richard Quick—a man always searching for the next big thing—became a devotee. As the women's coach of the 2000 Olympic team, Quick insisted that Boomer accompany him to Sydney, ultimately paying for the trip out of his own pocket.

Nelms, too, would eventually team up with Quick, but not until he had officially given up on coaching. In 1996, Nelms was hired by the Phillips Petroleum Company to coach its prestigious Phillips 66 Swim Club. The job promised state-of-the-art facilities and every resource imaginable. However, the location—Bartlesville, Oklahoma—was far from ideal. "There were 35,000 people and 85 churches," Nelms says. "It was definitely a cultural adjustment for a secular and skeptical retreat from Eastern Oregon."

During his 4-year stint there, Nelms's swimmers did well—but as he developed his theoretical teachings, he also came to terms with his limitations. "I know what people are thinking," he says. "If I'm so goddamned smart, why don't I have 30 world-class kids in the pool every single day? And the answer is, because I suck at coaching. Or, to be fair, the economics and sleep-deprivation of the lifestyle."

So Nelms stopped. Instead, he decided, he'd impart his out-of-the-box philosophies to any *real* coach who was receptive. The scary thing was, there were so few of them. In Nelms's words, "I need to have some sense that the coach I'm working with is forward thinking. I don't want to help somebody put an ornament on some crap that they do that isn't what I believe in. I've seen some stuff that's really disturbing. I turn people down all the time."

In 2001, Quick persuaded Nelms to be a "volunteer assistant," but he spent most of his time crisscrossing the world, doing conferences and instructional videos and the like. In May 2002, Nelms spoke at the

Australian Swim Coaches and Teachers Convention on the Gold Coast and was introduced to Shane Gould, that nation's most famous swimming champion—or, at the very least, until Ian Thorpe starred at the Sydney Olympics. At the '72 Games in Munich, Gould was the Australian Mark Spitz, a 15-year-old sensation who won three gold medals, along with a silver and a bronze, in *individual* events. (Whereas Spitz picked up three of his record seven gold medals in relays, Gould, with a far less powerful crop of teammates, had no such luxury.) Throughout 1972, Gould, amazingly, held world records in all five freestyle events, with distances ranging from 100 to 1,500 meters.

Then, shortly after Munich, Gould walked away, burnt-out physically and emotionally. "She still loved swimming," Nelms says, "but not the public life associated with fame." She married a Christian fundamentalist who disdained competitive sport, and she basically stayed out of the water for 2 decades. After divorcing in 1997, Gould became reacquainted with her former world and grew convinced that the grueling way she'd been trained was unhealthy and improper.

Gould and Nelms connected on that level—and many others. Soon they were live-in lovers in Australia, with Nelms regularly traveling back to the States and other continents as duty called. Gould, at 47, would ultimately compete in the 2004 Australian Olympic Trials—mostly as a symbolic gesture, for the event she chose, the 50-meter butterfly, was not an actual Olympic race—while Nelms would help bring about the revival of one of the few swimmers as phenomenally talented and driven as his famous girlfriend had once been.

On a warm afternoon at Spieker Pool, Coughlin, now a Cal senior, is swimming a couple of laps for Nelms and McKeever—a scene strikingly similar to the one that took place upon her arrival at Berkeley years ago. This time, all of her teammates have long since finished practice, and Nelms, having arrived from Australia just an hour or so earlier, a backpack over his shoulder and a Diet Coke in his right hand (to deal with the jet lag), is only mildly disturbed by what he sees. He is talking to McKeever about the technical adjustments in Coughlin's underwater backstroke start, using words like *atlas* and *axis* as McKeever nods knowingly.

Coughlin stops, removes her goggles, and looks up at Nelms. "The mass behind your buoyancy makes you go too deep," Nelms says quietly. "Try keeping it the same, but as you're going in the water, make a spoon out of your back." Coughlin nods. "Shane was talking about this with some kids she was teaching the other day," Nelms continues. "She says, 'Pretend you're a cat hiding in the garden. Now pretend you see a bird.' See how you raise your neck like this"—he elevates his head suddenly, as if preparing to pounce. "That enlivens your nervous system. It feels good to raise your head like that. It's a primal act, but we rarely do that any-more as humans—maybe if I see a cute girl on campus or in a bar."

McKeever smiles, as does Coughlin. Nelms moves on to an adjust-ment he'd like Coughlin to make with her hands—holding her thumbs outward to "activate your center." He suggests she try the start again while conjuring an imaginary ball resting between her knees. "It should feel like there's a triangle inside your thighs that's pulling up."

Immediately, Coughlin begins nodding. "We've done this before in Pilates," she says.

Next, Coughlin moves on to freestyle, showcasing a newly adjusted stroke, and when she finishes and looks up at Nelms, he is smiling approvingly. "You were carrying speed," he tells her, "rather than trying to make it."

"It didn't feel like I was trying as hard," Coughlin agrees, "but it felt faster."

Nelms lets the thought hang for a while before adding, "I don't think you're very good at making things happen, Natalie. You're better at letting things happen than making things happen."

Therein lies the central premise of Nelms's philosophy: With someone who can *feel the water* as viscerally as Coughlin can, less is more. The best thing a coach can do is to help get her in touch with her inner dol-phin—and then get the hell out of the way.

"What she needs is a lack of instructions," Nelms says. "When I first saw her that day in Berkeley, she was imposing the instructions of others on a process that is natural to her. I told her, 'Use your body like you think you should use it. Try to get your body to do what it feels like it should do, rather than what people have told you to do.' Swimming, to her, is a pleasurable physical experience, and she gets it in her gut."

This is how, despite her relatively petite frame, Coughlin can succeed in events that have typically been dominated by amazons. Coughlin, who isn't a hair taller than 5 foot 8, might weigh as much as 140 pounds during a peak training period, but from looking at her, you'd probably peg her for about 125. Certainly, she is ripped, although during breaks from swimming her muscles begin to atrophy at an alarming rate. She has relatively thin wrists and long fingers, and because of her shoulder injury, McKeever has always shied away from having her bench-press or do pushups.

To put it in more colloquial terms, Coughlin, in a fight, could probably kick a lot of people's asses, if only because of her relentlessness and determination. But if you wanted one of your swimmers to try to throw a bicycle across the pool, she would not be your first choice.

"Natalie's not a very powerful person," Nelms says. "US Swimming has administered all the strength tests, and she's off the charts—the bottom of the charts. According to them, she can't swim very fast. Look at it this way: She can't impose herself on the water; she has to relate to the water. What happens to most people in the water is that a big part of them is still relating to being on land, so a part of their movement includes land-based reactions. But Natalie uses her body in the water the same way that people walk on land. She begins most of her movements from balance, not from being off balance. Her movements are more curvilinear. Everything that lives in the water lives in curve circles, or curvilinear patterns; linear movements are land based. People that have a very good relationship with the water, like Natalie, can generally figure that out. She's just negotiating the environment.

"When Teri first saw Natalie swim as a freshman, with all those linear angles, she intuitively knew those movements are wrong. As a swimmer, her body can remember that."

This is just one of the ways in which the McKeever/Coughlin

partnership—and, for that matter, the McKeever/Coughlin/Nelms theoretical triumvirate—is perfectly cast. "When Natalie swims, you can see a relationship with the water," McKeever says. "It's a calming thing for her. She's at her most comfortable in the water, and I understand that, because I was that way. I wasn't extroverted. I wasn't especially pretty. But in the water, I felt right."

The end result is that to the naked eye, Coughlin looks as lovely in the water as a mermaid, even while expending energy and enduring pain at a rate that would make most people scream in agony. Longtime Georgia coach Jack Bauerle has said that Coughlin swims "like she's in the womb," while Stanford's Richard Quick simply calls Coughlin "the most talented swimmer I've ever seen."

Though understandably biased, Coughlin's close friends and former Cal teammates Marcelle Miller and Lisa Morelli offer no argument. Morelli marvels at how Coughlin appears to be "dancing through the water"—indeed, this is an athlete who can, during one of McKeever's funky drills, take off from 10 yards across the deck, break into a dead sprint, launch herself forcefully into the air, and, as she lands horizontally, make only a tiny splash while projecting herself forward into a silky smooth freestyle sprint.

"I've seen her do things that are just incredible," Miller says. "People may not realize it, but I think she's more talented than even Michael Phelps. Her feel for the water and her movement set her apart. If you watch her swim, it's flawless. It looks like she's not trying at all. Underwater, her body is so incredibly flexible, and she moves so gracefully, like no other human does."

It's not merely a convenient confluence of comfort and grit, either. Coughlin possesses some physical advantages, beginning with those uncannily flexible limbs. Before races, she does a series of warm-up exercises that include reaching both arms behind her back until her outstretched palms touch; she also does shoulder windmills that evoke images of twin blender blades. Further, she has an otherworldly lung capacity that, when she was 9 and suffering from pneumonia, caused X-ray technicians to believe there had been a mistake—that they were looking at someone else's photos. Put the ability to hold her breath for long periods while exercising furiously together with a powerful underwater kick, and you have the equivalent of a Ferrari Testarossa on the starting blocks.

"Her lung capacity is just freakish," Coughlin's friend and ex-teammate Haley Cope says. "I'm really good underwater, but Natalie just blows me away. In the backstroke, there are times when I can go off a start and beat Natalie the first 15 meters, but it doesn't take as much out of her as it does out of me."

Yet Coughlin, for all her intuition, intensity, and efficiency, still can't separate herself from the very best swimmers in the world with those qualities alone. To do that, she has to beat them with attention to detail— knowing what makes herself go, for how long, and what precise movements best help her achieve that flow. Even then, there are times when her preferred technique defies the experts. "Underwater, she's a model for what we'd teach other kids," says Irvine Novaquatics coach Dave Salo. "But she's not a model of what we'd teach kids in the backstroke. We've all looked at her backstroke and said, 'If she could get her turnover rate up a little more, she'd *shatter* records." By "turnover rate," Salo means the speed with which Coughlin completes a stroke cycle: The higher the turnover rate, the greater the number of strokes in a given lap. In the 100-meter backstroke, Salo says, she fluctuates between 1.4 and 1.5 seconds per stroke cycle; most other elite backstrokers are around 1.2.

Nelms, of course, would tell Coughlin to ignore such information and focus on the speed-per-stroke cycle that feels most natural to her. His gifts go beyond understanding and diagnosing; his true talent may be an innate ability to relate to the athletes he counsels. Whereas Coughlin was confused by Bill Boomer's assessments and struggled to comprehend his explanations—they sounded vague and convoluted to her—Nelms, from the first time they met, spoke her language. "He's so artistic," she says. "His eye is so incredible. You can tell he used to be a sculptor. He draws perfect body diagrams in about 2 seconds; you look at one and say, 'Wow, that's a work of art.' He picks up the most subtle things that can make a huge difference. Some of it sounds crazy, but it really does work."

In a 2004 article in *Time* magazine's Asian edition, Tracey Menzies, who coaches the great Australian freestyler Ian Thorpe, said of Nelms, "You've heard of horse whisperers? Milt is like a swimming whisperer. He observes and manipulates, and the results come quickly."

With Coughlin, as Nelms discovered the afternoon they first met, results tend to come at warp speed. He likens the process of working with her to "playing with a Barbie doll. Watching her make an adjustment is like watching time-lapse photography. What a good athlete will process in 6 hours, she'll process instantly. Give her the cause, the effect, and the relevant information, and she fixes things. Nowadays, it's like the three of us will go to a pool, spend little bits of time tinkering, and then Teri and I go home and write down stuff like mad. There are lots and lots of female athletes that are far beyond Natalie physically, but she is so intelligent. And when it comes to physical intelligence—an understanding of what her body does and how to make it behave in a desired way—she's a flat-out genius."

Yet when others start crediting Nelms for his impact on Coughlin's career, he gets uncomfortable. "Over a 3- or 4-year period, I may have had some influence, but it was only informational," he says. "We're talking about someone I saw maybe 10 days out of 4 years. Really, it comes down to what she and Teri did during all those other days. When I made those first suggestions, the two of them latched on to the concepts right away. It all just made total sense to Teri, too. There was a 30-minute encounter, and then I didn't see Natalie for a year. I gave them really good information that made sense to the two of them, and that's all it took."

There were tenuous moments, to be sure. At first Coughlin grew extremely frustrated with the changes, as she was failing to make interval times she'd reached when she was 14. To strengthen her back and other muscles, she'd used resistance exercises prescribed by San Francisco physical therapist Lisa Giannone; at McKeever's behest, Coughlin applied the same principles to a rigorous weight-training regimen that took a while to produce tangible results.

If McKeever's physical justifications made sense—harnessing the energy of the previous stroke by working with the water, rather than fighting it by aggressively driving the arms forward and thrusting them backward—it was her keen ability to tap into Coughlin's emotional state that made an even bigger impact. "She did things that US swimming coaches just don't do," Nelms says of McKeever. "If she saw that Natalie was exhausted or not into it, she'd tell her, 'Get out of here. I don't want to see you for a few days. And don't go near the water, unless it's the ocean.'

"Natalie's a kid who'd been dragged through the knothole backward by her sport, and it was no accident that she came to Cal. I mean, she can go anywhere in the country coming out of high school, and she chooses that program and that coach, with all Teri was dealing with at that moment. Whether or not she understood it as such at the time, Natalie knew it was her best chance—it was the best person at the best place. She beat every odd to get to this point. She's a cat that somehow got through all those years of being worked like a dog. Thirty or 40 years from now we're going to look back and say, 'What we were doing then was so damn primitive, and how that kid navigated her way through the madness was just a miracle.' Anyone else would've been chewed up by the sport, and the only coach who could have saved her was Teri McKeever."

McKeever acknowledges that when Coughlin began to thrive during what became a record-setting freshman season, she had to expand her base of knowledge to meet the challenge. "When Natalie arrived, Teri was scared to hell," says Salo, a longtime friend of McKeever's. "All of a sudden, she had this amazing athlete coming to Cal, and it made her step up to the level she's capable of. That's what makes a good coach. She'd always had the confidence to turn a swimmer no one had heard of into an overachiever. Now she had to reclaim her confidence and, with an athlete of that caliber, take that skill to the next level."

By the summer of 2001, the rest of the world was forced to take note of Coughlin's remarkable revival. Sure, many traditionalists ascribed her success to the residual benefits of Ray Mitchell's training regimen, but the people closest to the situation knew that McKeever had also played a major role. At the 2001 FINA World Championships in Fukuoka, Japan, Coughlin proved she was not merely a short-course supernova, winning the 100-meter backstroke in 1:00.37 seconds despite her having spent much of the second lap rubbing up against the lane line. Later, in leading off the victorious 400 medley relay, Coughlin had a 100 back time of 1:00.18, only .02 off the 7-year-old long-course world record set by China's Cihong He in what many experts suspected was a drug-tainted effort.

What Nelms remembers about that meet is not so much Coughlin's remarkable swim but the way she seemed to stalk him for several days without actually approaching. He'd be locked in a conversation, and out of the corner of his eye, he'd notice Coughlin several feet away, looking directly at him but making no attempt to inject herself into the proceedings. *This kid's weird*, Nelms thought to himself. It had been a year since their first and only meeting, and he wondered whether she even remembered who he was.

Finally, when Nelms was walking through the Ready Room, in which swimmers congregate before their races, Coughlin walked up to him and reintroduced herself. "I just wanted to let you know we had a couple of mornings this year that were really cold, and my shoulder started to hurt," she told him. "But I did exactly what you said, and it stopped. It doesn't hurt anymore, and I just wanted to thank you."

Nelms smiled, and as they continued their conversation, he couldn't resist the impulse to close one eye and examine Coughlin's drastically altered physique. One year later, there was nothing grotesque about it.

CHAPTER SEVEN

BLOWN OUT OF THE WATER

W e're gonna do a song I wrote after a night I spent right here on this block," the bespectacled man with the dreadlocks said, wiping the sweat from his brow. "I was out with a good friend of mine at a bar that used to be right across the street called the New Amsterdam, and we were getting really drunk and watching his dad play flamenco guitar, and it was a really cool night . . ."

Seconds later, Adam Duritz and his band, Counting Crows, broke into a stirring rendition of "Mr. Jones," the 1993 hit that propelled the San Francisco group into the national consciousness. A Berkeley native who later attended Cal, Duritz has made the most of his rock-star reality and reveled in many of the spoils of celebrity. The singer's most cherished perk, however, is the access he enjoys as the world's most conspicuous Bear Backer, and his love for Cal goes far beyond the traditional pursuits. He is as likely to show up at a women's soccer game—or, for that matter, a volleyball practice—as he is at a football or basketball event. Thus, it was no surprise that at this private show for roughly 100 friends (and, eventually, America Online subscribers) at Bimbo's 365 Club in San Francisco's North Beach district just before Halloween 2003, Duritz had invited several Cal athletic luminaries to the gig.

One of them, Teri McKeever, sat motionless in a folding chair near the stage, alternately mesmerized by the music and tormented by a tumultuous blow she had absorbed earlier that afternoon. She tried to immerse herself in the moment—partly because she doesn't get out much; partly because of the unique opportunity to experience a popular band play its trade in a behind-the-scenes setting. For McKeever, the real magic lay in the between-song asides and the backstory Duritz provided to songs like the one to which she was now grooving.

I was down at the New Amsterdam staring at this yellow-haired girl
Mr. Jones strikes up a conversation with this black-haired flamenco dancer
She dances while his father plays guitar
She's suddenly beautiful
We all want something beautiful
I wish I was beautiful
So come dance this silence down through the morning
Cut up, Maria! Show me some of them Spanish dances
Pass me a bottle, Mr. Jones
Believe in me
Help me believe in anything
I want to be someone who believes

When the show ended, Duritz drifted into the audience to schmooze with friends and acquaintances. McKeever and her assistant coach, Whitney Hite, thanked him for the invitation, and he responded with the utmost sincerity, "I'm *really* glad you guys could come. How's Natalie? Tell her I said hello."

I brought my wife, Leslie, over to introduce her to Hite and McKeever. In the 2 months since I'd been hanging out with the team, I'd already learned that McKeever tends to act awkward in situations such as this, but she seemed unusually rattled, even for her. Eventually, the two of us ended up off to the side, and she revealed the source of her misery: "Haley's leaving." Long pause. "She told me earlier today."

The woman looked shell-shocked. Suddenly she was as vulnerable and exposed as Duritz had ever been onstage, and I didn't have to draw her out to understand how big a hit she'd taken and on how many levels: She felt betrayed by Cope, who'd been like a daughter to her; she feared this would derail her dream of being the first woman to serve on a US Olympic coaching staff; she worried that Coughlin was losing the training partner and friend who could most relate to her pre-Olympic pressure; and she was questioning everything from her abilities as a coach to the direction of her program. "I wasn't going to come," she added, "but Whitney dragged me. He said I needed to get my mind off this; what I *need* to do is get a life. Or maybe I just need to get drunk."

She was kidding—at least, I assumed she was. As far as I knew, McKeever avoided alcohol, an understandable stance given the tragic role it had played in her father's death. Her voice quivered. "She told me, 'I'm leaving because you're not as good a coach as you were 2 years ago,'" McKeever added. "That one hurt."

Five minutes later, she was gone. Fourteen hours later, she was still reeling.

❧

The Kleenex box was a bad sign, albeit a melodramatic one. "I thought we might need this," Cope told McKeever as the swimmer pulled the box from a plastic bag, placing it between them as they sat on the grass at a park just west of campus.

Cope had gotten into a tiff with McKeever at practice the previous Thursday—Cope had been showing several younger swimmers an arm-rotation drill, which the disapproving McKeever called "stupid"; it turned out the drill had been conceived by Cope's husband, Brian Clark. For the next several days, Cope had been absent and incommunicado until finally she contacted McKeever and told her, "We need to talk." Now here they were, with 7 years of bonding in the bank and less than

10 months until the Olympics, about to have the conversation McKeever dreaded.

McKeever had come to the meeting believing she and Cope could talk through their problems and preserve the relationship. But a few minutes into the discussion, she realized Cope had already decided to leave. One of Cope's main complaints centered on what she perceived as a change in McKeever's coaching style. "Some of the things that got you here," Cope told her, "you're not doing now." Specifically, Cope cited a decline in the openness of McKeever's communication with her swimmers—less of a willingness to solicit their input. She also bristled at a gradual increase in yardage and what she believed was an abandonment of her coach's alternative philosophies.

"There's some truth in what you're saying," McKeever told her, "but *come on.*"

"The faster we got, the more attention we got, and the harder Teri fought to hold on to (the program's newfound success)," Cope would explain months later. "As an athlete, I felt like we had less input and control than in the past, and the yardage was getting higher and higher. I understand it, to some degree—she's a college coach, and she has to produce in those 4 years. That's a whole different perspective. I had a much different set of needs and less than a year to address them."

McKeever's perspective: As the program's profile rose, she started attracting more decorated swimmers, many of whom came from programs where traditional approaches were employed. In the process, she became more hesitant to mess with their tried-and-true methods than she had with the less accomplished athletes she'd coached in the past.

Had Cope's beef been primarily a philosophical one, McKeever might have kept her cool. But things degenerated as the conversation continued, and after a while it became clear: This was a divorce, and a particularly messy one at that.

"I've been unhappy for years," Cope told McKeever. "I love my teammates, I love the school. You're *okay*. Everyone on the team thinks you're mean."

Now McKeever was angry. "Haley, you don't know my relationship with Flora (Kong) or Cheryl Anne (Bingaman) or Ashley (Chandler). You don't know the stories behind some of the things that go down between us or how hard I try to help them. My job is to set a standard of excellence for the entire team."

McKeever was taken aback at what she considered Cope's lack of loyalty. "You don't know how hard I've had to go to bat for you in your career," she said. "Do you realize how committed I've been to your success? A lot of the dreams you've been able to realize—getting married, having a chance to start a family—I don't have those things, whether it was by direct choice or otherwise."

At that point, Cope went to the Kleenex box.

The conversation also featured a couple of classically caustic Cope moments. At one point, she said, as if taunting McKeever, "Just because I'm doing this, I don't want things to change between us."

"Haley," McKeever replied, "are you *kidding* me?"

Toward the end of the discussion, as Cope began breaking down the motivations behind some of McKeever's actions, the coach snapped, "Haley, don't psychoanalyze me. I pay someone to do that."

"Yeah," Cope shot back. "I know."

A day later, McKeever clutched a can of diet cola while walking across the lush north side of Cal's campus, still visibly reeling. Near tears, cursing every 30 seconds or so, she recounted the incident and pondered its ramifications. "This wouldn't have happened between two guys," she said. "Guys would've ridiculed one another mercilessly or fought each other and gotten over it—girls keep score. Haley was keeping score, and I fell behind without even knowing there was a game. The bottom line is that I was having a relationship, and she wasn't."

McKeever's voice cracked. "I mean, what am I doing? Maybe this is a sign from God. I need to start having a life, make some friends, meet a guy, have kids. And here I am, going to pieces over someone who apparently didn't care as much about me as I thought she did. I mean, nobody died. No one's house burnt down."

She stopped walking and leaned against a wooden bench overlooking a gorgeous hill of grass. "This is the closest I've ever come to just saying 'screw it' and quitting," she said. "I talked to my brother Mac on the phone last night, and I told him, 'Screw this. I'm done.'" Like every coach I've ever met, McKeever had an escape fantasy all mapped out: She'd move back to Southern California, get a job substitute teaching, hang out with her brothers and nieces and nephews, and regroup. "I told Mac, 'I just need to be close to my family right now.' He said, 'Teri, I won't let you do this. You've worked too hard. You care too much.'"

A few seconds later, McKeever, for the first time in an hour, turned to me and smiled. "Well," she said, "this'll be great for your book. Lots of drama."

"Yeah," I replied. "It's *great*." We both laughed, and then McKeever said, "Well, there goes my best chance for Athens."

She was only half kidding: She knew that should Coughlin swim as expected at Trials, it would behoove US women's coach Mark Schubert to include McKeever on his staff, if for no other reason than to keep his most important swimmer in her comfort zone. But the fact was, with Coughlin *and* Cope on the US team, McKeever's selection was a no-brainer. Now, with only one swimmer likely to make it, McKeever would have to sweat out her candidacy to the bitter end.

That was merely a secondary worry. As McKeever began walking back across campus toward her office in Haas Pavilion, it dawned on her that what most alarmed her about Cope's defection was that Coughlin, one of Cope's closest friends, might feel similarly frustrated with McKeever—perhaps even enough to leave. It wasn't a fear born of rationality; Coughlin, by all indications, was both loyal to McKeever and thrilled with her coaching. Said McKeever: "The first thing I thought after I left Haley was 'Oh my God; does Natalie know? Does she feel this way, too?' When I saw Natalie today we talked about it, and Nat said, 'Hey, I'm closer to her than anyone, and I didn't know anything about this until Sunday.' Then Natalie said, 'I *need* her.' And I said, 'I know, and that's what bothers me so much about this.' Though, if you really break it down, that's one of the reasons Haley's leaving—because Natalie needs her."

~

As McKeever began to process the situation, she became resolutely certain of one thing: She wouldn't let Cope or anyone else question her coaching. If nothing else, her own coach wouldn't allow it. Since the height of the Mike Walker messiness, Kathie Wickstrand-Gahen, perhaps McKeever's closest friend, had devoted a great deal of time and energy to keeping McKeever in a healthy frame of mind. This was hardly the worst crisis they'd confronted.

"Teri was always a phenomenal coach," Wickstrand-Gahen says, "but sometimes we're the last to see our own gifts and talents."

For much of her life, Wickstrand-Gahen has been on a quest for self-awareness and improvement. "I've always been a restless God seeker," she says. "I did EST (Erhard Seminars Training) in high school." Back then, as Kathie Wickstrand, she was an Indianapolis-based middle-distance free-styler and butterflier with Olympic potential as the 1976 Games in Montreal approached. Three months before the US Trials, her club coach, Gene Lee, was diagnosed with cancer.

Emotionally distraught, she tanked at Trials, then went to Indiana University to swim for the legendary Doc Counsilman, to whom she had been referred by the dying Lee. One afternoon in 1981, shortly after she'd graduated from IU, the 6-foot-1 Wickstrand emerged from a workout at Illinois State University, where her fiancé was an assistant football coach, and walked toward his office to say hello. "I was all sweaty, wearing my nylon shorts and bandanna, looking like Olivia Newton-John," Wickstrand-Gahen recalls. "The women's basketball coach, who was also the interim athletic director, stopped me in the hall and said, 'Do you have any eligibility left?' I told her I didn't, and then we started talking, and I said, 'You know, what'd I'd really like to do is coach.' I told her how I'd swum for Doc Counsilman and worked in his camp for years, and her eyes got huge. She said, 'Do you have a résumé? Our swimming coach just retired, and the search committee's meeting right now to name his replacement.'"

It turned out Wickstrand did have a résumé in the trunk of her car. She brought it inside to the athletic director, who told her, "I'd like you to come in and talk with the search committee."

"Great," said Wickstrand. "When?"

"Right now."

So the sweaty, utterly unprepared college grad in an Olivia Newton-John getup went in and lit up the room. "It was a rough situation," Wickstrand-Gahen recalls. "The former swim coach had been there for 35 years, and he had groomed his longtime assistant for the job. But I got a call that night offering it to me."

An uproar ensued, especially given that a woman had been hired to coach both the men's and women's swim teams. "This one parent, Chip Smith, was a legislator for the state of Illinois," Wickstrand-Gahen says. "He called me and called the AD and told each of us, 'No son of mine is going to swim for a female.' I said, 'Mr. Smith, give me 1 month with your son, and see what he says. That's all I ask.'" She apparently did all right: After her first year with the team, Wickstrand received a framed declaration from the statehouse in Springfield granting her the key to the State of Illinois.

Later, Wickstrand followed her husband to Purdue, where, upon her nighttime arrival in West Lafayette, "literally the first thing I saw was some drunk pissing on the sidewalk of the main street." Looking back, she considers it an omen. Unhappy at Purdue, Wickstrand took a job at Northwestern. It was a period of transition: She got divorced, and decided to seek help for what she says was a problem with alcohol. Then, in 1991, was diagnosed with malignant melanoma. "I used to say, 'This job is killing me'—now, all of a sudden, I had to confront the possibility of death," Wickstrand says. "Being a coach is too much like drinking—it's addictive, and you're totally insulated. You don't watch TV or look at the newspaper; you just go to the pool and back, and nothing else exists. It's a lifestyle."

So, in 1994, having beaten the cancer and successfully gotten sober, Wickstrand walked away. She moved to Esalen, the picturesque "alternative education center" chiseled into the central California coast. She had no TV, no phone, and sometimes—like many of Esalen's other residents—no clothes. She began grad school at the University of Illinois at Chicago, with designs on becoming a social worker, but dropped out, picking up cash by giving private lessons to competitive swimmers. By the mid-1990s, she says, "life coaching had started to explode. There were articles about it in *Newsweek* and *Time*. People would hand me articles and say, 'This is you.'" Then a friend introduced her to a life coach named James Gahen, the man who is now her husband. They moved to San Diego and went into business together, and the first person to hire Wickstrand-Gahen was McKeever.

"Teri was seeing a therapist at the time," Wickstrand-Gahen recalls, "and when she'd talk about how much stress she was under, the therapist would say, 'Just take a week off. Don't go to the meet.' Obviously, that's just not something a coach can do. She got frustrated with the process. With me, she could talk about coaching to someone who understood the lifestyle. If you think about it, it makes sense: Swimmers have coaches. What do coaches have?"

McKeever had first noticed the outgoing Wickstrand at swim meets—partly because she was one of the rare women in the profession and partly because her athletes always seemed to be smiling. When they finally connected on the phone that day in the early '90s, their friendship formed quickly. Wickstrand suggested McKeever come to an experimental workshop in Lake Delevan, Wisconsin, and McKeever accepted on the spot. A month later, they spent 3 days immersed in self-exploration with a group of women—a weekend Wickstrand-Gahen says was "like a year's worth of therapy for Teri. She wasn't really ready for something that heavy; she probably thought she was going to a spa when she agreed to come out."

The most revelatory moment occurred late in the weekend, when, in an attempt to illustrate the amount of responsibilities each participant was shouldering, the women were asked to hold out their arms and identify the people and entities in their lives for which they were accountable. A corresponding number of pillows would then be placed into their arms. "When it was Teri's turn," Wickstrand-Gahen recalls, "they kept stacking more and more pillows, and people around us were stunned. They didn't realize how swim coaches are. It was like, 'We're gonna need some more pillows.' So they keep putting more and more pillows on the stack, until eventually it reached the ceiling—and still, Teri held on. She didn't get it."

Finally, McKeever started crying and let go of the stack. As the pillows came crashing to the floor, the other women converged on McKeever, offering hugs and encouragement. "It was a defining moment," Wickstrand-Gahen says. "Teri has been a caretaker her entire life, and it's her nature to try to take on so much."

Yet McKeever's willingness to accept responsibility—combined with her sincere desire to impact the lives of her swimmers, not only as athletes but also as people—is what has helped her ascend to a level few of her peers believed was possible. "I think that's what makes me a good coach," she says, "but I think it's exhausting at times, and I wish there was a way to—not disengage, but to manage it. Because I know what kind of person I am: I will kill myself before I fail. That's the way I'm wired. It's not always a good thing. But that's the only way I could've ever made it here—being too stubborn to fail."

There are numerous stories of McKeever's displaying deep sensitivity when confronted with a swimmer's personal crisis. Leah Monroe, Coughlin's old Terrapins teammate, remains grateful for the way McKeever handled her departure from the sport. "We were very open with each other," Monroe says of McKeever. "I would tell her everything, and she was always very supportive. During my sophomore year, a family emergency came up, and I decided I wanted to deal with that and focus more on school, maybe go study abroad in Peru. I went in to tell Teri, and she was really understanding. She said, 'I just want you to you to be happy—and if you're not happy swimming, you're not going to be happy, period. So yes, you *should* take a break, and maybe quit altogether.'"

Conversely, McKeever expects her swimmers to display a great deal of dedication to their craft—not only in grueling workouts but also by devoting intense focus to the task at hand. When she believes that someone is slacking mentally, emotionally, or physically, she is not shy about jumping down the person's throat. "They've expressed to me that they have certain goals and will make certain sacrifices to reach those goals," McKeever explains, "and I am very serious about holding them to that, every day. I hold them accountable 100 percent of the time."

Watching McKeever become riled during a practice underscores the central paradox of her personality—at times her greatest strength as a coach can also be her downfall. Both hypersensitive and profoundly committed, McKeever can't hide the fact that she cares as much as she does. "She still takes things really personally," Wickstrand-Gahen says. "She'll tell me about a conflict within the team or someone's behavior, and I'll say, 'That's not personal.' But she has a hard time letting things go."

At those moments McKeever is like an open wound, and to some swimmers she can come off like a demanding, guileless mother figure. And oddly enough, she has something in common with Haley Cope, at least when she loses her temper—tact is not always her strong suit. Breaststroker Marcelle Miller would graduate from Cal in 2005 as one of McKeever's biggest devotees, but the walk-on from Massachusetts didn't feel that way at first. "I almost quit my freshman year," Miller says. "I felt she was degrading me in the pool all the time. We have a really good relationship now, though. I can talk to her about anything, and I feel like she'd do anything for me—not only to make me swim faster but to help me as a person."

While it's true that McKeever is one of those coaches who tend to be appreciated after the fact, she's no Vince Lombardi or Bill Parcells, control freaks who manipulated their charges in an effort to prod them to greater heights. With McKeever, there's nothing calculated or contrived. She vents not because she's trying to toughen up her swimmers, activate their inner fire, or help them learn how to deal with pressure. She simply does it because she cares a lot and (like most coaches) is under a great deal of stress, and that's how she responds to it.

And in the fall of 2003, even before Cope's departure, McKeever felt a tremendous amount of pressure—to get Coughlin ready for the Olympics and help boost her program to the next level.

~

Back in her office after our walk across campus, McKeever's immediate issue was how to break the news of Cope's departure to the team. She didn't want to overdramatize the event, but she knew her swimmers weren't stupid; they would soon hear the news and talk about it among themselves. McKeever's nature is to discuss things openly and honestly, but the mere act of mentioning the loss stressed her out—telling the other swimmers would make it more real.

A few minutes before the start of practice, McKeever grew distracted. Nike, with whom Cope had an apparel deal, had called earlier that day, wanting to know what was going down. "Whitney took the call, and he handled it really, really well," McKeever said. "Instead of getting all freaked out or gossiping, he just said, 'Hey, I wasn't there. You need to talk to Teri.'"

She was less pleased with a US Olympic Committee official who had called to deliver an "urgent" message to Coughlin. It turned out the message was from a sports agency, IMG, that was pursuing Coughlin as a client, and the caller was hoping to collect some background information. "It was completely unprofessional that he called to deliver that message," McKeever said. "I told him, 'Look, they've been in contact with her and her parents and me, and it's not your job to facilitate that communication.' He said, 'All agent signings have to go through us.' I said, 'That's not true. I've had professionals under my care, and they didn't go through you when they signed.' It's just ridiculous."

It was easy to see why McKeever hoped to shield Coughlin from such dealings. Her star swimmer still seemed weakened by the virus that had sidelined her in Barcelona, wasn't looking particularly good at practice, and was feeling overwhelmed. In less than 2 weeks, Coughlin would move into a condominium she had purchased in Emeryville. McKeever said as she left her office, "I'm worried about Natalie."

McKeever made the walk through the Haas Pavilion hallway, down a flight of stairs, and into another corridor, which housed the locker rooms leading to the pool. When she got out on deck, 20 of her athletes were already in the water, taking warm-up laps. It was 95°, and the workout bikinis most of them favored were skimpy and flattering. The coach called everyone together at one end of the pool and said, "I just wanted to let you all know that Haley talked to me yesterday and informed me she's going to be training elsewhere. She's played a big part in the building of this program, and we wish her well. This doesn't change any of our goals or what we're trying to accomplish."

Emma Palsson, a junior sprint freestyler and butterfly specialist from Sweden—and probably Coughlin's best friend on the team—rolled her eyes. No one else reacted visibly. After a 5-second pause, McKeever called out a freestyle set, and everyone was back in the water, speeding off toward the opposite end.

Three weeks later, Coughlin sat at Fatapple's, a casual restaurant in north Berkeley—famous for its olallieberry pie, which, the locals claim, rivals Pitocin in its ability to induce extremely pregnant women into labor—having devoured another tasty breakfast special, and voiced some frustrations of her own. "Well, apparently I'll have to take a full class load this spring—and I'm not happy about it," she said. It seemed one of the athletic department's compliance officers had told McKeever the previous spring that Coughlin, if she returned to school, could take as few as three units in the spring of her senior season while remaining eligible and preparing for the Olympics—thanks to a rule designed to help athletes who were prospective Olympians. "Then," Coughlin said, "a week ago, he told Teri, 'I was wrong.' Teri jumped down his throat, and rightfully so. I mean, that was a huge factor in my decision to come back."

Coughlin figured she'd sign up for 13 units but drop all but a single four-unit psychology course immediately after competing in the NCAA Championships in mid-March. "It'll leave a mark on my record," she said, smiling, "but so what?"

In other words, Coughlin expected to be a well-known Olympic champion—not to mention a psychology major with a bachelor's degree and an otherwise sparkling academic record—by the time any prospective employer or grad school admissions official got around to asking, "What about those incompletes in the spring of 2004?"

The Olympics were squarely on Coughlin's mind, and until recently, she'd have bounced her thoughts off Cope, the one person in Berkeley who could at least partly relate to her pressures. When Cope left, Coughlin's initial reaction was panic: Not only were the two friends; they were also training partners. "It's a big loss for me," she said a few days after hearing the news. "Haley and I went through so much together, and I couldn't have done what I've done without her. There were times when everyone else was gone and it was just the two of us here training with Teri—before the Worlds, before the 'Duel in the Pool' with Australia last spring after NCAAs. That time, everyone else was on spring break, and it felt like we were the only people in Berkeley."

Now, with Cope having landed an hour east at the University of California, Davis (where Natalie's sister, Megan, was a freshman), to train under Pete Motekaitis, the coach of that school's men's team, Coughlin was starting to adapt to her friend's absence. She took comfort in the presence of another postgraduate swimmer, ex–UCLA all-American Keiko Price, a sprint freestyler who was attending graduate school at Cal. "As long as I have Keiko," Coughlin said, "I'll be okay." It helped that Price, a native of Hawaii, was relentlessly cheery and kind, devoid of the abrasiveness that Cope sometimes displayed.

A few days after Cope's departure from Berkeley, Coughlin and the Bears had flown north to compete in the nonscoring Colleges' Cup in Vancouver. Coughlin, continuing a frustrating pattern—Cal had previously trounced the University of the Pacific and Washington State in dual meets—hadn't been particularly pleased with her swims in Canada. After returning to Berkeley, she got a call from Cope, who asked about the Vancouver trip.

"It was fun," Coughlin told her. "It was a good team-bonding experience, but a bad meet. The pool was terrible, and I swam like crap."

"Yeah," Cope agreed. "I saw the times."

"Haley," Coughlin said, seething, "I've gotta go."

CHAPTER EIGHT

SCIENCE FICTION

Stranger things have been seen in Berkeley, though, to be fair, many of them can be ascribed to the sensory enhancement caused by psychedelic drugs. Yet *this*, to the unaltered mind, is nothing if not trippy, for Natalie Coughlin seems to be going back in time.

Cruising slowly atop the water while on her back, Coughlin lifts her right arm upward, as if throwing a baseball, reaches forward, and slaps her outstretched hand down below the surface, just to the right of her thigh. She makes a similar motion with her left arm, all the while kicking in a counterintuitive downward-upward chop. Ten yards behind her, in the same lane, teammate Micha Burden is doing the same thing—as are the rest of the Golden Bears in various lanes at Spieker Pool on a brisk early-December morning.

The drill is known as reverse swimming, and seeing it from the deck is like scrolling through a televised swimming event on a TiVo rewind cycle. It is bizarre and intriguing and utterly Teri McKeever, a teacher who insists that her students not only complete her lessons but also understand the inherent value of what they're learning.

If the typical college swim practice is as monotonous as a statistics lecture, McKeever's workouts are more like extension-course seminars, with an emphasis on communication and experimentation. Unlike most coaches, McKeever makes a point of giving her swimmers the rationale behind her drills. When introducing them to reverse swimming, she talks about the deconstruction of their strokes as a means of erasing muscle memory and enhancing cognitive awareness of the body's behavior during the various movements in each cycle. Further, the drill requires them to tune in to the principles of buoyancy by learning how to stay afloat when moving unnaturally.

"It helps with balance," McKeever explains. "Things that you do to propel yourself forward when you're unbalanced, like kicking, don't work if you're going backward. You have to figure out how to hold on to the water while going in an opposite direction—some people get it right away, and some struggle with it. Haley Cope could do every single stroke in reverse; it was uncanny. There are also elements of breathing involved: You learn to breathe with your body, rather than with your head. And really, it's about achieving balance and body awareness by learning how to be centered and firm. Think of it like pushing a piece of spaghetti across a table. If it's an uncooked piece of spaghetti, it moves the way you want it to. But if it's a cooked, wet piece of spaghetti, you're going to have a hard time getting it to go anywhere."

Sometimes the explanations are far less involved. During a drill in which the swimmers use a pull buoy—a white cylindrical flotation device that rests between the upper thighs—McKeever is asked to describe its purpose. "It keeps your ass up," she says, adding that by forcing a swimmer not to kick, it simulates flotation and allows her to concentrate on her upper-body movements; additionally, having her legs on the surface assists with body positioning. "It's cheating," she says, "but it allows you to focus on your upper body and not worry so much about the rest of the stroke during that period."

Though not every Cal swimmer is sold on every drill, there isn't much complaining when McKeever mandates something unique or unprecedented. If nothing else, the variety is welcome, for swimming is a sport in which the boredom of constantly chasing a black line at the bottom of the pool challenges the attention span. Because McKeever not only questions the effectiveness of such an approach but also disdains it on philosophical grounds, she devotes a lot of time and energy to keeping her workouts fresh—whereas someone like Irvine Novaquatics coach Dave Salo, who shares her sensibilities, is prone to improvisation, McKeever maps out virtually every lap of every practice.

The result is that even with a relatively traditional drill, there's usually an experimental twist. For example, while the typical approach to interval training calls for short breaks between intense sprints, McKeever sometimes asks her swimmers, in lieu of heavy breathing, to take five "underwater bobs" before their next set. By inhaling deeply, sinking to the bottom of the pool, and then floating to the surface, typically exhaling just before they reach the top, the swimmers, McKeever feels, can reset their systems and achieve a purer form of rest before continuing the workout. "It's relaxing for some people," she says. "It evokes that same feeling you have when you're a kid blowing bubbles in the water; it allows you to mentally and physically refocus."

Underwater bobs force a swimmer to become comfortable with water falling over her face—a condition analogous to breathing during races. It also makes her more aware of the breathing process in general, so she uses her whole diaphragm rather than just her upper body.

Conventional coaches are most interested in output and intensity—above all, compelling swimmers to meet certain time standards and carry them out over extended periods—but McKeever focuses more on getting them to understand body mechanics and to feel those principles at work. She is fond of using props, many of which are housed in each swimmer's mesh storage bag at the end of her practice lane. There are arm paddles (to increase strength and enhance the feeling of planting freestyle strokes under the surface and "holding" water), snorkels (to help create awareness of one's "body line" during kickboard drills), and long pull cords that attach to a swimmer's waist and are held by a partner on deck.

At first glance, the cords' primary value appears to be resistance, and it's true that attempting to reach the wall while being held back by a teammate 25 yards away is a serious strength builder. But it's what happens after the turn that in McKeever's eyes provides the greatest benefit.

"I'm trying to illustrate that coming off the wall, it's never going to be any better," McKeever explains. "That is the biggest push they'll have during a race, and they'll never be able to create more acceleration than that, no matter how much energy they expend. Then, after the turn, when they're being pulled toward the people holding the cords, they'll be going faster than they'd be able to on their own. I want them to feel the sensation of being that fast, to understand that it's possible, and to achieve a comfort level at that pace."

Similarly, the paddles accentuate the rotation of an arm into the water during the freestyle cycle—and, McKeever hopes, help to underscore another of her basic tenets: Instead of pulling backward with the arm as if to jet-stream the water back behind one's body, the proper technique is to hold the position while letting the other arm propel the body forward. "It's like walking," she says. "You don't slide one foot back while you move the other forward; you plant it and let the other side do the work. Ideally, you put your hand in the water and exit at the same spot."

Balance is another of McKeever's guiding principles—she advises her athletes to "swim from your core" or "swim from your middle," language similar to that used in the yoga and Pilates classes in which the Bears are required to participate. During various drills, she asks the Bears to "breathe from your lower ribs, instead of your chest," and likens the body's core to an engine that, rather than the arms or legs, should be the primary force propelling them through the water.

Instead of beginning every drill from a wall, McKeever might have the swimmers float on their backs or stomachs and, midway through a lap, break into a stroke—all so they'll experience the sensation of swimming from the core. "This forces you to check in with your body position," McKeever explains. "When you start from a floating position, you have to figure out a way to propel yourself in a more organic way; you can't just kick or use your hands or do something that might work off a wall.

Natalie does this really well. She's great at generating propulsion and keeping her line while moving from her center."

McKeever attempts to accomplish something similar with rotational kicks, in which a swimmer places her hands on her thighs while propelling herself forward or backward. Sometimes, to combat the sensory overload that occurs during turns, she'll mandate rapid-fire stroke changes in the middle of the pool. This often takes the form of a "3-3 transition"—three strokes of one discipline followed by an abrupt switch to another—which makes swimmers aware of their head and body positions, flotation, and breathing patterns. Sets are frequently interspersed with "balance up" turns in which swimmers, after pushing off a wall, float passively for a count of 10 "Golden Bears" before resuming. During the takeoff, McKeever reminds them to "lengthen your necks…feel the length as you start swimming…make sure not to hunch your shoulders."

Similarly, a "board roll-off"—the swimmer places her torso on a kickboard, rolls sideways into the water, and then swims a few yards, using only her arms before starting to kick—is designed to help McKeever's charges feel what their bodies are like when perfectly balanced. It also helps with hand positioning among freestylers, especially those who don't dig deep enough. "Ideally, you should swing your hand to a position below the water's surface," McKeever says. "A lot of swimmers tend to come in too high when they're swimming normally, but when you lay on a board, it forces you go low."

Conversely, keeping the feet from sinking too far under the water is an objective of McKeever's snorkel-kickboard drills. "The way you normally kick with a board is really unnatural and bad for your shoulders," explains distance-freestyler and butterflier Erin Reilly. "Kicking with the snorkel, and just holding the bottom of the board, helps you control your body line and kick with your whole leg."

McKeever is also a fan of "one-armed swimming," in which a swimmer completes only half of a stroke cycle and floats passively in the interim. "So many coaches just tell you to do drills and never tell you what the point is," says Jen Strasburger, a former North Carolina standout who, while attending graduate school at Cal, served as McKeever's volunteer assistant during Coughlin's senior season. "One-armed swimming helps with balance and rotation, but I never knew that. I've never seen someone who's as technically precise as Teri. She understands technique and explains how to use it. She's willing to listen and to try new things, and she keeps it interesting. These swimmers are used to variety, so maybe they don't appreciate it, but I came from a world in which a set was, like, '10 × 400—go.' With Teri, there's a lot more variety, and it's for a purpose, too."

This is not to suggest that McKeever's sole purpose is to provide her swimmers with some sort of touchy-feely oneness with the water. She obviously wants them to go fast during races, and she shares many of Salo's race-pace sensibilities. Often, while her swimmers are in a floating position, McKeever will blow a whistle, summoning an immediate sprint from a dead stop. This, too, teaches them to accelerate from their center. "A lot of it is about energy level and being able to tap into that energy when it's needed," Whitney Hite explains. "It's like a light switch that you can turn on and off, instead of the old model, which is 'Let's turn it on and see how long we can burn it.'"

Similarly, McKeever uses the concept of "hand hits"—rapid, race-sharp bursts—to help her swimmers learn to manage their breathing during races. Since breathing in or out of a wall is a strategic no-no, McKeever will mandate, for example, three hand hits just after a wall so the swimmers accelerate coming out of a wall without breaking stride for needless breaths.

McKeever, more than most of her peers, gives individualized instruction during group workouts and insists on involving her swimmers in the process. For example, when working on turns, she often requires each Bear to pick a partner: One turns while the other trails behind and observes, then provides instant feedback.

"Teri's very specific," Hite says. "With her, it's all about pinpoint accuracy. It makes sense, because that's how she lives her life."

There is an intensely psychological component to McKeever's approach. She may not pound swimmers into submission the way many of her peers do, but she does push them to the brink and create a race-tough mentality that they carry into competition. One obvious way to do this is through the dreaded hypoxic exercises, the very mention of which has been known to provoke tears, yelps, and even panic attacks among the Bears. A set might consist of the following: 75 yards of freestyle, with three breaths; two 50s under/over, each with an underwater lap followed by a 25-yard sprint with no breath; then an easy double-arm backstroke length followed by another 25-yard, no-breath sprint. Then, without rest, the whole set is repeated—again, and again, and again, and yet again. If anyone breathes, the entire team might be asked to repeat the set.

This not only engenders mental toughness but also helps the swimmers to understand the difference between wanting to breathe and needing to. McKeever hopes that the hypoxic work will also help swimmers plow through taxing periods when racing and, for those final strokes at the end of races, understand that furious sprints are possible when out of breath.

Even when the Bears *do* breathe, the process may be unconventional. Another of McKeever's favorite devices is "alligator breathing": When a swimmer gets to the wall, she opens her mouth wide and takes in water while breathing through her nose. This allows her nervous system to adapt to a foreign feeling—to become comfortable breathing with water in the back of her mouth. Breathing with only half of one's mouth out of the water is an efficient race strategy. "It teaches you to read where the water is on your face," McKeever says, "to learn when you can and can't take a breath in a race." According to stroke guru Milt Nelms, alligator breathing also has a theoretical purpose: to combat the brain's primitive need for air, thus instilling a sense of comfort in situations when oxygen is scarce, such as at the end of a race. (It also kills any germs that may have entered her mouth during the previous 24 hours, but the chlorine-induced oral cleansing is merely an ancillary benefit.)

~

Put all of this together and you have what might be termed the McKeever Model, an approach to coaching competitive swimmers that even the most charitable of her peers would deem highly unconventional. Yet to Coughlin, who had experienced both extremes, McKeever's teachings made perfect sense—it was the Ray Mitchells of the world who espoused a philosophy that belonged out on the fringe. "The swimming mentality is so stupid," Coughlin says. "So many people are so worried about yardage—who trains harder than who—and they just mindlessly go back and forth and beat themselves into the ground. People will say, 'I swam so-and-so yards today.' Big frickin' deal! It's so frustrating, because so much of the swimming community is focused on yardage, yet that's just one piece of a big puzzle. A lot of coaches are arrogant and won't step outside the box. There are very, very few coaches willing to look at it from a different perspective."

As Coughlin made her push for Athens, it became clear that striking Olympic gold wasn't merely a quest for personal glory. She felt she'd also be striking a chord for change—making a statement about the pathology of the predominant swimming culture and sending a message that an alternative approach such as McKeever's could be successful on the grandest of stages. That meant a great deal to Coughlin, who resented the unquestioned tenets of the culture and the way in which dissenters were marginalized. She hated competing in a world in which, in the words of former Southern Methodist University swimmer McCall Dorr, "coaches throw eggs against the wall, and the egg that doesn't break is the fastest swimmer."

The truth was that Coughlin, by the end of her time with Mitchell, had been perilously close to cracking. Only with McKeever's careful and thoughtful handling did she rediscover her love for the sport and once again summon the intensely competitive will that had made her a star in the first place.

Coughlin knew that especially after her physical breakdown in Barcelona, there were legions of traditionalists quietly looking forward to the day she would fall flat in Athens, thus reaffirming their more-is-better training tenets. She understood that those people regarded her early successes at Cal as a carryover from her hard-core yardage at Terrapins, which they now theorized had begun to wear off. Hell, even some of her *teammates*, bothered by Coughlin's penchant for begging off drills she felt weren't helpful to her preparation, were in this camp. So yeah, a lot would be on the line during these next 8 months. She was swimming not just for herself, her coach, her school, and her country but also for the legitimacy of an entire philosophical shift.

Fail in Athens, and the revolution was dead.

This, more than anything, was the reason Coughlin couldn't try to overextend and chase history like Michael Phelps: Too much was at stake. Win the 100 back, and she'd be smiling, waving proof that her and McKeever's approach works, and her critics could kiss her gold medal until the end of time. But it wasn't just about proving she was right: Coughlin already knew that, win or lose. More than anything, she felt a gnawing pressure to serve her sport, specifically those who would follow her into swimming's highest echelons, by validating a divergent path to glory.

"As much as I love swimming, and as great a lifestyle as it can provide for a child in so many ways, there are moments when I think I'd have a hard time telling someone's kid to join a competitive swimming club, because the culture is so messed up," Coughlin says. "It's all about accumulating yardage and practicing 11 times a week—arrogant coaches saying, 'We do 10 grand a day, blah, blah, blah'—and who needs to get your ass kicked like that when you're 12 years old? No wonder so many kids quit swimming and become water polo players.

"It's frustrating, because so many coaches act like, 'This is the only right way to do this, and if you don't do it this way, you can't succeed.' They're not as open to new ideas as they should be."

To Coughlin, it wasn't just that swim coaches told kids what to do and when to do it; coaches tend to do that in any sport. What truly offended her was the utter certainty with which they espoused their theories, regardless of whether or not there was any scientific basis behind them. For example, one morning over breakfast at Fatapple's in Berkeley, Coughlin, sounding exasperated, brought up the universally accepted concept of a swimmer's aerobic base. "Some people would tell you that the reason I'm able to go so fast now is because of the aerobic base I built up when I was younger; that because of all the yardage I put in then, I can draw on that in my races now," she said. "I mean, give me a break—how long does an aerobic base supposedly last? Five years? Seven years? Longer? Is anything that I'm doing now responsible for my success, or is it all because of how hard I worked as a kid?"

To Milt Nelms, the problem wasn't that the notion of an aerobic base had no validity—it might, for all he knew. The problem was that this and other tenets espoused by most coaches were presumed true unless a preponderance of evidence indicated otherwise. In his eyes, not only did the prevalent training model have no scientific basis, but based on what he'd learned from scientifically trained peers, it was the antithesis of science. "The scientific method holds that everything is doubted until proven true," Nelms explains. "But many American swimming coaches, even when they acquire scientific information, don't apply science as scientists should. They operate from a premise that their method is the right one unless proven otherwise—and sometimes, even when science *does* prove it's not the right way, they disregard that knowledge."

Salo, who has a doctorate in exercise physiology, also bemoans the lack of scientific basis behind the preachings of his peers. "They argue that you need what they call an 'aerobic base,' but if you ask them to define it, they can't," he says. "The assumption is that if you have this basic training, you can swim fast later on. My argument is that you can develop your aerobic base without lots of volume. If I go out and run 10-meter sprints with 30-second breaks, my metabolism is still riding high, and those are more like race conditions. You engage all of your fibers with short, fast stuff, but only some of them at a time when you go long and slow."

Yet most prominent coaches insist on volume at all costs, even for sprinters. It's as if Carl Lewis or Marion Jones were being asked to run a pair of 10-Ks daily to prepare for their 100- and 200-meter races. Coughlin, while attending a ceremony in Dallas to accept the 2002 Honda Award as the nation's best collegiate swimmer, recalls swapping training stories with USC track star Angela Williams, a sprinter: "She was blown away by what they ask us to do. The thought of her running a mile, even, to prepare for one of her races was just preposterous."

Asks Salo: "If you're only doing an event that lasts 2 minutes and you're essentially doing a marathon every day to prepare—why would you do that?"

There are many answers to that question, but the most significant one is this: because some exceptionally fast swimmers tried it, and it worked for them.

~

Back in the 1930s, the Japanese had designs on taking over the world—the swimming world, that is. Competitive swimming had been around since the middle of the 19th century, and training had focused almost exclusively on technique, with trial and error being the prevalent strategy. Then, after photographing world-class swimmers underwater to study their stroke mechanics, Japanese coaches augmented that focus on technique by instituting an intense conditioning program, one that included daily swims of up to 5 miles. During the 1932 and 1936 Olympics, Japanese men proceeded to win 19 of the possible 30 swimming medals. There were few imitators, however, and World War II effectively destroyed the Japanese swimming program.

Then, 2 decades later, the Australians began what Nelms calls the Arms Race: After intensive interval training, the host Aussies utterly dominated the swimming events at the 1956 Melbourne Olympics, winning 14 medals after having captured only one at the previous Games 4 years earlier. Among the medals were gold-silver-bronze sweeps in the men's and women's 100-meter freestyles, as well as gold medals and world records in both relays (800 free for men, 400 free for women) contested at the time. In the men's race, Australia beat the US team by nearly 8 seconds.

This time, imitation was the sincerest form of flattery. By instituting interval training, the Aussies had borrowed a track-and-field concept that called for a specific number of brisk runs at a set distance, without enough rest to allow for recovery. In that sense, their model was similar to the one Salo employs today, but with much higher volume. The Americans were the biggest copycats, and many US experts turned to science in an attempt to gain an edge. In 1959, the book *Swimming and Diving*, by James Armbruster, Robert Allen, and Bruce Harlan, detailed a comprehensive approach that included year-round training, pace work, and core body-strength exercises. That was followed, in 1968, by Indiana coach James (Doc) Counsilman's *The Science of Swimming*, which heralded interval training but cautioned against overkill. Counsilman, the US Olympic coach in 1964 and 1976, was a trained scientist who explained how the laws of physics govern stroke mechanics and espoused a three-stage approach to understanding swimming from a scientific perspective: curiosity, confusion, and comprehension. He began analyzing stroke mechanics via underwater motion camera in 1948 and later used the technique to illustrate the "Bernouli effect"—that swimmers propel mainly by means of lift propulsion.

Counsilman's star swimmer at Indiana University, Mark Spitz, became a worldwide celebrity after his seven-gold-medal performance at the 1972 Olympics, with Australia's Shane Gould emerging as the Southern Hemisphere's superstar. As the sport's popularity increased, so, too, did the obsession with volume. During the mid-'70s, Mission Viejo Nadadores coach Mark Schubert created the infamous "Animal Lane," in which world-class swimmers such as Brian Goodell, Shirley Babashoff, Jesse Vassallo, and Casey Converse covered unprecedented distances on a regular basis. "We knew we were doing things no one had ever done before," Goodell told *Swimming World* magazine in July 2004, noting that the group was training 15,000 to 20,000 meters a day, 6 days a week. "It gave us an edge going into races—we always knew we'd be strong at the end."

There's little doubt that some athletes, especially those in endurance events, respond to massive amounts of preparation. But it's also true that other athletes, particularly those asked to make rapid-fire, explosive bursts, aren't suited to such a model. I'm reminded of a comment made by NFL Hall of Famer Jim Brown, probably the greatest running back in football history. As we stood on the pool deck of his picturesque backyard in the Hollywood Hills, he was telling then rookie halfback Ricky Williams, the reigning Heisman Trophy winner, why he'd never felt compelled to display his skills as a blocker during games: "If you get a Thoroughbred horse," Brown said, "are you gonna have him pull a milk truck?"

Nelms, who often likens Coughlin to a cat or a cheetah—she saves up energy for the hunt and thus is less able to devote it to nonessential pursuits—offers an analogy similar to Brown's: "She's not a 1-ton pickup. She's a Ferrari. A Ferrari can't pull a wagon, but it can still race."

Yet swimming coaches, like their counterparts in other sports, tend to see value in pushing their charges to physical exhaustion. "Pounding is a way to make coaches look good," former Cal star Cope says. "If you think about it, you bring the greatest amount of people from a mediocre level to a less mediocre one. Of course, you burn out some people that way, but the ones who don't tend to get faster. Athletes don't help, either. They're proud of the fact that they can hold a certain time for this many thousand yards—they get reliant on that, instead of learning the way their own bodies function."

The result is that coaches, even in the face of evidence to the contrary, are deeply resistant to change. When Salo's race-pace ideas began translating into tangible success—in the form of internationally prominent swimmers like Amanda Beard, Aaron Peirsol, Jason Lezak, Gabrielle Rose, and Colleen Lanne—it's amazing how few of his peers grasped the significance. "You would've thought he'd have created a revolution in swimming," Nelms says, "but he hasn't. Partly, that's because he won't talk about what he does. But it's also because people aren't open to changing the paradigm. Any science that flies in the face of the culture is rejected."

What infuriates Nelms is that the hallowed tenets of the mainstream swimming culture are so specious. After all, it's not as if the model is based on some sound theoretical premise. The American swim-club system, in Nelms's eyes, "is a cultural product. It came from nonworking mothers of middle-class families sitting around the swim club and staging bake sales so they could pay the aquatics director an extra $300 a month to be the coach. Age-group divisions were arbitrary, not based on development. Even into the '70s, we had a bunch of mostly mom-and-pop swim clubs being coached by pool managers and part-timers and volunteers. We don't have a designed, developmental system, and now there's so much inertia that the system is incredibly resistant to change."

As with any sport, says Nelms, "the culture is conservative. There tends to be this incestuous thing—athletes become coaches, who turn out the next wave of athletes, and everybody protects one another's interests. I figured this out from observing my own patterns and tendencies—I found I was repeating what I had done and been taught to do. People are scared by any new way of thinking, and every shift comes from within the swimming culture and will reflect the aberrations and distortions within that culture."

What makes swimming particularly egregious is that the culture is so undeveloped. "Really, the sport is at the beginning of its evolution," Nelms says. "It has only been broadly, professionally coached for 30 or 40 years. Compare martial arts, which have been around for thousands of years, with swimming, which takes place in a much more complex environment. Yet swimming has developed culturally more than scientifically."

One telling indication of the culture's lack of scientific legitimacy is the ease with which anyone can pass off him or herself as a swim coach. "You can't get a bachelor's degree in swim coaching," Nelms scoffs, "but you or I can pay $50 to USA Swimming and pass a multiple-choice test to become a certified swim coach. There's also a so-called professional organization, ASCA (American Swimming Coaches Association). There are many well-meaning and sincere people working as coaches, but there's no way to differentiate them from the dubious ones. If you take a test and can flog enough little kids to make them swim fast enough, you can move through the ranks."

This is a culture, then, that is both unevolved and undiscerning. Yet so many coaches within it have no problem coming up with pseudoscientific justifications for their training techniques. "The people in it want to tell you they're using science," Nelms says, "but if you just go buy a little pamphlet, 'Science Process for Dummies,' you can challenge all the science that they're supposedly citing. The research is fundamentally flawed: When you research a population trained with the same method and told to perform the same way, what kind of results are you going to get? The fact is, and I include myself here, we don't know anything about the human body—how it operates underwater and what really happens when it moves in that environment. We don't even know how some *fish* move as fast as they do—look at Gray's paradox, which holds that fish don't seem to have enough muscle power to propel themselves at the speeds they do. So most of us pick anecdotal bits of information, but mostly what we do is imitate whatever the mythology is that jumps out from our best athletes. It's like, 'What did Ian Thorpe do?' or 'What did Michael Phelps do?' But if the methodology of training Michael Phelps is what made him great, well, he isn't training alone. There are 30 other people in his training group. Where are the other multiple gold medalists and world record holders?"

Nelms is the first to remind anyone who'll listen that he himself is not a scientist. But he does understand enough about physiology to harbor some serious concerns about the way the majority of young people in his sport are handled. "From what I've been told, there are several growth phases in a natural sleep cycle. Studies have shown that at 1:30 or 2 a.m., kids begin to secrete the growth hormone," he says. "If somebody interrupts that secretion cycle to get you up to train at 5 in the morning throughout your childhood, what does that do to your body? Somebody, explain to me how that's good for us." According to Nelms, a New Zealand coach observed a pair of identical twins, both of whom were swimmers. One quit and, within 5 months, grew 4 inches taller; the other kept swimming and did not experience a similar spurt.

Even scientific principles that seem grounded in fact bother Nelms. For instance, when asked about the notion of an aerobic base, he concedes that "there's scientific evidence that points to the fact that your aerobic potential is shaped during childhood." Yet he finds the conclusion that high-volume training is the best way to maximize that potential to be absurd. "Swimming is an aggressive, monolithic activity," he says. "What a child is designed for is variety. To go after your aerobic base with the same continuous activity 4 hours a day is probably not the best for development. The fact is that if there's an aggressive, assertive stress in the environment, we will borrow resources from other qualities to meet that stress. It's a survival mechanism, not a developmental one. The coach says, 'Whoa, it works; hit 'em again.' But what appears to be adaptation is in fact a survival mechanism.

"In terms of a young girl's actual swimming potential, it probably would be better to dive for rings at the bottom of the pool or play Marco Polo than to do what these girls are doing. It's nice to have an aerobic base, but you need a sensory base, a base of skeletal strength, a base of rhythm, and a neurological base—all of which are compromised by doing a single activity like swimming. What youth sports do is not what Mother Nature wants done. Just look at the typical case of a female swimmer. She borrows until there's nothing left to draw on, and one day you get a drawn, puppy-dog-looking 14- or 15-year-old girl who says, 'I quit.' She doesn't even know why, but some mechanism of the organism says, 'You will die, or you will not be healthy enough to procreate, unless you change environments.' That's not an adaptive base. That's a maladaptive one."

Similarly, Nelms looks at Mitchell's reliance on cutting-edge physical data—when Coughlin was there, he constantly measured her and the other Terrapins' heart rates and ordered frequent lactate and blood tests—as another implementation of "science as convenience."

"From what Natalie has told me, Ray kept meticulous heart-rate records on his kids. But really, I suspect it was all about measuring work or effort over time," says Nelms. "It was used to support his opinion of how kids should be trained. He had them wear heart monitors"—Coughlin and her friends referred to these as Big Brother—"to bed that would download information, the idea being that one of the effects of overtraining is that your heart rate won't go down at night. Looking at it generously, he didn't want Natalie to overtrain for her own well-being. Looking at it cynically, he didn't want her to overtrain and fail to perform because of it. I speak from personal experience here—I did many similar things as a coach, because the performance of the kids I coached impacted the respect I received in the swimming community."

Coughlin, too, suspects that Mitchell had his own interests at heart when he administered the tests. Because of that and other experiences, she is often suspicious when coaches or officials cite science to justify a certain training approach. Certainly, there are times in which scientific study has enhanced competitive swimming—for example, the instant ear-prick tests that measure lactic acid in the blood during warm-down swims, thus alerting swimmers to the optimal number of laps they need to put in after competition to avoid lingering pain. Though Nelms is mostly dismissive of the bureaucracy at USA Swimming, he cites physiology director Genadijus Sokolovas, a former Soviet (Lithuanian) modern pentathlete with a PhD, as an "expert on the symptoms of overtraining. He supplies responsible information. He is also an undisputed, nationally recogized expert on appropriate levels of stimulation for children in various stages of development. He is the consummate scientist because he considers all information and constantly challenges his own assumptions, and even his own research."

Yet along with scientific feedback, McKeever and Coughlin had come to place great trust in their instincts. Says Nelms: "Both are intuitive people who are skeptical of being told how you should swim. There's a lot of abstract in swimming, and swimming is a pleasurable physical experience—Natalie gets it in her gut. For her it's an activity that's dynamic and movement oriented, and all the statistics and data dispensed by USA Swimming and ASCA and other swimming beaurocricies around the world, when not analyzed properly, take away from that."

Both McKeever and Coughlin rejected the prevalent training model to such a degree that they quarreled even with some of its standard language. Unlike her peers, who swore by the time-tested strategy of "tapering" before big competitions, McKeever chose not to use the term. Rather than pushing the body beyond its limits and then drastically reducing yardage to simulate rest, McKeever simply viewed her equivalent strategy—tipping the training scales further toward the mental realm as a major competition neared—as fine-tuning a group of healthy, well-trained athletes. She wouldn't even say the "T word" at workouts or in meetings, instead talking about being "fine-tuned—with more rest, and sharper and crisper workouts that are more intense and race ready."

After an unimpressive performance in a big meet, a swimmer would often rationalize her disappointment by saying "I missed my taper," meaning that the coach had failed to reduce workout volumes at the appropriate time. McKeever loathed that; she considered it the epitome of unaccountability. "A taper isn't just in the pool," she says. "It's about getting race ready in all phases: How are you sleeping? How are you eating? It's a partnership between athlete and coach, and the athlete has a responsibility to be interactive and communicative. It's not about magically performing better because your coach reduced your distance by the prescribed amount."

To McKeever, the intense cardio work favored by traditionalists certainly had its place, but she had come to believe that such preparation need not be water specific. Spin classes and sustained, fast-paced dry-land workouts, she felt, could be substituted at times for marathon swimming sessions; that way, the preparation in the water could be more race specific and technique oriented. "The idea is that you're training the engine," McKeever explains. "The engine—your body—doesn't know if you're biking, running, or swimming; it just knows it's being pushed."

This philosophy had been partly shaped by the realities of coaching at Cal. "Going to school here, you can't train 100,000 meters a week," McKeever muses. "The schoolwork is too intense. Besides, we don't have the pool that long, because we share it with the men and both water polo teams. So we have to find a different way to stress the organism. This is good, because my overall philosophy is that there are a lot of ways to be successful, and we're trying to expose people to as many of them as possible. The idea is to have as many tools in your chest as you can when it's time to go out there and compete."

Coughlin, for her part, was so down on the culture that she innately identified with anyone presumed to be part of the counterculture. She found herself both rooting for and defending sprinters Gary Hall Jr. and Anthony Ervin—and, for that matter, her friend Haley Cope—because their idiosyncratic personalities and unconventional training methods caused them to be branded as rebels. "Look at Gary Hall," she said following the 2004 Olympics, when Hall, at 29, became the oldest American swimmer to compete in the Games since Hawaiian sensation Duke Kahanamoku in 1924. (Incidentally, Coughlin's maternal uncle—her mother's brother—is married to a woman who is a descendant of "the Duke.") "People like to portray him as a slacker, but maybe he's just an amazing athlete who has an interesting way to train."

She also came to view the way she had been trained as a child as somewhat dysfunctional. "I remember a conversation I had in 2001 with Cristina Teuscher, who had won a gold medal at the '96 Olympics (in the 800 free relay) and a bronze in 2000 (in the 200 IM)," Coughlin says. "When I was younger, people would always ask things like 'What's your average of 10 × 400 back-to-back?' as if that were important. Christina said, 'You can't do 10 × 400 as fast as you used to, but you can do one 400 faster.' That comment has stuck with me ever since. The sad thing for kids is, if you train at that level I used to train at all the time, you can only go one gear."

Eight months removed from potential Olympic glory, Coughlin was tantalized by the possibility of achieving a platform that could help change the paradigm. She didn't merely want to be a role model for kids; she wanted to play a role in helping to improve the old model, by creating a more complex, saner paradigm in its place.

Something had to be done; that was nonnegotiable. Otherwise, when Coughlin looked into the eyes of those awestruck kids begging her to sign their swim caps, how long would she be able to resist the compelling urge to tell them what she sometimes felt: *Get out, now, before this sport devours your body and spirit. Trust me. I know.*

CHAPTER NINE

COMING TOGETHER, FALLING APART

On a frigid New Jersey morning in early December, seven young women lay in a cramped hotel room, only one of them sleeping—and another sobbing in the predawn darkness. The sleeping swimmer, Cal junior Lisa Morelli, was catching a couple of hours of shut-eye before the Bears' early-morning flight back to San Francisco—and simultaneously preventing anyone else from doing so. Morelli was snoring, loudly, while the others—Micha Burden and Marcelle Miller in one double bed, Coughlin next to Morelli in the other, Flora Kong and Keiko Amano on the floor, and Emma Palsson in the bathtub—stirred restlessly amid the unrelenting buzz saw.

Shivering under the thin blanket she shared with Morelli, Coughlin was in desperate need of sleep. After Cal's wildly successful performance at the Princeton University Invitational, she and the rest of the Bears had piled into vans and taken a trip through driving snow to New York City, where they'd checked out the Christmas tree at Rockefeller Center, had dessert in the restaurant popularized by the film *Serendipity*, and cruised Times Square. Now, at 2:30 a.m., they were finally back at the hotel, only 2 hours from the dreaded predawn wake-up call, and Coughlin could feel a cold coming on—her throat was sore, her sinuses throbbed, her heart raced, and now tears stung her swollen eyes.

Coughlin hadn't been right since Barcelona. Over the past 5 months her immune system, normally impenetrable, had been compromised by a variety of colds and viruses, and she felt generally sluggish. Coughlin had yet to have what she considered a top-quality workout since she'd returned from the World Championships, and until the past couple of days, she had struggled to approach her typical form in races. Even worse, other than from Teri McKeever, she wasn't receiving much sympathy at the pool. The rest of the Bears saw a tired swimmer who skipped occasional sets and missed practices and spin and weight sessions whenever she felt under the weather. *Yeah, like I'm* not *sick*, some would think to themselves as they gutted out another workout with depleted, sleep-deprived bodies of their own.

As important as Coughlin was to the team's success, some of her teammates resented her—which said as much about the culture as it did them. The swimming world is so grounded in the tenet that longer, harder workouts lead to faster times that any perceived shortcut is frowned upon, especially by those doing the bulk of the suffering. Yet when word spread of Coughlin's mini-breakdown in the snore-infested hotel room, even some of Coughlin's close friends on the team had trouble relating.

The reality was, no one else on the roster could truly understand the pressure-packed existence she experienced on a daily basis. In 8 months Coughlin's entire athletic career, and possibly her financial future, would be decided by her performance in one meet.

Though amiable and deeply committed to the program, Coughlin, because of her immense talent and notoriety, had never really been "one of the girls," and now she was truly living a separate existence. She had just moved out of her North Berkeley apartment and into the condominium she had purchased in nearby Emeryville, using "medal money" from past national and international meets that she'd been allowed to pocket while retaining her amateur status. She was being wooed by agents, doing interviews and photo shoots for national publications, getting intermittently tailed by an NBC television crew, and speaking at university functions. Through all of this, the psychology major maintained her 3.5 grade point average while taking her heaviest course load at one of the toughest academic institutions in the country.

Every decision Coughlin made carried overtones that escaped most of those around her. Many college swimmers, including some of Cal's, partied heavily when no major competition loomed. Coughlin, by contrast, wouldn't even take vitamins or sip an "immunity boost" at Jamba Juice, fearing the hidden ingredients could lead to a positive drug test. Each lap she took at practice was viewed within two contexts: how it would help her prepare for the collegiate meets and how it would affect her Olympic prospects. Some Bears questioned Coughlin's dedication, but hers was a focus to which they could not relate.

To McKeever, such carping was blasphemy. She remembered experiencing a similar sensation when Staciana Stitts came home from Sydney with a gold medal and what the swimmer called "post-Olympic depression." McKeever had told the team then to be forgiving of Stitts, asking, "Do you know what it must feel like every time you get up to swim to have someone say, 'She's an Olympic champion'? Even if it's not in your best event, you're still an Olympic champion, so the expectation level is there. You don't have the luxury of not being at your best, ever."

With Coughlin, McKeever felt, it was degrees worse: "She is on an island. She has to be at her best at all times, in and out of the pool. She has the responsibility of being asked to help carry her sport in the United States." Thus, the coach had little patience for Coughlin's internal critics. "If these people understood how much she's done for this program and for this university, they'd kiss her feet," the coach had said while eating a frozen yogurt on a Durant Avenue bench the afternoon before the team left Princeton. "What they don't realize is the emotional responsibility of being Natalie Coughlin. When they're older, they'll look back and realize what a privilege it was to have been on a team with her, and they'll view these issues much differently."

And yet, despite the building tension within the team fabric, the Bears had surprised themselves and their coaches with an astonishing performance at Princeton, a meet that changed an entire team's perception of where it belonged and what it might accomplish. The Bears had cruised to lopsided victories in all four of their early season dual meets against overmatched teams, yet there was a general lethargy to their efforts that had McKeever and Hite questioning their own coaching approach. The Princeton meet, which Cal figured to win, would at least provide some tougher competition; it was also the last time the Bears would compete against anyone for another 7 weeks, until the opening of the brief Pac-10 dual-meet season against powerful Arizona in Berkeley.

Often, with a break like that looming—one that in this case would include a winter training trip to Australia—coaches push their swimmers in practice and try to keep them in shape for the season's pivotal stretch. But McKeever and Hite were so frustrated and flummoxed by what they'd been seeing that they made a tactical decision: They would ease up in practice and give the Bears some rest before Princeton, a move they hoped would lead to improved times. That, in turn, would give the swimmers some much-needed confidence.

The two coaches had no idea how much their ploy would pay off.

"When I got to Berkeley in July, things had been miserable, and I hadn't seen enough in those 5 months to convince me things would get that much better," Hite says. "But Princeton showed us how good we could be. That was the single most important meet I've ever experienced."

That's a pretty heavy statement from someone who won three national championships as a Georgia assistant coach and another as a Texas swimmer. Yet that's how transformational the Princeton meet was. It was as if the Bears, suddenly, were a different team.

Coughlin, despite her various physical maladies, won the 100- and 200-yard backstrokes and the 200-yard individual medley, an event that triggered memories of her former life as a teenage phenom. The 200 IM was the event in which she'd finished fourth at the 2000 Trials, and the time she recorded at Princeton (1:55.46) was a personal best. She had all but abandoned the event since she'd come to Cal, yet McKeever had designs on her swimming it at the Pac-10 Championships, where USC's Kaitlin Sandeno, a former and future Olympian, would provide some intriguing competition.

More significant was Coughlin's presence on Cal's 800-yard free-style relay, an event she didn't figure to swim at the NCAA Championships because her anticipated schedule (she had won the 100 back, 200 back, and 100 fly in each of the past three NCAA meets and had swum on four relays) wasn't particularly suited to adding another 200 free on the meet's second night. Yet in Princeton, Coughlin led off a relay that included breakout freshman Erin Reilly, senior Micha Burden, and junior Lauren Medina, and they proceeded to set a school record with a time of 7:09.37.

When Hite saw the time, he suspected a scoreboard malfunction. He and McKeever later went online and began comparing it with other times around the country; it was the best in the nation to that point, by far. "No one else was within 5 seconds," Hite recalls. "We started saying, 'Hey, we could *win* this event at NCAAs.'" The statement was significant because of recent history. Whereas the balance of swimming power had once resided in the Pac-10—usually with Richard Quick's Stanford jug-gernaut—it had shifted in recent years to the SEC, where Georgia and Auburn had developed powerhouse programs. So thorough was those two schools' dominance that in the previous three NCAA meets, they had combined to win all 15 relays. Breaking up that dual dynasty, even in a single relay, would be a momentous accomplishment—and to do it, the Bears would need their best swimmer onboard. So Hite launched a lob-bying effort that would persist all the way to March.

The most memorable swim of the Princeton meet, however, was provided by Cal's other Natalie—senior cocaptain Natalie Griffith. That she was swimming at all was a minor miracle: Three months earlier she had sat in McKeever's office and told her coach she was quitting.

McKeever wasn't totally shocked: Griffith, though a valuable contributor to the team's success in each of her three seasons, had thus far had a career defined more by what she hadn't accomplished than by what she had. Not only was she constantly overshadowed by her luminous namesake, but this Natalie, whom teammates called "Nut" to avoid confusion, was haunted by her illustrious past. While not quite as decorated a high school swimmer as Coughlin—hell, who *was*?—Griffith had been a big-time recruit when she accepted a full ride to Cal. The Newport News, Virginia, native had qualified for nine events at US Nationals while still in high school and, with her versatility and aptitude for the rigorous butterfly, seemed perfectly suited to collegiate swimming stardom.

But Griffith, it turned out, was that rare swimmer whom McKeever couldn't push to greater heights. Griffith had had a decent freshman season and then leveled off, and her enthusiasm for the sport waned to the point where her ascendancy to the captain's position—by a vote of her teammates, who also picked outgoing junior Amy Ng—was viewed by some swimmers as a nod more to her longevity than to her motivational impact. So when Griffith told McKeever in September, "I can't do it anymore," the coach was understanding. "Look, let's not b.s. each other," McKeever said. "The fact is that you need me, and I need you. So let's try to figure out a way to make it work."

What McKeever meant was that Griffith, as an out-of-state resident on a full scholarship, was taking up a hefty share of the Bears' money pool. Already underfunded—the NCAA allowed 14 scholarships for women's swimming and diving; Cal had only enough capital to offer 11—McKeever could ill afford a hit like the one she was about to suffer. With 11 scholarships, many of which were split between two or more swimmers, McKeever knew her mistakes were costly. Defections, on the other hand, were downright deadly. Were Griffith to leave the team, McKeever could take away her scholarship, but that would hurt both of them—for McKeever, there was no one with whom to replace Griffith this year; for Griffith, a year of out-of-state tuition while completing her degree would run about $20,000.

So McKeever's immediate response was to figure out a way to keep

Griffith in the fold. "Let's not look at 'how do we get to March,'" McKeever told her. "Let's look at 'how do we get to November.'" If Griffith's motivational malaise seemed like a daunting force, McKeever's inclination was to attack the problem by breaking it into smaller, more manageable issues. For example, Griffith had signed up for an afternoon class and consistently missed practices to attend it, instead making up the lost time with individual workouts. "How about this?" McKeever suggested. "I won't question it if you miss those practices altogether. But when you are here, you have to be engaged in the process. If you're going to be a captain, I need you to be focused when you're at the pool."

An agreement was forged, yet there was no epiphany. Over the next few months, Griffith seemed to be making an honest effort in the pool, but her race results hinted of no transcendent transformation. Then, at Princeton, something incredible happened. She got in the water for the 400 IM and, unbelievably, turned back the clock and swam like the carefree kid she used to be. Four hundred yards later, she touched the wall well ahead of the second-place swimmer and looked up at the clock in amazement. Her time was 4:15.86, the fastest she had gone since she was 16. Griffith was so overcome with emotion, she began to cry. Then a few of her teammates started crying, and then some more, and then McKeever cried, and the whole team was hugging. Later that night sophomore backstroker Helen Silver related the story on the phone to her best friend on the team, injured breaststroker Gina Merlone, who was trying to recover from a pair of ACL (anterior cruciate ligament) tears in the same knee. "When you really want to quit swimming, it's stuff like that that makes you remember why you do it," Merlone told me later. "God, I miss it so much."

To McKeever, it also provided her swimmers with an invaluable lesson: that, in the coach's words, "the payoff doesn't always come when you want it to come. If you're enjoying the process, rather than trying to force the payoff, then sometimes great things will happen when you're not expecting them to."

It was probably the most emotional moment of Griffith's Cal career, and had she never again set foot in a pool, she could have walked away with pride and satisfaction over what she had accomplished in that race. Yet in a little more than 2 months' time, Princeton would no longer rate as Griffith's crowning moment.

In fact, it wouldn't even come close.

~

There was also one not-so-golden moment at the Princeton Invitational, so scary it caused everyone who witnessed it to gasp. Six laps from the completion of the 500-yard freestyle, Cal's Lauren Medina, who was swimming the best race at that distance of her life, stopped in the middle of the pool and began waving her arms wildly. A lifeguard jumped in and helped her to the wall, and when she got out of the pool she was practically hyperventilating. McKeever, who had come running over, feared that Medina might have choked—or, perhaps, been stricken by something even more frightening.

"I can't breathe," Medina told her. The swimmer was shaking; her eyes were filled with fear.

Suddenly, McKeever understood. "Lauren, you're having a panic attack," the coach told her. "It's okay; you're gonna be fine. Trust me."

McKeever had experienced her share of anxiety attacks, most of them in the year before Coughlin arrived in Berkeley, when the Mike Walker situation had reached its nadir. She remembered every wretched symptom: the shortness of breath, the rapid heartbeat, the overwhelming feeling of despair. Later, after calming down, Medina was completely embarrassed. Her explanation, months later: "I was swimming so fast that I just freaked out. All of a sudden I couldn't breathe."

Over the next few months, however, the problem would persist: Every time Medina would become overwhelmed by the magnitude of her accomplishments in the water, or by what she hoped to accomplish, the panic would return, and she'd have to try to remain calm for the sake of her teammates. And make no mistake—Medina loved her teammates. Fun-loving, effervescent, and relentlessly competitive, Medina, better known as "Salsa," might have been the team's most popular swimmer. Though they ran in different social circles, Coughlin adored Medina as a teammate, partly because she emblemized everything laudable about McKeever's program.

Of all the McKeever Overachievers, Medina was the current poster child. If Haley Cope's ascent to world-class status was a miracle, the muscular Medina was the poor woman's version, a low-priority recruit whose drive and ability to respond to coaching had spurred her to increasingly impressive heights.

Raised in the modest suburbs southeast of LA, Medina, a third-generation Mexican-American, was the only girl out of four kids, and the only one for whom music was not a main passion. When Medina was 11—an age at which most of her teammates were already well-established swimmers at various competitive levels—she was visiting her aunt Stella in Pico Rivera on a summer afternoon and fooling around in the backyard pool. "Lauren, you're a good swimmer," her aunt noticed. Lauren's cousin, Chris, told her she should try out for a swim team, and soon she was swimming for a local club called Santa Fe Springs. "I was so happy to be on a team," Medina recalls. "I would go to practice and then wear my swimsuit and cap around the house the rest of the day."

Medina's work ethic helped propel her through the ranks, and while swimming for the Industry Hills Aquatics Club, she ended up with a new coach, Rick Shephard, who drastically upped the training volume. Suddenly Medina, primarily a sprint-freestyler at that point, was doing hard-core distance work and practicing twice a day, 6 days a week, and again on Sunday morning. One day when she was 13, a blond-haired, blue-eyed boy on the team, a high school sophomore with whom she had been friendly, got into an argument with Medina and made a rude and crude comment about her ethnicity. She retreated to the locker room, found a toilet stall, and bawled. When she got home and told her parents, she recalls, "they had a fit. My mom is not someone to mess with. She went ballistic."

That was it was for Industry Hills. Medina switched to a more prestigious club in Pasadena, Rose Bowl Aquatics. Unfortunately, the twice-daily ½-hour commute each way from her home in West Covina was a killer. By the time she was attending St. Lucy's, a strict, all-girls Catholic high school in Glendora, Medina was locked into an exhausting schedule: Wake up at 4 a.m., drive to Pasadena for a 2-hour workout, get back in the car for the commute to school, return to Pasadena for a 3½-hour workout, drive home, eat dinner, and collapse. The regimen didn't do much for her study habits; Medina simply skipped most homework and got by on what she learned in class.

Swimming, as she got older, became more and more of a struggle. "A lot of swimmers peak at 13, then get mediocre and go progressively downhill," Medina says. "I thought for a long time that I was one of them, and so did my mom. So many times I just wanted to quit. I felt like I was beginning to burn out. People I used to beat were now beating me, I swam lousy in meets, and my parents started getting down on me: 'You just don't want it bad enough.' At least twice a day I would think about quitting."

As she entered her senior year of high school, however, Medina discovered at least one good reason to continue: She might nab a scholarship, at least a partial one, to swim in college. The big-time programs weren't recruiting her, but she had attracted attention from Arizona State and some lower-profile swimming schools: Notre Dame, Pacific, the University of San Diego, and several Ivy League colleges. Encouraged by her mother, Medina emailed McKeever and UCLA coach Cyndi Gallagher, though she didn't expect responses. "I knew it was kind of a reach," she says. "That night my mom answered the phone, put her hand over the mouthpiece, and said, 'Oh my God; it's Teri McKeever!'"

Sitting in her Berkeley office, McKeever was mildly intrigued by what little she knew of Medina. "I hadn't ever seen her swim," she recalls. "I talked to her club coach, and he told me, 'She's a nice girl. She has some talent, but she's been a little inconsistent.' I saw her as a depth person, someone who could possibly fill out our relays."

Medina, meanwhile, was "blown away" by McKeever's interest. "I didn't think I was good enough," she says. "Haley Cope sent me an e-mail, saying, 'I really think you'd be a good fit,' and I e-mailed back, 'Honestly, I don't feel like I'm on that level.' Haley responded, 'Don't be ridiculous; we wouldn't be recruiting you if you weren't.'" Medina enjoyed her visit to Cal and was especially taken with McKeever. "A lot of the reason I wanted to go there so badly was because she was a female," she says. "I was at the point where I just didn't want to deal with being coached by men."

In February of her senior year, Medina was on the verge of committing to Cal, when one night she got a phone call from UCLA's Gallagher. "We don't know how we missed you," an apologetic Gallagher said. "Why don't you come take a visit?" Now Medina was confused: She had always dreamed of attending UCLA—but why was Gallagher suddenly calling *now*? The reason, she learned much later, was that her mother had called Gallagher and, pretending to be her daughter, left a message touting her credentials. In the end, Medina decided she felt most comfortable with McKeever, who had been interested from the time she got the initial e-mail, and accepted a partial scholarship.

As a freshman, Medina became an immediate contributor, swimming on Cal's 800-yard freestyle relay that finished ninth at NCAAs and scoring points in freestyle events in dual meets and at the Pac-10 Championships. Academically, however, she was completely under water. The combination of poor study habits, a sudden onslaught of social activities, a renewed commitment to swimming, and the transition to an academically challenging university was too much. "I was so naive," she says. "I had older friends who had told me, 'College is so much easier than high school'— but they were going to junior college. I had always done well in high school but hadn't done any work. I'd also never gone out much in high school—I never had a boyfriend, and I had to ask people to go to my proms. Now, all of a sudden, I had a ton of social options. Meanwhile, I was working so hard in the water. It was so intense. They're giving you money to come here, and you feel like it's your job to perform."

By the end of her freshman year, Medina was on academic probation, perilously close to flunking out. "Teri was so supportive," Medina recalls. "She recommended I come up and do summer school and take a class that teaches you how to study, and it was a great thing for me. She was just very nurturing. She said, 'Everybody makes mistakes. You're not the first person this has happened to. You just need to change your approach and get back on the horse.' I felt really comforted by that. I come from a nurturing family. It's not like I need to be babied, but I do well in this type of environment. She understands we get stressed with school. She understands we're girls. She knows when we're PMS-ing, that sometimes we're in a bitchy mood."

Medina got it together in the classroom, and in the pool she continued to improve. *Maybe I didn't peak at 13*, she thought. As a sophomore, she finished seventh in the 200 free at the Pac-10 Championships and qualified for NCAAs, where she also swam on the 800 free relay. But she had a disappointing swim in the 200 free prelims, and the relay finished out of the top 16, the cutoff point for honorable-mention all-American honors (anyone in the top eight is an all-American), which she had earned as a freshman. As the NCAA meet's final events played out, Medina sat seething in the stands with her teammates at the Martin Aquatics Center in Auburn and had an epiphany: *That's it—I'm tired of being mediocre. I can be better than this, and I refuse not to be.*

Adam Crossen, McKeever's assistant at the time, noticed how visibly peeved Medina was and walked her down to a corridor outside the pool area for a private discussion. "She had trained hard that year, but it hadn't been validated," Crossen says. "She had gotten nervous and flopped at the meet, and she felt like she had let the team down. She said, 'Adam, I'm bummed. I'm never gonna do well.' There were mental barriers she had to overcome."

Recalls Medina: "I think I was jealous—of Auburn, which won the championship in its own pool, and of Natalie. I knew I was never going to be on her level, but I wanted to be in that area."

"I'm fed up with this," Medina told Crossen. "I don't want to sit here next year in this same position, having regrets, wishing I had trained harder and gone faster."

"Then you need to make that happen," Crossen told her. "You need to be consistent. You need to want it. You need to push yourself and the people around you, all the time."

"I'll do it," Medina told him, glaring. "This will *not* happen again."

∼

That Coughlin would become such an unabashed fan of Medina's was hardly a shock. It was no coincidence that each of her best friends on the team—Emma Palsson, Marcelle Miller, Micha Burden, and Lisa Morelli—was a hardworking overachiever. Palsson, a sprint-freestyler from Skanor, Sweden, was a former member of that country's junior national team who decided to attend college in the United States. "We didn't even see her swim before we offered her a (partial) scholarship," Crossen recalls. "We just made the offer and took a chance." Miller, a breaststroker from Portsmouth, New Hampshire, also arrived at Cal sight unseen; she had been recommended by her club coach and joined the team as a walk-on. Burden, an amiable and attractive Alaskan, was swimming at Golden West Junior College in Southern California when McKeever showed up at one of her meets. Burden was so stunned and excited that she started to cry. Morelli spent most of her life on the East Coast until the summer before her senior year, when her family moved to San Diego. She, too, was surprised to have Cal as an option; her distaste for the snobby environment of Torrey Pines High School helped her gravitate toward Berkeley's unpretentious campus, where she wowed teammates with her radiant smile, dogged work ethic, and, on occasion, amazing capacity for chugging beer.

Watching women like this grow as people and swimmers and reach their potential in the team context was what Coughlin loved most about college swimming. But this was no typical college season; everything Coughlin experienced had to be viewed under the Olympic microscope as well. And while the Bears beamed over what had gone down in New Jersey, Coughlin fretted over her inability to return to pre-Barcelona form.

Sitting in her office in Berkeley shortly after the Princeton meet, McKeever was asked if she believed Coughlin was nervous. "Oh, yeah. Definitely," the coach answered. "I mean, she's had 4 years of being a sure bet to win a bunch of medals, and now that we're getting close, her body isn't right. I think stuff from the last Olympics is coming up, but it's a delicate situation, and I'm not sure what the best way is to handle it. I don't want to rip off the scabs by probing too deeply. First of all, I don't know what the issues are. Secondly, I'm not sure *she* even knows what they are. I mean, she's only 21.

"So, she's nervous because of that, and because of what happened at Worlds, and because of what's going on out here every day in practice. In Barcelona, her body failed her, which is what happened before the last Olympics. And I think that worries her. Today, she said to me, 'I haven't had a good practice in 3 months.' I said, 'Nat, you haven't had a *great* practice in 3 months, but you've done some good things.'

"I've started keeping a journal for her, to show her how she's made progress. And I'm trying not to make it so much of a grind. About 3 weeks ago I took her out of spin and told her to stop coming into the weight room for a while. Today, I let her write her own workout—and the workout for the whole team. Now, did she *really* write it? Not really. I asked her what she wanted to do, right before practice, and then I said, 'Here's what I was thinking.' She basically took that and made up the workout. So, hopefully, that's close enough for her to think of it as hers.

"There's so much pressure going on in her life right now," McKeever continued. "She's taking her biggest academic load ever, and she's not a student who's going to settle for Cs—that's not her personality. She just bought a condo. She's been there a month, and she wants it to look a certain way. And it disrupted her routine. It's different not being a few blocks away—that's why, instead of going home and taking a nap, she's been hanging out in my office all day."

The departure of Cope, her longtime training partner, served as another disruption to Coughlin's world. "I worry about how Natalie is with that," McKeever said. "She says she's fine, but Haley said she was fine, too. They'll turn on you *fast*." McKeever laughed, then went on. "I mean, is Nat concerned because she lost a training partner? Does she feel like she's getting shortchanged here, too—like it's hurting her preparation? Does she feel all alone? The saving grace is Keiko (Price); she is just such an awesome person. But still, I think about it."

On the other hand, McKeever seemed more at peace with Cope's decision than she'd been in its immediate aftermath. "Haley tried to make it personal, but I'm not going to let it be about that," McKeever said. "She's a person who has always done unusual things when she's nervous. I mean, let's face it, she was practically unknown when she came here, and she's realized almost all of her dreams. If she gets to the Olympics, it won't just be because of what she'd done over the final stretch; it will also be because of her time here, plain and simple."

Yet being blindsided by the departure of a swimmer with whom she'd once been so bonded clearly weighed on McKeever as she tried to contend with Coughlin's winter blahs. "I want to make sure Nat's okay with what we're doing, and it's hard sometimes, because we are so close," McKeever continued. "Will she tell me if it's not good, or does she not want to hurt my feelings? Similarly, I don't want her to feel like I'm getting on her. But I'm trying to be more proactive, to ask her how she's doing more, and to be more 'on it' with her workouts. And you know what? Maybe this is for the best. Maybe Haley leaving will help Natalie, because now she has even more of my attention."

There was one Coughlin-related responsibility McKeever couldn't wait to shed: her unofficial role as manager, interview arranger, and agent. That wouldn't happen until March at the earliest, after Coughlin's collegiate career officially ended. But the more legwork she and Coughlin could do before NCAAs, the more quickly the swimmer could close a deal and turn pro. That said, this was a huge decision, and McKeever was intent on helping Coughlin make the right choice.

"The agent thing is a real stress, too," McKeever said. "We wanted to get interviews done in November, but there was no way we were prepared enough. I want her to go into the interviews with a game plan, and we weren't ready. We're going to try to get them done in January, and then hopefully she'll make a decision pretty quickly in March, right after NCAAs. I told her, 'I think we need to limit the number of interviews. It's like college recruiting. You can't talk to everyone.' And I think ultimately she'll approach this like she did when she was choosing a college. She'll feel comfortable with someone and won't be afraid to think outside the box. Just as, on paper, Cal wasn't the logical place to sign, but she had a feeling that she'd fit in here."

It's just that now, even as the Bears began to gel into a cohesive unit, Coughlin was very much in a realm of her own.

CHAPTER TEN

SHARKS AND MINNOWS

I n January 2004, most Cal students were either chilling at their parents' pads or shredding at Lake Tahoe's ski resorts. But when you're a member of a big-time collegiate swim team, one of the perks of your existence—a sort of compensation for the many hours spent toiling in practice—is the annual training trip before the start of the winter break. The trip's purpose is twofold: to prepare for the most important portion of the NCAA season and to facilitate team bonding. The locations vary, though the goal, for the most part, is to go someplace *warm*.

This year, McKeever had planned a doozy. The Golden Bears would fly to Sydney, Australia, in the heart of the Aussie summer, and sharpen their skills in a swimming-obsessed country. Largely because of Coughlin's notoriety, the Bears would get to hobnob with 2000 Olympic hero Ian Thorpe, a cross between Elvis Presley and Michael Jordan in his country, as well as 1972 multi-champion Shane Gould, her country's version of

Mark Spitz. There was an ancillary benefit, of course, to meeting with Gould—her boyfriend, Milt Nelms, would be there, too.

When the Bears' long flight touched down at Sydney Airport, Nelms and Gould were there to greet them. When the stroke consultant saw Coughlin disembark, he was startled by her appearance. "I was shocked when she came off the plane," he says. "She always looks so vibrant, electric, and springy, but this time she looked like crap. She was kind of wan, soft looking, and exhausted. I knew she wasn't right."

Over the next 9 days, McKeever allowed Coughlin to spend her mornings with Nelms in an adjacent pool while she and Hite put the rest of the team through its typical workout. It was a boon to Coughlin's mindset and pre-Olympic preparation—the most extended stretch of quality time she'd had with Nelms. Other than McKeever, Nelms was the only person Coughlin trusted to assess her technique, and even with the Games closing in, she was open to trying new things. "Teri had her do a lot of aggressive downtime, and we got to spend more time in the water than we ever had in the past," Nelms says. "That's when I really started to pick up some information. I learned a lot about how she learns, and I came to the conclusion that the less you say, the better. It's mostly her asking questions and me trying to get her to a place where she's comfortable."

Yet not everything was hunky-dory Down Under. The anti-Coughlin sentiment had swelled among her teammates in the weeks leading up to the trip, and now her presumed preferential treatment became the prime topic of discussion. The team was bonding, all right—united in its censure of the Bears' star swimmer.

"Everyone was saying stuff in the locker room," backstroker Helen Silver recalled several months after the trip. "We were doing all these things as a team, and Natalie would be off with Keiko (Price) or Milt. It kind of felt like the things she and Teri were working for were separate from what we were doing as a team."

Coughlin's close friend Marcelle Miller admits that she, too, began to get caught up in the "Why isn't Natalie here?" feeding frenzy. "Natalie was working with Milt, missing practices, and it bothered me at first," she says. "Then I thought about it, how she was spending her whole day in the water while the rest of us would go out and have fun. She didn't get to enjoy Australia at all. She was there to seriously improve her technique. I finally decided, 'I'm not gonna get worked up about whether she's here or not.' But I was in the minority. No one was talking about it in front of Natalie, but everyone was thinking it. They were all mad at her. We had a bad team attitude."

So, while Cal swimmers were shopping, sightseeing, sunning, and sampling kangaroo meat, Coughlin was playing the role of visiting celebrity, meeting and greeting various Australian luminaries. She did get to join the team on its breathtaking climb to the top of the Sydney Harbour Bridge, complete with a resounding, back-and-forth "Go Bears" cheer at the apex. Coughlin was also present for the trip's most memorable encounter, which began one afternoon as the swimmers were kicking back on the beach outside their hotel in Cornulla, about 45 miles south of Sydney. In a prearranged bit of scheduling magic, up walked Ian Thorpe, the country's biggest sports celebrity. He hung out for a while and chatted up Coughlin and many of the other Cal swimmers. Then, to their surprise, he said, "Hey, why don't you come up to my house for a barbecue?"

That *hadn't* been part of the plan. Soon there was shrimp on the barbie—as well as steak and chicken and sausages—and the freshly tanned swimmers, now sporting skirts and dresses, rolled up in cars driven by Thorpe's friends. "It was a huge, perfect party house," Silver recalls. "There was a dock with a boat, a pool and hot tub, and a pool table. We played pool, hung out with his friends, and had fresh fruit for dessert. It was an amazing night."

The swimmers hit the dance floor, grooving to tunes like "Beautiful" by Snoop Dogg and Pharell, and Justin Timberlake's "Rock Your Body." They cooed over Thorpe's new Labrador puppy—until the diminutive dog ate so much barbecue that he threw up. The only collective moment of regret came when Thorpe, standing behind a full bar, asked, "Your coach is cool with you having a drink, right?" Remembering that this was indeed a training trip, the swimmers declined.

Most of the time in Sydney, though, Coughlin could sense the intra-squad tension—and she wasn't the only one picking up on the negative vibes. "Teri is very intuitive and aware," Miller says. "A lot of girls on the team don't give her enough credit for that. She really does know everything. At times, she might seem a little bit paranoid, but she has a better handle on what's happening than most people realize."

McKeever called a team meeting one afternoon after practice, gathering the Bears in a trailer next to the pool. When she began talking, some swimmers expected her to try to smooth things over and convince them Coughlin was working as hard as they were. Instead, she angrily addressed the complaints and patently dismissed them, saying, "Natalie is the reason we were able to come to Australia in the first place, and she's the reason we have a lot of things we have. So if you don't agree with her approach, you're just going to have to deal with it. She's working on some things that are important to her training, and how she prepares is none of your business. You guys need to stop worrying about what she's doing and focus on yourselves."

McKeever teared up as she spoke; so, too, did Coughlin. Sitting in a chair near the back of the room, Coughlin thought to herself, *It feels like the whole team is against me. Don't they realize how hurtful they are?*

Finally, McKeever turned toward Coughlin and said, "I'm not sure if Natalie would want me to share this with you, but she confided in me the other day that she wants to have the best Olympics of any swimmer in history. So, believe me, she's not slacking off. She's trying to set world records and win gold medals."

The meeting didn't resolve the situation—Coughlin still felt stung by the in-house criticism, which didn't totally subside. But the air had been cleared, and that alone relieved much of the pressure that had been building for weeks. "I respected Teri for getting it out in the open," Silver says. "It wasn't unspoken anymore, and that allowed us to move forward. One thing I realized is that I don't understand the pressure of being Natalie Coughlin."

Says Miller: "I give Teri a lot of credit: She talked about the big pink elephant in the room. Overall, it helped the team bond. Because it wasn't just ignored, and because it came from Teri, people were able to get over it and loosen up."

Freshman Erin Reilly, for one, felt a strong surge of empathy for her celebrated teammate. "I felt so bad for her," Reilly says. "She gave up so much to stick around another year, and to have her teammates not even embrace her must have been really tough. I can't even imagine what she put up with all season, and through it all she just carried herself so well. She'd do something amazing in the pool and it was like everyone expected it. It sucks for her that her own teammates wouldn't even get that excited."

So much of McKeever's coaching philosophy centered around team bonding, a curious approach, given swimming's innately individualistic setup. Yet McKeever believed chemistry could go a long way toward improving a team's collective standing, and she did her best to facilitate it at every turn. At the start of the fall semester, the Bears had gone on a "team retreat," spending a weekend at a Lake Tahoe cabin during which they laid out their goals, sang Cal fight songs, and engaged in role-playing games designed to forge togetherness. In September they all swam the Tiburon Mile in the frigid Pacific Ocean. In January, after returning from Sydney, they would do a series of exercises with Kathie Wickstrand-Gahen, involving behavioral tests that grouped McKeever, Hite, and the swimmers according to preset categories.

Then there were the exceptionally well-planned recruiting weekends, which inevitably included team outings and gatherings at McKeever's house. And those efforts paid off in a big way.

In early November 2003, Emily Silver called to tell McKeever she would be attending Cal. Then she phoned her sister, Helen, who had several Cal teammates in her apartment at the time. Helen began screaming joyously; then she and her jubilant friends took to the streets to spread the news to others on the team, and an impromptu celebration ensued.

Emily Silver's signing, in McKeever's eyes, was the difference between a subpar recruiting class and a terrific one. That's how good McKeever thought the sprint freestyler was, with the potential to become even better. The Bears had lost out to Texas in the battle for backstroker Diana

MacManus and failed to attract Candace Weiman, a swimmer from nearby Castro Valley who had considered coming home to the East Bay after starring at Alabama; instead, she chose to transfer to Florida. Two other highly rated swimmers, Brooke Bishop and Erica Liu, chose Stanford over Cal. The Bears had signed some intriguing swimmers for the '04–'05 season, including backstroker/IMer Emily Verdin and breaststrokers Genna Patterson and Jenna Rinaldi, but there was no instant star in the mix. Emily Silver, Helen's smooth, ever-smiling, 5-foot-11 kid sister, changed all that. The fact that a sprint-freestyle star was exactly what the Bears needed most made it an even bigger coup.

Silver had briefly considered Auburn, the defending national champion, and Arizona, whose already strong program was on the rise, before settling on the Bears. McKeever had been cautiously optimistic about landing her, but it was a tricky proposition. Not only did she have to convince Emily that she was interested in *her*, and not merely in tapping the family bloodline, but she also had to make sure that Helen didn't feel overshadowed by her immensely talented sister. For all the times McKeever had grown frustrated with Helen, she also was exceedingly proud of the backstroke specialist, who had surprised observers throughout the nation by emerging as a standout freshman the previous year. At one point, out of respect for Helen's status and contributions to the program, McKeever called the sophomore into her office and said, "Helen, you do realize that you are my number-one priority, right? I'd love to have Emily come here, but if you feel uncomfortable with that in any way, I'll stop recruiting her right now."

It was hardly unpredictable that Helen, the third of four kids in the Silver family, told McKeever that wouldn't be necessary—she wanted Emily at Cal more than anyone. In October, when McKeever sat down to dinner with Emily and her folks in their home in Bainbridge Island, Washington (near Seattle), and said to the high school swimmer, "I want to offer you a full scholarship," Bob and Mary Sue began to cry with joy.

Emily was a good bet to succeed as a collegian: Like Helen, she hadn't been overtrained while under the tutelage of a reasonably restrained youth club coach. She was also very serious about her craft, as evidenced by her decision to forgo the second semester of her senior year of high school to move to Southern California and train with Dave Salo at Irvine Novaquatics (while doing independent study to complete her coursework). Then again, projecting the contributions of incoming recruits is not an exact science. Abrupt quitting is so endemic to swimming that losing one or two signees is almost inevitable; indeed, breaststroker Jenna Rinaldi, from North Carolina, would last a week with the team the following August before deciding to walk away.

"It's so funny when you recruit," Coughlin said one morning at Fatapple's in North Berkeley. "You hear, 'This person's gonna be good. That person's not that good,' but you never really know. We've had big-time recruits who really struggled their freshman year. Then you have someone like Erin Reilly, who no one's expecting anything from, and she's terrific. She trains so hard, and even when she's tired, she can do amazing things."

From her first few practices at Cal, it was apparent that Reilly, a superskinny strawberry blonde from Sacramento, had been drastically undervalued in the recruiting process. "I wish we had more than 11 months to work with her," Whitney Hite told me during a practice in late August, gesturing toward the freckled stick figure who was gliding through a protracted freestyle set in the far left lane at Spieker Pool.

"What do you mean?" I asked. "She's only going to be here for one season?"

"No. I mean, more than 11 months until the Olympic Trials."

"Wow," I said. "She's that good?

Hite nodded and said, "She could be."

The only problem was, Reilly would've been the last person to believe him.

Actually, it was a multifaceted problem, beginning with the fact that Erin was never supposed to be a star—her older sister, Brenda, was. Ever since they were a pair of redheaded pool rats tooling around Westchester County, a suburb of New York City, the Reilly girls had clearly defined roles—Brenda as the driven future Olympian, Erin as the shy, supportive younger sibling. "I was on a team since I was 4 because of my sister, but back then, to me it was a joke," Erin recalls. "Everyone was nice to me because my sister was there, but I didn't take it very seriously. My friends and I would go to the bottom of the deep end and take long showers."

By the time she was 16, Brenda owned most of the New York State age-group records in the sprint-freestyle events and was still harboring Olympic aspirations. She moved from the Westchester Middies to the prestigious Badger Swim Club in nearby Larchmont, New York, where coach John Collins, a former American record holder in the 200-yard butterfly, had a stable of renowned swimmers. Erin, who was 10 at the time, was on the verge of quitting the sport and taking up soccer. "My mom told the coach at Badger, 'Erin's pretty much done; she hates it,'" Reilly recalls. "But they convinced me to give it a try."

Swimming for Badger assistant Carlie Fiero stirred something in Erin, who began to view practices in an entirely different light. "Carlie was really tough and strict, but she was fair and honest, too," Erin says. "No one had ever really said that I'd be good before, and she made it worth it to work hard. I remember at the end of every practice, we'd swim a 50 for time with fins. If you beat the preassigned time, she'd give you one of these sour watermelon-wedge candies, and I was very motivated by that."

As Erin was blossoming as a distance freestyler and butterfly specialist, Brenda was experiencing the harsh side of swimming that afflicts so many young standouts. Early in her junior year of high school, she tore cartilage in her left knee, had surgery, and struggled to regain her prior form. She was good enough to get a scholarship to Notre Dame and have a commendable collegiate career but, says Erin, was "burned out" by the time she arrived in South Bend, Indiana.

Conscious of their elder daughter's plight, John and Mary Jane Reilly were especially careful with Erin as she rose through the youth ranks. "My sister started lifting weights at 12 and doing doubles (two workouts a day) in sixth or seventh grade," Erin says. "She was thinking Olympics, and she ended up getting so burned-out on the sport. So my parents were super, super protective when it came to me. They wanted five practices a week and nothing more, and they battled my coaches all the way through high school."

By then John had taken a job in Sacramento—the family of six (Erin has older and younger brothers) packed up and drove west before Erin entered the seventh grade, dropping off Brenda for her freshman year at Notre Dame along the way—and Erin had endured a coaching switch at her local club, Arden Hills, which soured her on the sport once more. She wanted to swim with the Sierra Marlins, a club that was a 40-minute drive from her home, but, she recalls, "my parents were not very supportive. They said, 'If you love the sport enough, you'll get it done where you are.'" She stayed at Arden Hills, where her new coach demanded she practice twice a day. Reilly's mother told the coach one practice a day would be fine, thank you, and finally relented in Erin's junior year of high school.

It was during that season that McKeever went to a high school sectionals meet to watch a recruit named Cheryl Anne Bingaman, who had signed a letter of intent to attend Cal out of Lodi High and would, as a freshman, earn all-American honors by swimming on the Bears' third-place, 400-yard freestyle relay at the 2003 NCAAs. While scouting Bingaman, McKeever kept noticing the slender junior who was breaking sectional records and, more important to the Cal coach, appearing to exert very little effort in the process.

"I was like, 'Who's *that*?'" McKeever remembers. "I said, 'Move that girl up the list; she's good.' Her sister had a Stanford sweatshirt on, which wasn't very encouraging, but I was definitely going to give it a try."

Up to that point, Reilly had envisioned herself swimming at a lower-level program such as Boston College's or Northeastern's—or, perhaps, following in Brenda's footsteps at Notre Dame. Georgia and Auburn, the nation's top two schools, each sent her questionnaires, neither of which she bothered to fill out. "I'd had a good run, and I had been getting better every year, but I still didn't think I wanted to go to a top team and have it be just swimming," she says. "I didn't know if I was that good, or if I wanted to make that much of a commitment."

When McKeever called Reilly's club coach to inform him of her interest, Reilly's reaction was far from positive. "I said, 'There is no way I'd ever go to Berkeley,'" she recalls. "I had been down there, and my feeling was 'I hate Telegraph Avenue. It's gross. I don't care if it's a good academic school. It's not for me.'" At the end of Reilly's junior year, McKeever showed up to watch one of her practices on a brutally hot Sacramento afternoon. "It was 110°, and Teri was dressed in nice clothes, just dying during my practice," Reilly says. "She came over for dinner, and my little brother, just to be stupid, wore a huge Notre Dame shirt. I remember that she had such a nice feel about her and the way she talked about swimming. I could tell I would be comfortable swimming for her, and my parents loved her. She said, 'You need to be at a top school. You're that good.' So I took a visit and was weirdly blown away."

Buoyed by McKeever's interest, Reilly ended up taking trips to Notre Dame, Northwestern, Texas, and Virginia, none of which compared to her Cal visit. "It was so well organized, and they treated us so well," she says. "I was sold."

When McKeever and Hite saw Reilly swim up close, they were beyond sold. They knew they had landed a sleeper recruit who had a chance to get better each year; now they had to convince *her* of that. Whereas Ashley Chandler, Cal's other talented distance freestyler/butterflier with that kind of talent, seemed to drive herself with an inner fury, the ever-amiable Reilly was almost compliant in her approach. The two would push each other, lap after endless practice lap, but while Chandler was upping her game to meet the challenge of a raw newcomer, a typical occurrence in sports, Reilly sheepishly marveled at the notion of keeping up with the former national champion. At first, Reilly admits, "I was really shy and nervous around everyone. They'd make weird jokes, and I didn't know how to respond." Mostly, Reilly kept quiet, put her goggles on, and swam, her efforts getting more and more impressive. Qualifying for the NCAA Championships was her only goal, and she did so with more than 3 months to spare, hitting her "A" cut, as part of the 800 free relay, in the Princeton Invitational.

When she got to Australia, Reilly was still coming to terms with her burgeoning potential. During one of the Bears' first practices there, she caught the eye of Milt Nelms, who later pulled her aside for some individual instruction. "The first time Milt saw her was during a full-team practice, and he noticed her immediately," McKeever recalls. "She has a nice relationship with the water. Sometimes she lets that get in the way. She gets real effortless. It looks easy, efficient. She has to see herself at a higher level and push past that."

In Australia, Reilly also began to adjust her head position during the freestyle stroke, moving it from an more upright stance to one more in line with the rest of her body. Over the next few months, Hite helped rid her of another bad habit—breathing into or out of a turn, an inefficient no-no in racing. Every time the coach noticed Reilly taking an ill-advised breath in practice, Hite would make her do five pushups.

What Reilly needed most of all, though, was some Coughlinesque drive and swagger. In Coughlin's words, "It's almost like Erin's scared to be good. Because she really could do some awesome things." With so much riding on her senior season—her dream of beating Stanford, a chance to win a national title in the 800 free relay—Coughlin was going to do everything she could to stoke Reilly's competitive fires.

As the Bears returned from Australia and began preparing for the stretch of five dual meets against Pac-10 rivals they hoped to sweep, the internal criticism of Coughlin subsided. Such was the paradox of her place on the team—at times some swimmers might have groused about her perceived perks, but they damn sure *loved* her come race day.

The more important the meet, the more the other Bears appreciated the three individual victories Coughlin guaranteed—usually not in her best events—along with the single relay she'd propel to an enormous lead. Some team members might have wished she'd been more engaged or overtly involved in motivating the other swimmers, but in the heat of battle, nobody was in a position to complain.

Other than a couple of throwaway races as a freshman, in nonconference meets that had already been decided in the Bears' favor, Coughlin had never lost a race for Cal. This was true not only in dual meets but also at the NCAA Championships. It might have been tempting to attribute that incredible run to talent alone, but to do so would have been an injustice. Every athlete, no matter how skilled, has a bad day at some point—that Coughlin had endured hers without losing was a testament to her relentlessly competitive nature.

That, too, was something her teammates understood better than anyone. The rest of the world saw her all-American looks and graceful manner, both of which obscured the fire within. Like Michael Jordan, Jerry Rice, and so many other champion athletes, Coughlin won most of all because she absolutely refused to tolerate the horrific alternative.

Haley Cope recalls being stunned by the sight of Coughlin's perpetually bloody lower lip during big meets. "I came to realize that when it really starts to hurt, Natalie bites down—so her legs will hurt less than her mouth," Cope says. "You could tell how hard she was working by the way she looked. If she had blisters on the bottom of her lip by the end of the meet, you knew she'd been pushed. I think she has a bizarrely high pain tolerance, and a lot of that is pure will. Her pain tolerance is somewhere the rest of us won't go."

Even amid her highly competitive teammates, Coughlin's aversion to losing was on an entirely different level. Some accused her of cheating during the games of Scattergories the Bears played while hosting dinners for recruits at McKeever's house; at the very least, Coughlin was guilty of getting intensely involved in the board game, exhorting those on her team to share her determination to win. In the pool, Coughlin could be similarly passionate, bristling when teammates left early at the start of sets.

"As much as Natalie likes to win, she hates losing much, much more," Cope says. "If she gets beat in anything, the relationship dynamics change pretty quickly. There's a difference between the piddly people like me who break the occasional world record and Natalie. I'm a like-to-win person; as long as I did fairly well, I'm pretty happy with myself. If Natalie went under the former world record in a race and still got beat, she'd be pissed. "

Even something seemingly as innocuous as a game of sharks and minnows, one of McKeever's rewards for enduring the rigors of practices—which at the same time honed hypoxic skills—had the potential for combustion. The game, in which some swimmers are "sharks" who try to force the "minnows" to the pool's surface, calls for captured swimmers to reenter the water and join the sharks. When the Bears played toward the end of a practice shortly after they'd returned from the 2002 NCAA Championships, assistant Adam Crossen decreed that the last remaining minnow would be allowed to skip the rest of the workout. Coughlin, not unpredictably, was intent on winning, and eventually a gang of inspired sharks darted toward the bottom of the pool to foil her.

Coughlin failed to honor Berkeley's tradition of nonviolent resistance. Marcelle Miller, one of her best friends, took a vicious kick to the chest; other teammates ended up with punches and scratches. Coughlin's freshman roommate, Kyoko Yokouchi, punched her in the mouth. By now Coughlin had won as the last remaining minnow, but out of principle, her teammates wanted her brought to the surface. Natalie Griffith took the lead in doing so, and she and Coughlin—and virtually everyone else—ended the game with scowls on their faces.

That was the last time the Bears played sharks and minnows.

CHAPTER ELEVEN

SWIMMING NOT TO LOSE

T he statement stunned her like the sound of a starting gun interrupting a daydream. The 2004 season was about to begin in earnest, with Cal hosting dual meets against Arizona and Arizona State, and they would mark the last time that the greatest swimmer in school history would perform at Spieker Pool. "Today and tomorrow are your final home meets," Coughlin's friend Mohamed Muqtar, the athletic department's director of student services, reminded the senior on the morning of Friday, January 23, as they sat in his office in Haas Pavilion.

"Whoa," Coughlin said. "Oh, yeah, I guess they are. Wow, that just snuck up on me."

The meets would take place concurrently with dual meets featuring Cal's men's team against the same schools, with the women and men alternating events—meaning more people than usual would be there to appreciate Coughlin's farewell performance. On paper, the Cal women were better than ASU, but the talented Wildcats presented a major challenge to the Bears' goal of going undefeated in dual meets. With standout swimmers like Emily Mason, Marshi Smith, Jenna Gresdal, and freshman Whitney Myers, Arizona was the nation's sixth-ranked team with a bullet.

The eighth-ranked Bears, meanwhile, would have to rely on a winning formula of Coughlin's comprehensive excellence, teamwide precision, and overall toughness. "We'll lose the first relay," Coughlin said, "but if we can win the first two or three individual events, they'll fold. That's the kind of team they are. But if they have some early success, they'll get into it, and then we might have problems winning the meet."

Coughlin's own mind-set was not ideal for such an intensely competitive competition. For one thing, she was distracted by the impending end of her collegiate career and the big decisions that go along with turning pro. The first and biggest was whom to hire as an agent. He or she would not only immediately negotiate what figured to be her most lucrative deal—an apparel contract with Speedo or Nike, or perhaps a wild-card entry into the swimwear sweepstakes—but also relieve McKeever of many of her responsibilities as Coughlin's first line of defense from the outside world. Additionally, as Athens approached, Coughlin's agent would play the central role in the marketing of this potential crossover personality who insisted upon being heavily involved in the shaping of her own image.

As Coughlin and McKeever assessed the swimmer's many options, they were fortunate to receive guidance from a pair of Cal swimming fans, former Olympic medalist Steven Clark and Leland Faust, who worked for a San Francisco financial firm called CSI Management, to which many prominent athletes had entrusted their investment dollars. Clark and Faust met with McKeever and Coughlin, helped them understand the agent-selection process, and would ultimately join them in interviewing candidates. Among the logical possibilities: Octagon, led by Peter Carlisle, who had already signed Michael Phelps (that agency's Tom Ross had arranged for Coughlin to throw out the first pitch at an Oakland

A's game in September); New York–based Peter Raskin, who had previously represented Janet Evans; and Evan Morganstein, whose Premier Management Group represented 20 of the nation's top swimmers and at the time also happened to rep McKeever.

Then there was a woman named Janey Miller, a former IMG employee who, after having moved to Boulder, Colorado, had left the business to start a family. Now with two young children, Miller, whose former clients included track star Michael Johnson, speed skater Apollo Anton Ohno, and swimmer Amy Van Dyken, was starting her own firm and looking for a marquee client with whom to launch her business. "I've talked to her a couple of times on the phone, and we've really connected," McKeever had said of Miller in December. "She's the first person who suggested that Natalie could drive the process, rather than the other way around. I'm looking forward to talking with her more. She just had a good feel about her."

In addition to the business-related distractions, Coughlin had emotional ones. It had been a traumatic week in Berkeley, as several days earlier Cal basketball player Alisa Lewis had died from bacterial meningitis after suddenly falling ill. The Cal athletic community was overcome by grief—and by paranoia. Lewis's teammates and coaches were given the antibiotic Cipro as a precaution, and everyone who trained in or near Haas Pavilion, including the swimmers, was lectured on the importance of maintaining sanitary environments. The day before the Arizona meet, Coughlin and many of her teammates went to a memorial service at Haas that left most attendees in tears. "I didn't know her," Coughlin said, "but by the end it felt like I did, because they really brought her to life. It was so tragic."

What Coughlin and her teammates didn't realize was how sharply the tragedy resonated with their assistant coach. Nine years earlier, Whitney Hite had nearly died from a similar illness—and only his love of swimming, along with his intestinal fortitude and the grace of God, had pulled him through.

A Denver native, Hite had arrived at Texas as a 6-foot-4, 140-pound stick of a swimmer good enough to earn scholarship money for his books and little more. Asked to describe himself as a swimmer, Hite says, "*Slow.* I tried real hard, but I certainly wasn't anything special."

Following his junior year at UT—his sophomore season of swimming, thanks to an earlier redshirt year—Hite returned home to Denver for Memorial Day weekend. He had planned to run the Boulder-to-Boulder 10-kilometer race on Memorial Day and went out for drinks with friends on Saturday night to…carbo-load. He woke up on Sunday, he recalls, feeling "kind of hungover. I had just come back from training with the team in Colorado Springs and was in peak physical condition, but I felt so lousy that I stayed in bed and slept most of the day."

His fever worsened as the evening went on, and by 10 p.m. it had shot up to 106°. Ice baths reduced his temperature to 102°, but it kept spiking to 106°. At 4 a.m. Sunday the phone rang at the Hite household—Hite's grandfather had died while coming out of surgery. Hite's father headed to Colorado Springs to attend to his father's funeral arrangements. At about 5 a.m., Hite began throwing up repeatedly, lying prone on the bathroom floor between heaves. His body ached, especially his head. His skin was covered by blood blisters—the meningitis, which had begun in the brain, had progressed down his spinal cord and entered his bloodstream.

At that point Hite's mother insisted they go to the hospital. "I couldn't put on my own clothes," Hite recalls. "I had started to bleed into my joints. It's by far the most painful thing I've ever been through."

It was very nearly the last thing he ever experienced. Upon Hite's arrival at St. Joseph's Hospital in Denver, doctors placed the patient on intravenous penicillin and braced for the worst. "It was pretty touch and go," Hite says. "They told my father to drive back from Colorado Springs because I wasn't going to make it. When you're sitting there in bed and you see that your blood pressure is down to 60 over 40 and your heart rate is 25, knowing that you have no control, you get pretty scared."

Soon a priest arrived to perform last rites. The patient, however, was strangely defiant. He kept asking his doctors about going home even as he endured the most brutal pain he'd ever experienced. "I kept wanting more morphine, but that lowered my heart rate, so they had to stop giving it to me," Hite recalls. "The ibuprofen was making me throw up, so I couldn't take anything for the pain. They wouldn't let me sleep, because my heart rate was so low that they were scared I'd fall into a coma."

The day after Hite was admitted, he got a visit from his boss at a local pool and insisted he be placed on the lifeguard schedule for the following week. "I wasn't worried about how sick I was," he says. "I was worried about getting back home and getting back to normal. I kept pushing the doctors to let me go home, and one of them said, 'I don't think you understand—you're lucky you're not pushing up daisies.' They had told my parents, 'You need to make preparations. He is going to die.' And they later said I was a million-to-one shot. There had been six cases in Colorado that year—four people died, one was a paraplegic, and then me. I could've been blind, deaf, an amputee, a paraplegic, afflicted with seizures for life. I was very lucky."

Hite's determination to get back to the pool certainly didn't hurt. Leave it to an exceptionally driven athlete to insist on getting up and going to the bathroom, even when the painful process took half an hour. "Every time I sat up, I got a huge migraine," he recalls. "Every joint in my body killed; I couldn't bend my legs. They took me to get a chest x-ray one day, and I told the nurse, 'Whatever you do, don't touch my legs.' She did it anyway when she was trying to lift me off the gurney, and I let out a primal scream that was so loud it even surprised me."

After 4 days in intensive care and another 4 days in a regular room, Hite decided that was enough. He told his doctor, who wanted him to stay at least another week, "I'm leaving whether you check me out or not." Finally, his doctor agreed to let Hite go if he could walk 30 yards during his rehab session later that afternoon. It took him an hour, but Hite passed the test and went home. He had lost 24 pounds and had to learn to walk again, but he was dead set on making it back to the pool.

"When someone takes something away from you, and then you get it back, you have an incredible appreciation for it," Hite says. "Looking back, I say it's the best thing that's ever happened to me." He was grateful to Texas coach Eddie Reese for allowing him to "start over," and the story ended happily, with Hite's being part of the Longhorns' NCAA Championship team in 1996. "I did get back to where I was before," Hite says, "but I was still slow as hell."

Hite also changed his outlook on the sport, becoming more attuned to technique and motivational strategies. "As a teammate," he says, "when you know your contribution's not going to be in the pool, your challenge is, how are you gonna make everyone around you better?"

It was that mentality that led Hite to coaching, though his quest to enter the profession wasn't especially well conceived. After graduating from college in 1998, Hite drove from Denver to US Summer Nationals in Clovis, California, crashed on a friend's hotel-room floor, and hoped something good would happen. On the last night of the meet, it did— Hite was introduced to Georgia coach Jack Bauerle, who mentioned he might have space for a volunteer assistant. So Hite, without having formally accepted the position, "packed up everything I had, put it in a trailer, and just showed up." He worked at an Athens, Georgia, bagel shop and spent mornings coaching high school kids at a local club, landing a paid position with the Bulldogs—at $9,000 a year—after 4 months, when another assistant left the program.

Five years and three national championships later, Hite landed in Berkeley, where his steely toughness and motivational majesty jibed with McKeever's technical excellence to create a killer coaching combination. "Whitney is so intense, so hard-core, and so fired up about swimming," freestyler Lauren Medina says. "I think we needed a change, someone to come in and say, 'Stop whining and get the job done.' His philosophy is that you need to work your ass off, day in and day out, if you want to get better. At first, I was intimidated by him. I felt I was never gonna be good enough for him. I wanted to prove to him I was as dedicated and driven as the swimmers from Georgia."

Says backstroker Helen Silver: "What's nice about the program is the

Teri-Whitney mix. You get the relentless intensity from Whitney and the teaching and nurturing from Teri. It is a very family-oriented program, just because we are like her kids. I've talked to people in other programs that are successful, and it's not a team thing for them at all."

～

As the Arizona dual meet was about to begin, Hite had already played it out in his mind, time and time again, and broken it down to a pair of pivotal efforts. "The two backstroke races are the key," he said as he confidently paced the deck. "We need to come up big in both."

The good news was that the greatest backstroker of all time was standing 2 feet away, wearing a blue cap with gold Cal script and the name "Coughlin" inscribed in block capital letters. The bad news was that, as usual, she wouldn't be swimming the backstroke for the Bears.

That's because, in Helen Silver, McKeever and Hite felt they had another swimmer capable of beating almost anyone. The almost-6-foot sophomore's effort could be uneven in practice, but in meets her competitive fire emerged, and she had made a habit of defeating higher-ranked swimmers in dual meets during her Cal career. Today she was especially primed because her sister Emily—Cal's star signee for the following season—was in attendance. In the end, Emily had chosen Cal over Arizona, and Helen felt the Bears could validate that decision by prevailing.

As Coughlin had predicted, the Bears were beaten in the first relay, the 400 meter medley. (Because this was an Olympic year, NCAA meets were being staged using short-course meters, rather than the usual yards, though this was not a uniform implementation. The Pac-10 Championships, for example, used yards.) But freshman Erin Reilly outkicked Arizona's top swimmer, Emily Mason, to win the 800 free, and Medina took down fellow junior Jessica Hayes in the 200 free, staking Cal to an early lead. Then came the essential 100 back, with Silver battling a pair of powerful sophomores, Jenna Gresdal and Marshi Smith, in a taut affair. Surging out of the last turn, Silver put away the competition and won comfortably, and the Bears looked capable of fulfilling Coughlin's prophecy.

Yet there was no reason for the Wildcats to fold; because of the inherent disadvantage of having a perpetually feeble diving program, the Bears were essentially 26 points down. This was the case going into every dual meet against a strong opponent—and for similar reasons, Cal would be all but mathematically eliminated from competing for the Pac-10 Championships at that meet in late February. Such was the curse of Cal swimming: You had to beat any legitimate opponent by 27 points or more simply to win a dual meet.

Why was diving such a disaster in Berkeley? The most obvious target of blame was longtime coach Phil Tonne, who in 20 seasons of coaching the men's and women's teams had contributed alarmingly little to the Bears' overall success in important competitions. This was especially true on the women's front—only one of his divers, back in the '91 and '92 seasons, had even qualified for NCAAs. McKeever was so frustrated by the situation that she would gladly have given away one of her 11 scholarships for a diver who could at least score points in dual meets, let alone Pac-10s and NCAAs. Tonne, however, couldn't attract anyone of that caliber. By way of explanation, he would complain that Cal's facilities weren't as attractive as those of many of its opponents. Stanford, for example, had a state-of-the-art platform in its pool, while none existed at Spieker, where the divers shared the pool with the swimmers.

There was also the philosophical question of whether diving belonged in a swim meet in the first place. "Other than the fact that it takes place in water, it is so far removed from what we do," Coughlin says. "It would be more logical to stage a water polo game between races and count the goals toward the point total than to do what we do now." Indeed, collegiate diving had a judging setup that made international figure skating seem steeped in integrity. Each dive was judged by the two diving coaches of the competing schools, meaning Tonne, at least technically, was half-responsible for quantifying his athletes' dismal showings in competition.

There were two diving events and 14 swimming races (12 individual contests bookended by relays) in each dual meet, meaning that diving essentially counted for a whopping eighth of the point total. In dual meets, quality opponents would finish first, second, and third in each diving event to capture a total of 16 points, while Cal would be relegated to the fourth and fifth positions and the three points that came with them. Often, in fact, Cal's best diver would finish worse than fourth, but the rules mandated that a team could accumulate no more than first-, second-, and third-place points for any one event. Thus, in theory, McKeever could have entered a pair of discus throwers from the women's track team, instructed them to do pikes (the most basic of dives), and *still* received the exact score: a guaranteed 32–6 deficit overall.

All of this was why, when the 1-meter diving scores were posted midway through the meet, there was a giddy sense of excitement among the Bear swimmers: Five-foot-one freshman Lila Korpell had taken third place, meaning Cal's deficit in the event was 15–4 rather than the customary 16–3. While it's possible that some of Arizona's divers had simply faltered, the Bears weren't about to question Korpell's unlikely breakthrough—that two-point difference might decide the meet.

It was going to be close. Coughlin had done her job, leading 1-2-3 sweeps in the 50 and 100 freestyles and cruising to victory in the 100 fly. But Helen Silver, in her best event, had been dusted by Hayes in the 200 back, one of the races Hite felt the Bears had to have. As the meet played out, it became perilously clear that Erin Reilly would probably have to defeat Mason again, this time in Mason's specialty, the 400 free.

Though game as always, Reilly would come up 2 seconds short— and it wouldn't matter. That was because Ashley Chandler, she of the disappointing freshman season, showed a measure of grit that both surprised and delighted McKeever. Maybe it was an Arizona thing: Chandler, who hailed from the Phoenix suburb of—no lie—Chandler, was suddenly swimming like the decorated teenager who people joked must have had her town renamed in her honor. She utterly overpowered Mason down the stretch, winning by nearly 2 seconds, to keep Cal in contention as the meet wound down.

Silver had sulked for a couple of minutes after her defeat in the 200 back, but McKeever made sure she understood the importance of her performance in the final individual race, the 200-meter individual medley.

"You have to take at least fifth," McKeever urged. "If you do that, and we go 1–3 in the relay, we can at least tie." Silver took fourth, by 0.32 second, to put the Bears in even sweeter position: Win the 400 free relay, and the meet would end in a 150–150 deadlock. Take first and third, and Cal would win by a 152–148 score.

With Coughlin leading off Cal's A relay, McKeever liked her team's chances of finishing first. When Coughlin swam her 100 in a sizzling 54.01 seconds—far faster than her time of 55.52 in winning the 100 free an hour earlier—it was effectively over, with seniors Danielle Becks and Micha Burden, along with Medina, cruising from there. So Cal had a tie in the bag—the victory would come down to whether its B team could edge Arizona's B relay for third. With Chandler and Reilly providing solid opening legs, the B Bears were still in fourth, until junior Emma Palsson made a move during the third leg. That meant Cal's fortunes would be decided by its unlikely anchor, 5-foot-2 junior Keiko Amano.

Not only was Amano by far the shortest swimmer on the team, but she was also the quietest. So unassuming was the Japanese-born sprint-freestyle specialist from Camarillo, a small town 50 miles northwest of LA, that the Bears had managed to *lose* her on her recruiting trip.

McKeever, then-assistant Adam Crossen, and about a dozen team members had been walking through San Francisco's Pier 39, a popular outdoor shopping area that backed up into the Bay, on a Friday night in the spring of 2001 and left to make the 20-minute walk to Ghirardelli Square for ice cream sundaes. They were almost there when McKeever suddenly looked around and blurted, "Wait—where's Keiko?" A dozen swimmers shrugged in unison. "Oh my God," one blurted out. "We left her!" The Bears' Katherine McAdoo ran back to retrieve the recruit outside the Pier 39 bakery where she'd last been spotted. Amano, it turned out, had gone inside to use the restroom and was standing there, looking lost and forlorn, when McAdoo arrived to rescue her.

"Well," McKeever said to Crossen at night's end, "I guess we blew that one."

The coaches were able to laugh at their faux pas. The valedictorian of her private high school, Amano was intrigued by Cal's prestigious bioengineering department and had contacted them in the first place. McKeever and Crossen had regarded Amano as a project who might someday help with relay depth. When it came time to take inventory of the incoming class, McKeever told Crossen, "She's not coming. It's fine. Call her and get it over with."

So Crossen called Amano, asked if she'd made a decision, and nearly dropped the phone when she answered, "Yes. I think I'm coming to Cal."

What? Crossen nearly blurted out. At conversation's end he ran to McKeever's office and said, "Teri—she committed!" It was the first verbal commitment he'd secured as a collegiate coach.

Once in the fold, Amano confounded McKeever by behaving as if she were unreceptive to coaching. *This girl is incredibly bright,* McKeever thought to herself. *How can she be so intelligent and yet be so blocked when it comes to swimming?* During hypoxic sets, Amano had been known to cry because she was so unnerved by the specter of oxygen deprivation. By the end of Amano's freshman year, McKeever figured, *That girl's only gonna make it a year. She's chosen the most academically demanding thing you can do, and she's not getting any better when she does swim.*

Amano's sophomore year was nothing special. She stayed in Berkeley for summer school, kept working out with McKeever, and, as she competed in various long-course events, underwent a remarkable transformation. Her swims were cleaner, more technically precise, and *faster.* "How come you can't do that during the year?" McKeever asked.

"I'm too tired," Amano answered. "I'm up late studying all the time."

Many coaches would have scoffed and told Amano to reevaluate her commitment to swimming. McKeever responded that fall by amending Amano's schedule, allowing her to skip certain workouts to allow her some rest. That did wonders, as did Amano's suddenly improved ability to assimilate McKeever's lessons on technique. "Sometimes she's too smart, too analytical about things," McKeever says. "I tell her, 'Let it go—just let your body take over and see how it feels. There's not a right way and a wrong way. It's a concept.' Sometimes she just has to work through it on her own."

One afternoon in May 2004, I sat with Milt Nelms and McKeever at Cancun, a taqueria in downtown Berkeley, when the coach posed a question to the stroke guru. "I've always wondered," McKeever said, "can you teach someone how to be talented? What do you think?"

"Yes," Nelms replied. "Especially in a sport that's so sensory."

"I didn't used to think so, but I do now," McKeever said. "Do you know who taught me that? Keiko Amano. It took a long time for her to get it, but eventually she decided she wanted to be coached; she wanted to listen. I had to reprogram her, and once I did, it was like she had a whole different skill set."

Nelms took an enormous bite of a chicken burrito and laughed. "I see her in the water and say, 'Look at that little thing. How can she go that fast?' It defies everything we know about physics," he said. "How can someone that short go 22.8 (in a short-course 50-yard freestyle relay split)?"

This was not as insulting as it sounded—Nelms and McKeever loved Amano as much as they did virtually any swimmer on the Cal team, partly because she was a testament to McKeever's penchant for milking the most out of her swimmers and partly because the swimmer by that time had already carved out a place in Golden Bear lore with several transcendent performances.

Amano's second-biggest moment as came at the end of that relay against the Wildcats. Given a slight lead over Arizona's B team by Palsson, Amano briefly lost it before powering back into third after the first turn. She kept charging, setting off a wave of euphoria in the Spieker stands. Cal's male swimmers and coaches stopped what they were doing to behold the spectacle—Amano not only was going to win the meet, but was making a run at Arizona's star-studded A team! In the final 25 yards, she closed on the Wildcats' Lisa Pursley, finishing a mere 0.93 second out of second place. Had the race been 5 yards longer, there was little doubt the pint-size piranha would've run Pursley down.

If Amano had emerged as the swimmer McKeever would most want anchoring a B relay, the A equivalent unquestionably was Lauren Medina. With Coughlin preferring to swim the leadoff leg for several reasons—it made for less choppy water, the better for her faultless technique to pre-vail over physically stronger swimmers; it allowed her to set records by producing a pure time from the starting gun; and it usually so demoral-ized the opposition that they psychologically gave up—Medina's bravado and fortitude made her the perfect closer.

There was no closer route to McKeever's heart than to swim a deciding relay leg against UCLA, a Pac-10 rival also coached by a woman, Cyndi Gallagher. Of the school's three biggest rivals, UCLA ranked a distant third on the animosity scale, behind Stanford and USC, for the vast majority of Cal students and student/athletes. McKeever, however, still had some of that old USC undergraduate in her—the thought of losing to the Bruins tormented her. Medina, who had once dreamed of swimming for UCLA, was determined to make sure that wouldn't happen.

The 10th-ranked Bruins had served notice that they were a major force by throttling 4th-ranked Stanford, 151–92, in Los Angeles on January 30. The Bears, who had cruised over Arizona State, 185–110, the previous Saturday (the day after the Arizona meet), had just completed a surprisingly easy 180–80 rout of 9th-ranked USC across town and were dining with family members and supporters at LA's famed Mexican res-taurant El Cholo when they heard the stunning UCLA-Stanford score.

When the Bears entered UCLA's Student Activities Center pool (more commonly known as "Men's Gym Pool") the following afternoon, the atmosphere was electric. An overflow crowd cheered as the Bruins opened the meet with a victory in the 200 medley relay, only to have the Bears capture the next four events. Coughlin again won the 50 and 100 frees and the 100 fly, and Helen Silver (100 and 200 back) and Ashley Chandler (400 and 800 free) also came up huge with two victories apiece. Yet UCLA got the obligatory 32–6 diving edge and stayed in the meet, and with one event to go, the 400 free relay, it was 142–141 Cal, meaning the winner of that race would win the meet.

The Bears had Coughlin leading off, but the Bruins, a team known for its sprinters, had depth and a roaring crowd to their advantage. Coughlin, with a swift 54.40 opening split, gave Cal a lead of a body length and a half, but the Bruins steadily closed the gap, and Kim Vandenberg nearly caught Micha Burden by the end of the third leg. That left Medina and senior Malin Svahnstrom, whose adrenaline-fueled surge in the first 50 meters nearly matched Coughlin's time over the same distance.

The UCLA swimmers and fans were going nuts—they had seen this type of race hundreds of times. Svahnstrom had all the momentum, and Medina would soon surrender the last vestiges of her lead and succumb. As the two swimmers came off the final turn, Medina slowed for a moment—it was as if time stopped so the fans could appreciate Svahnstrom's closing burst.

It turned out Medina was just getting started. She flashed back to her days as a recruiting afterthought, when Gallagher called to woo her long after McKeever had expressed interest. *No way we're losing this meet,* Medina thought as she pulled back in front, the apparent leader vacillating with each swimmer's stroke. The knot in McKeever's stomach began to dissipate—Medina smelled the wall like a shark smells blood. *Thwap!* Medina outtouched Svanhstrom by 0.41 second, setting off a wild celebration on the Cal end of the deck.

McKeever's Overachievers had done it again.

"Teri has an incredible knack for bringing the best out of people," says her friend Dave Salo, the Irvine Novaquatics coach. "Too often we get credit for the good athletes that come out of our programs and do well on a national or international level. But a better test of coaching ability is, what do the nonstars do? When you take the Lauren Medinas and the Erin Reillys and turn them into impact swimmers, then you've got my attention."

Now, more than ever before, the Bears had become McKeever's Believers. Their goal of completing an undefeated dual-meet season had just one remaining obstacle—the biggest one of all.

∼

"We *have* to win this meet," Coughlin said as we sat in Barclay's, a restaurant/pub in Oakland's Rockridge district, 2 days before Cal's showdown with Stanford, sliding her pint of microbrewed beer across the table for emphasis. It wasn't as scandalous as it seemed, or at least it wasn't intended to be—we had tried to get ice cream cones across the street at the Dreyer's Factory Store, but a note on the door said "Back in 15 Minutes," so here we were. I was always a little self-conscious during my public meals with Coughlin, but this time, what with the daytime beers and the fact that we were perilously close to my 'hood, who knew what danger lurked? At any moment, I expected some hypervigilant mom I knew to burst through the door from the outside patio and make a major scene.

Coughlin was in a terrific mood. She and her teammates had been looking forward to taking another crack at the Stanford Cardinal since August, when she decided to return for her senior year. The Bears had actually beaten the Cardinal in swimming in each of her previous years, but the meets were swimming *and* diving competitions, and Cal had lost all three by narrow margins, the past two on the final relay. A year earlier at Spieker, Coughlin, having already swum the maximum four events (three individual races and a relay), had watched helplessly as the Cardinal's star sprint freestyler, Lacey Boutwell, predictably dusted breaststroke specialist Stacianna Stitts in the final leg of the 400 free relay to complete a comeback triumph. This year, Coughlin vowed, the Bears would finally end their 28-year drought against their archrivals.

She wanted to vanquish the red menace and win the Big Meet for many reasons: as a parting present to McKeever and validation of the coach's teachings, as a repudiation of a school and culture she fundamentally loathed. But the biggest driving force was the battle she'd waged more than 4 years earlier to attend the school of her choice. "I want to show my parents how wrong they were about Cal," Coughlin said.

Choosing Cal over Stanford had been Coughlin's first definitive move as an adult, and it was, in her mind, the sole reason she was now setting world records and being talked about as a multiple gold medalist. Hell, it was probably the sole reason she was still swimming, period.

"With the frailty she had back then, I don't think she would've made it to Christmas of her freshman year if she'd gone to Stanford," says Milt Nelms, who previously worked as a volunteer assistant for Cardinal coach

Richard Quick. "Richard just charges straight ahead, and she realized, maybe not consciously, that he was going to get her to do whatever he wanted to do—that he would have control—which was the opposite of what she needed at the time. I told him once, 'That kid would not have made it 8 weeks with you,' and he got really quiet, like he was visibly hurt I'd said it. A couple of months later he asked me what I'd meant by that, and I told him. I know athletes that are perfect for Richard, but Natalie Coughlin would not have been a good match. But I remember vividly when she signed with Cal—he was stunned. He could not figure out how that had happened. And, of course, everybody was waiting for her to fall on her face."

Now, after having proved so much to so many, Coughlin was going to throw in the faces of her parents something that they had long since come to understand and accept. After the Bears' meet against Stanford during Coughlin's freshman year, McKeever held a picnic for her swimmers and their families in the beautiful eucalyptus grove on the southwest end of Cal's campus. There Jim Coughlin approached her and said, "Teri, I want to apologize. I had a chance to watch your team and their team, and see you and Richard coach against each other and how each team behaved, and now I realize how wrong I was. I understand now why my daughter felt so comfortable being here with you. This is absolutely the best place for Natalie." McKeever was so touched she nearly cried. She and the Coughlins later became exceptionally close, and the coach cherished their involvement, with Zennie and Jim hosting dinners and making goodie bags for the Cal swimmers and raising money by selling snacks during home meets.

Rapping her long fingers on the wooden table at Barclay's, Natalie had the unmistakable air of a 21-year-old who knows more than anyone in the room. "I feel really good about this meet," she said. "It just feels like we're about to do something great."

Coughlin was excited that her longtime boyfriend, Ethan Hall, would be in Palo Alto to watch her swim. After graduating from UC Santa Barbara, Hall had returned to the Bay Area and was working at a mortgage-brokerage company. "He's had to work a lot of weekends," she explained, "so he hasn't been able to make it out to too many meets."

She certainly would welcome his emotional support, for there had been times that winter when she'd felt so alone. Relating an incident from the meet at USC, Coughlin told me she'd had "a breakdown" against the Trojans, a reaction to the pressure she felt to maintain her career-long winning streak in Pac-10 dual meets. It started before the 200-meter freestyle, when the Trojans' public-address announcer said during introductions, "Natalie Coughlin has *never lost* a race in her college career." The stat wasn't even accurate—Coughlin had failed to win a couple of throwaway races as a freshman—but what bothered her was the undue pressure she faced to stay undefeated throughout her senior season. She was also upset because in the lanes on either side of her happened to be the two American swimmers most capable of taking her down at that distance: 2000 Olympian Kaitlin Sandeno and American record holder Lindsay Benko, a former USC swimmer who was competing as a member of the Trojans' Swim Club. Technically, a victory by Benko wouldn't count, but Coughlin still felt pressured to win the race. She pulled out the narrowest of victories, outtouching Sandeno by 0.19 second, with third-place Benko less than a second behind the winner.

Three events later, McKeever sent Coughlin back out to face the formidable Sandeno again, this time in the grueling 200-meter butterfly. By then Cal had the meet in hand, and McKeever could easily have juggled the schedule so that Coughlin didn't have to swim that event. As she was walking to the blocks, Coughlin, in her own words, "became a total brat. I snapped at Teri, 'Why do I have to be the one who's thrown out there?'" She won handily, beating Sandeno by more than 2 seconds, then retreated to a nearby bench and began to cry. Her closest friends on the team, Emma Palsson, Marcelle Miller, and Micha Burden, went over to comfort her and calm her down. McKeever approached and said, "I hate to see you like this. By going out there, you won so much more than that race."

Looking back on the incident, Coughlin was not proud, but she understood the emotions behind her outburst. "For most of my college career I was able to revel in the joy of victory," she said. "But this year, as people have drawn attention to my streaks, it's been more of a fear of losing, and that's not nearly as enjoyable. I remember when I finally set my (long-course) world record in the 100 back in 2002. People had been expecting me to do it for a year and a half, so when I finally did, it was almost as if I couldn't really even enjoy the accomplishment."

McKeever, too, sensed Coughlin's tightness in the face of such constant attention, later saying, "After the thing happened at SC, when she was over it—or, at least, partly over it—I said to her, 'It's good that you were able to confront an uncomfortable situation. That's probably the one person (Sandeno) who could've beaten you, and you didn't let her.' Because of what she went through before the last Olympic Trials, I've been hesitant to put her in uncomfortable situations. But as the Olympics draw near, I probably need to think about pushing her more."

As excited as she was about the team's prospects for beating Stanford and achieving a top-five finish at NCAAs, a part of McKeever was eager for the collegiate season to end so she and Coughlin could get down to business in their preparations for Athens. The swimmer McKeever was coaching right now seemed geared toward getting through the next 2 months without absorbing any significant blows, rather than someone savoring the end of an amazing career. "College swimming is the first time that it's not about you, and that's what was so liberating for Natalie when she came here," McKeever said. "And that's also what's paralyzing for her now. It's become about her again, and she feels the strain."

Gliding her empty glass across the wooden table 2 days before the last and most important dual meet of her life, Coughlin conceded that she hadn't been having a whole lot of fun. "I was thinking last week that I'm not swimming as well as I should," she said, "because I'm worried too much about having to win—or, really, about trying not to lose. I'm stressing out about this Pac-10 win streak instead of just getting in the water and going for it. I need to get back to just looking at the girl next to me and thinking, *I'm gonna beat her.*"

Especially if she happened to have a red S on her swim cap.

CHAPTER TWELVE

BLUE VALENTINE

Sitting stiffly on a wooden bench, heavy head resting in her damp hands, the tired swimmer closed her eyes and wondered how, in a locker room full of teammates—beneath a packed swim stadium with thousands of eyes preparing to gaze upon her—she could feel so desperately alone.

She had never been this miserable, even during her darkest day with the Terrapins or the most acute stretch of shoulder trauma. The pain she felt right now was something worse, a hollow numbness that was equal parts depression and disbelief. *How can this be happening?* she wondered over and over. She hadn't slept more than an uninterrupted hour for the past two nights, and as much as her arms and legs hurt from her having exerted herself in the water, her heart ached even more.

It occurred to her that it was Valentine's Day, a thought so absurd it almost provoked laughter. Almost. Laughter would not have played well in this locker room, not with a group of swimmers who had been so sure they were ready to vanquish their archrivals and now were coming to terms with the brutal reality that it wasn't going to happen.

The final dual meet of Natalie Coughlin's unrivaled career had been playing out at the Avery Aquatic Center for nearly 2 hours now, and here, during the second diving break, the math was not in Cal's favor. Only two events remained, and Stanford's swimmers had already started openly celebrating a 28th consecutive victory in the Big Meet. For a few moments there was a sunken silence, a collective resignation among two dozen deflated swimmers. And then, from the lone man in the room, came a strange shout of defiance.

"They're out there acting like they've already won, but it's not over," Whitney Hite barked, his words reverberating through the room. "You can still do this. You *will* do this. We're just so damn close. Do *not* give up."

The Bears perked up, energized by the strand of hope that still existed, if only in a technical sense. Their insolent assistant coach began laying out the numbers, explaining precisely what they'd need to do to win. Finally, Coughlin opened her eyes, bit down on her lower lip, and marched quietly out of the locker room with her teammates. She wasn't sure she believed Hite, but at least his words had distracted her. And right now, anything that took her mind off her misery was far better than the bitter alternative.

Buoyed by a hearty cheer from the huge assemblage in the stands behind their side of the pool deck, the Bears congregated and psyched themselves up one last time. Senior cocaptain Natalie Griffith, who was about to swim the 400-meter individual medley, was wide-eyed as she walked to the starting blocks, looking as if, in teammate Lauren Medina's words, she had seen a ghost. Standing behind the blocks as she waited to lead off the meet's final event, the 400-meter freestyle relay, which would take place immediately after the 400 IM, Coughlin stepped forward and put her hands on Griffith's shoulders. The two Natalies had never been particularly close, but now, on the verge of suffering yet another disappointment against the team they detested most, their bond was palpable.

"I can't believe we're gonna lose to them again," Coughlin said between F-bombs. "But if we're gonna lose, let's go down swinging."

"Hell yeah," said Griffith, snapping out of her daze.

"Hell yeah," echoed Coughlin. "Go get 'em."

How had it come to this? The Bears trailed 140–124 with two events to go and Stanford needing a mere 11 points to clinch the victory, and none of the Cal swimmers, or their coaches, could figure out how it had happened. Sure, there was the diving disparity, and Stanford, in sisters Tara and Dana Kirk, had two of the best swimmers in the country. But the Bears, in the very fibers of their being, were convinced they were the deeper, tougher, more resilient squad that was destined to prevail. They had never been more motivated—they'd been talking about this moment for months, and their team meeting two nights earlier had been nothing short of surreal.

On a clear Friday night in Berkeley, the swimmers had gathered in the Grille Room at Haas Pavilion to make collages containing their favorite memories of the season, one of those touchy-feely activities of which McKeever was so fond. When they were finished, the coach stood up and told her swimmers how much she cared for them and admired the sacrifices they'd made to that point.

Then McKeever said, "I know how much this meet means to you, and I know that if we win, you're going to want to celebrate. You're going to want to go on and on until midnight, when we all know that would be inappropriate." She paused, and then, to everyone's amazement, added: "*When* we win this meet, you're going to have to celebrate a hell of a lot later than that."

Some swimmers howled in approval; others merely sat there open-mouthed. *Teri's telling us to party!* McKeever, a woman who didn't drink, whose father had been killed by a drunk driver, who normally would have implored her swimmers to get a good night's sleep a mere 12 days before the start of the Pac-10 Championships, was encouraging a celebration that had been a long time coming.

If the swimmers hadn't known before how much this meet meant to their coach, they did now. The older ones had seen firsthand how desperately she wanted to defeat Stanford—and the younger ones were well familiar with the story of Cal's last visit there 2 years earlier. The two teams were locked in a typically tight contest when Richard Quick, the Cardinal's legendary coach, engaged in a bit of gamemanship that enraged his Cal counterpart. Stanford's senior cocaptain Jessica Foschi, a talented distance swimmer from New York with loads of international racing experience, was swimming back-to-back events, the 1,000- and 200-yard freestyles. Foschi won the 1,000 free, but instead of getting out and walking to the warm-down pool with the other swimmers, she continued swimming in the competition pool and warmed down as the slower finishers completed their laps. This, McKeever felt, was clearly unfair; she also believed Quick, with whom she had a good relationship, had intentionally entered an exceptionally slow swimmer in the 1,000 so that the race would take longer to complete, thus ensuring that Foschi had ample warm-down time before the 200.

As she saw what was happening, McKeever boiled over. She started running up the pool deck, pointed at Quick, and screamed, "That's b.s., Richard!" (She might have included a profanity or two, but that was the gist.) Avery Aquatic Center grew quiet—swimmers, parents, fans, and even recruits of both schools were stunned by McKeever's rage. She couldn't help it. In a system she knew was already stacked against her team, the thought of Quick's resorting to such rule-bending tricks put McKeever over the edge.

Foschi finished second to Coughlin in the 200, and the Bears lost the meet by a 159.5-to-140.5 score as Cal's diving deficit once again proved to be the difference. The two coaches patched up their differences on deck, with Quick telling McKeever, "I didn't mean to do anything out of line," and McKeever responding, "I respect you too much to even get into this with you. The reality is that you have a better team than I do right now; you don't need to play games."

Rather than scorn their coach's emotional outburst, the Bear swimmers embraced it as a sign of McKeever's fallibility and competitiveness. Soon the coach cracked up at the sight of the team's latest T-shirt design—with McKeever's off-color quote embossed on the back.

It would be hard to imagine a similar display of frivolity at Stanford, where Quick's manic intensity set a daunting tone. Coughlin, in fact, had gleefully discovered a photo of Quick in one of her psychology text-books, included in the middle of a chapter on anger management. The caption began: "People with a type A personality—those who are impatient, competitive, and hostile..." It went on to note a correlation between those with type A personalities and heart disease. Coughlin quickly photocopied the page and placed it on Cal's growing locker room bulletin board.

Though cast as the villain, Quick wasn't a one-dimensional autocrat. His detractors (Coughlin and McKeever ultimately not among them) blasted his propensity for coaching to his stars and, they charged, ignoring the majority of his rank-and-file swimmers. They viewed him as a humorless taskmaster who cared only about results and failed to develop anyone who didn't share his swimming-is-life mentality. Yet Quick's coaching talent was undeniable: The man had won 12 NCAA Championships (six with Texas, six with Stanford), had placed in the top three every year from 1983 through 2002, and had been part of the past five US Olympic coaching staffs, including three times as head coach. To his credit, he was one of the few figures in his sport—along with McKeever—who looked outside the normal channels for means of improving their swimmers. It was he, remember, who had hired Milt Nelms in the first place, before the stroke guru became a confidant of McKeever. In fact, as Nelms and others would attest, Quick, if any-thing, was too far out there when it came to alternative approaches. The man was like an old-fashioned salesman, espousing snake oil as the wonder drug and actually believing in its healing power.

One afternoon in September of 2004, while dining at a taqueria near his Irvine, California, headquarters, Novaquatics coach Dave Salo picked up a bottle of Cholula Hot Sauce when asked to assess Quick's coaching style. "This makes you faster," Salo said, shaking the bottle. Then, picking up a glass of iced tea with his other hand, Salo said, "And this." He put down the hot sauce and the tea and picked up a salt shaker. "This, too. Put 'em all on you, and you'll be unbeatable."

Witnesses said that at the 2004 Olympics, when Quick was named to the US staff for the sixth time, as a women's assistant, he had his current and former Stanford swimmers sleeping underneath a magnetic triangle in an attempt to channel their energy. He would also cause a miniscandal after the 2004 Trials, when it was revealed that six Stanford swimmers in Long Beach had been spotted with small patches affixed to their shoulders, a practice that apparently had also occurred during the Cal-Stanford meet. In the wake of the BALCO steroid scandal, which had emanated from a laboratory just up Highway 101 from Palo Alto, the revelation about the patches was not welcome publicity for US swimming. The patch, known as the LifeWave Energy Enhancer, was said by one coach to contain testosterone. Quick denied that the patches were illegal, and no evidence was ever uncovered to substantiate the accusations. Quick explained to the *San Francisco Chronicle* that the patches were designed to electronically stimulate acupuncture points, inserting current into the body to help improve an athlete's stamina. "We're not trying to hide anything," Quick told the newspaper, "because it was out there in broad daylight." He said he was "known as a coach who tries to leave no stone unturned in how to improve in a safe, healthy, legal way."

Quick certainly had been aboveboard when it came to preparing for the Cal-Stanford dual. Earlier in the week, he had called McKeever and broached the subject of whether the teams should wear Fastskins, the Speedo-manufactured body suits that cut down on water resistance and theoretically produced faster times. Quick could simply have had his swimmers wear the suits and potentially caught the Bears unawares, but he wanted a level playing field. McKeever, mindful that only four Stanford swimmers had made their NCAA qualifying cuts, an alarmingly low total to that point, agreed that swimmers for both teams could feel free to wear the Fastskins.

To her, it would make the meet that much more special. She had played out various scenarios in her mind, trying to plot the optimal lineup for victory, and no matter which way she tried it, Cal's potential winning margin was thin. Coughlin had suggested she swim the 200 free as one of her events, but McKeever convinced her otherwise, instead penciling in her star for the 50 and 100 frees and the 100 fly. That meant Lauren Medina would have to beat Stanford's star freestyler, Lacey Boutwell, in the 200 free. "Lauren can do it," McKeever said. "She has to, because it's tough to see us winning otherwise."

If the Bears were to lose, it would not be for want of motivation. A little more than a month earlier, upon arriving in Australia, they had been a fractured unit rife with jealousy and internal backbiting. Now they were battle tested and united in a quest to make a historic and symbolic stand. Only twice had Cal defeated Stanford in women's swimming, and not since 1976. A victory not only would be a huge boost for the program but also would be heralded by the campus community in general.

On an across-the-board level, the Cal-Stanford rivalry, once reasonably civil, had heated up in recent years, especially as the Cardinal won seven consecutive football games from 1995 to 2001 and made a landmark Rose Bowl appearance in January 2000. As the millennium approached, it appeared as though Stanford had the upper hand in everything. At one point Stanford won 10 consecutive games in men's basketball, 15 straight in women's hoops. The Cardinal athletic department was being hailed as the model of comprehensive excellence augmented by academic accountability. The school had the greatest sugar daddy in the history of college sports, real estate magnate John Arrillaga, who gave millions to the athletic department. The school went out and hired the finest coaches in every sport and had won the Directors (née Sears) Cup—a points system designed to quantify across-the-board athletic success—each year of the award's existence.

Golfer Tiger Woods, the world's most successful athlete, proudly wore a bloodred shirt on Sundays of majors to honor his Stanford heritage—he had attended school there and played on the golf team for 2 years before turning pro. Chelsea Clinton, the president's daughter, had gone there. The school was in the heart of the Silicon Valley in the midst of a dotcom boom that was the modern-day gold rush.

For Cal fans, it was as if they had been forced to view the world through Cardinal-colored glasses.

Lately, however, the earth had begun to look a bit bluer. The turning point, most Cal fans felt, had come in the spring of 2001, when then-Stanford rugby coach Franck Boivert sent an e-mail to his Cal counterpart, Jack Clark, claiming his players had voted to forfeit the team's annual match because "they do not have the heart to play against a team vastly superior to them in size, weight, and speed." At the time the Bears and coach Jack Clark had won 10 consecutive national championships (en route to capturing 12 straight titles), but Stanford's refusal to play was appalling. The Cardinal had beaten Cal as recently as 1996, and the forfeit ended an unbroken 110-year tradition of annual meetings. More important to Cal fans, Stanford's wimpiness—especially in such a macho sport—spoke to everything they loathed about the institution. It was as if the Cardinal credo were, "If we can beat you, we'll play. But if we can't, we'll take our ball and go home."

Now Cal, under hot new football coach Jeff Tedford, had won two consecutive Big Games, giving the school ownership of "the Axe" and its fans a newfound swagger. Golden Bear teams were beginning to break through in numerous sports, and the end to the women's swimming streak would be another sign that the balance of power was tilting to the east side of San Francisco Bay.

To Coughlin, all of this mattered—and so much more. To her, Stanford was akin to the swimming establishment, a viewpoint bolstered by the school's state-of-the-art facilities and stable of former age-group champions and elite recruits. Cal, by comparison, was the heart of the revolution, a chaotic home to new ideas, free will, and self-motivated scrappers. It was private school versus public school; spacious, country-club-like campus versus thriving, diverse urban university.

It was no coincidence, she felt, that the most magical moment in the history of the spirited cross-Bay rivalry had been so singular, strange, and sublime: the legendary finish of the 1982 Big Game in Berkeley, in which Cal's Kevin Moen began and ended a five-lateral kickoff return by racing *through* the Stanford band, crushing a trombone player's instrument as he leaped over the goal line. "The Play" not only stood as the most thrilling finish in college football history but also spoke to the creativity, spontaneity, and out-of-the-box thinking that Coughlin loved about her university. If Stanford was a sheltered enclave of theoretical musings, Cal was the real world.

There is an old saying that sums up the differences between the two schools: At Stanford, they teach you to wash your hands after you urinate. At Cal, they tell you not to piss on your hands.

Stanfordites, Coughlin believed, were the type of people who'd walk into a party, linger near the back wall, and observe from a safe distance, judging the behavior of those in the center of the action. And Cal people? They *were* the party, decorum be damned. They were like her maternal grandfather, Chuck Bohn, an ex-Marine with a booming voice and an equally conspicuous stuffed-bear hat who was prone to screaming "*Go Bears!*" during those tense, quiet moments just before the sounding of the starting gun.

Cal fans, in short, weren't afraid to throw themselves out there, no matter how much they might be scrutinized. Nor, apparently, were Cal assistant coaches—as the swimmers were about to find out.

~

Whitney Hite's impact on the Bears during his 9 months in Berkeley had been significant, but sensitivity was not regarded as one of his prime assets. Hite had been tough, in both demeanor and assignments, and he hadn't acted particularly worried about whether his swimmers regarded him as overly brusque or demanding.

Now, however, as the Bears sat in the Haas Grille Room the night before the Stanford meet, they saw an unexpected vulnerability as Hite stood up to address the team.

Almost as soon as he started speaking, Hite choked up. "When I got here, you were a bunch of individuals," he said. "But you've worked hard for a common goal, and you've become a team. We've challenged you to put in the work it takes to be great, and you've stepped up to that challenge. This is the proudest I've ever been of any group of athletes in my life. I completely believe in you and what you're about to do." He paused, and his eyes got moist. *Oh my God*, Lauren Medina remembers thinking, *he has a soul!* No one on the team could believe it—Hite, the demanding deck demon, had started to cry.

The meeting broke up, and Coughlin drove home to Emeryville, where she fielded a phone call from Ethan Hall. From the second she answered the phone, Coughlin could tell that something wasn't right. The two were working through issues in their relationship, and the conversation put her in the deep funk that had carried over to the meet. The fact that it took place on Valentine's Day—and that Hall was not in attendance—only depressed her further.

The rest of the Bears were unaware of Coughlin's misery. To them, it was "Cal-entine's Day," the inscription on the homemade pins Coughlin's mother, Zennie, was passing out to the fans on the west side of the Avery Aquatic Center. A record 1,784 fans showed up for the meet, with spectators evenly split between the two teams: red-clad rooters on the east side of the stands, their blue-and-gold counterparts staring back from the opposite end.

Technically, it was Stanford's swim stadium, but that didn't stop the Bears from acting as if they owned the place. They strode into the pool with a boom box blasting Justin Timberlake's "Rock Your Body," dancing and strutting and having fun. Just before the meet began, the Cal swimmers, as was their custom, belted out an a cappella rendition of "Big C," one of the school fight songs—and marveled as hundreds of Golden Bear fans stood and joined them. "I remember looking up in the stands and seeing all the people and thinking, 'Do you really like swimming *that* much?'" Medina recalls. "It was Valentine's Day—I assumed people would be off with their honeys."

Stanford, however, struck the first emotional blow. It came at Medina's expense, in the 200 free, the event McKeever felt the Bears had to have. The Cardinal, as expected, had won the meet-opening 200-meter medley relay, with the Kirk sisters, in the breaststroke and butterfly respectively, providing a decisive edge. Cal struck back in the 800 free as Ashley Chandler, now swimming with authority, and Erin Reilly seized command from the start and finished 1–2. This marked another step in

McKeever and Hite's quest to get Reilly to face up to her potential as a swimmer. As a youth swimmer, Reilly had gone to distance camp with Stanford freshman Lauren Costella, who went on to become a two-time national champion in the 1,500 free. Yet when the coaches had scored out the meet beforehand, they had Reilly beating Costella in the both the 400 and 800 free. "Lauren Costella?" Reilly had exclaimed. "She's gonna be tough." McKeever grimaced—the last thing she needed was a star-struck freshman before the biggest dual meet of the season. "Erin," McKeever said, "you're going to beat her." Reilly did, by more than 8 seconds.

Then came the 200 free, which looked great from the Cal perspective for about 170 meters. Medina had charged to the lead and looked stronger than Boutwell, a terrific finisher, until the Cal swimmer headed into the final turn. Then, suddenly, the panic symptoms that had afflicted her at Princeton began to return. She breathed just before the wall, turned sluggishly, and gave an opening to Boutwell, who charged from behind and won by 0.34 second. Medina, convinced she'd let down the team, was crushed; senior Micha Burden, who'd swum to an under-whelming sixth-place finish, was even more visibly dejected.

Cal's spirits were quickly buoyed by Helen Silver, who rolled to a decisive victory in the 100 back. Silver had planned on racing Stanford's Kristen Caverly, a talented and versatile swimmer whom she had defeated in both backstroke events the previous year at Cal. The statuesque Caverly, who would make the 2004 Olympic team in the 200-meter backstroke, had been sidelined by a back injury, but she was suited up in a one-piece for the Cal meet—as a decoy, it turned out, courtesy of some borderline gamesmanship by Quick. Momentarily let down by Caverly's absence, Silver took out her frustration on Stanford senior Megan Baumgartner, winning by more than 2 seconds.

Then it was Kirk time—Tara winning the 100 breast easily and Dana capturing the 200 fly even more decisively, with Chandler and Reilly going 2–3. Finally, it was time for Coughlin to enter the water for the 50 free. More vulnerable in a short race, Coughlin removed all doubt by crushing Boutwell with a time of 24.60 seconds—an NCAA record and just 0.08 second shy of former Stanford star Jenny Thompson's American record. She dusted Boutwell again in the 100 free, and then Silver won the 200 back by nearly a second and a half.

Tara Kirk and Stanford teammate Kristen Gilbert finished first and second in the 200 breast, but Chandler and Reilly pulled off another 1–2 effort in the 400 free, with Cal sophomore Kate Tiedeman, a Palo Alto Swim Club alum competing in her hometown, sneaking past the Cardinal's Evins Cameron in the final few meters to capture fourth—and the two points (as opposed to one for fifth place) that went with it. Numerous Cal swimmers had ventured over to Lane 1, right beside the Stanford bench area, to cheer Tiedeman home, and with good reason: The Bears would need every point they could muster to have any chance of winning. Despite the slew of impressive efforts, Cal was losing the numbers game.

"I know we're going to win," Hite kept telling the Bears and McKeever. "I just don't know how."

Even after Coughlin held off Dana Kirk to win a surprisingly close 100 fly—her winning time of 56.64 seconds was an NCAA record and just 0.3 second off her world record—the Bears were in a bind. Stanford had mitigated the damage by finishing second, third, and fourth. When the 3-meter diving scores were added—the Cardinal (surprise, surprise) had finished first, second, and third, as it had in the 1-meter competition staged earlier—the home team had a 140–124 edge.

As they emerged from the locker room for the final two events, the Stanford swimmers looked elated and relieved. They had survived another stiff challenge from their rivals, and the streak was safe. There were hugs and high fives and hoots of approval from the Stanford side of the stadium. Needing just 11 points to clinch the meet, the Cardinal figured to get all of them in the 400 IM (individual events awarded nine points for first, four for second, three for third, two for fourth, and one for fifth), with juniors Tami Ransom, Cameron, Costella, and Coughlin's old Terrapins teammate Laura Davis as its entries. The Bears, meanwhile, would send a far less distinguished cast to the blocks: Griffith; fellow captain Amy Ng, a junior; struggling junior Jenna Rais; and Tiedeman, a moonlighting distance freestyler.

This was when the two Natalies, Coughlin and Griffith, were huddled together at the blocks, bemoaning their predicament. Up in the stands above them, a third Natalie was also coming to terms with Cal's imminent defeat.

∾

"Sweetie," I said softly, placing my hand on top of my 7-year-old daughter's blue Cal cap. "It's not looking too good for the Bears."

Natalie Silver was not so easy to convince. "You mean it's over?" she asked incredulously.

"No, sweetie, not yet. But almost. And I don't think there's any way we can score enough points to win."

Having indoctrinated my little girl into a life of Golden Bear worship from a painfully young age—one of the first phrases out of her mouth was "Stanford PU," the result of having a demented father and a fellow Cal alum for a mother too distracted to protest—I felt obligated to come up with a scenario to appease her. The best I could do was something far too radical to work: Throw Coughlin into the 400 IM as a desperation move and pray that the Bears could win the 400-free relay without her. On deck, Hite and McKeever were discussing another drastic possibility: splitting up the A and B relay teams in an attempt to take first and second. McKeever was also thinking about what she'd say to her swimmers after another piercing disappointment; it was tough to envision any other outcome.

Natalie Silver, however, had a plan. The little lady was having a grand old time at the meet, having heard her name (what with the two Natalies and Helen Silver, to whom she bore no relation, in multiple races) mentioned over the PA system every few minutes. She did not intend to have it end on a downer. "This is my lucky hat," she proclaimed, removing her Cal cap and waving it vigorously. "Remember, Daddy?" It was true: At the previous November's Big Game at Stanford, Natalie's decision to turn the same cap backward had coincided directly with Cal's comeback from a 10–0 halftime deficit for a 28–16 victory. "If I wave it," she said simply, "we'll win."

The gun sounded, and Stanford's Ransom, an accomplished backstroker, shot to the front. But Griffith stayed with her and caught her at the 100-meter mark, with the Cardinal's Cameron in hot pursuit. Ransom and Cameron pulled ahead, but Griffith remained close, and the Bears' Ng made a spirited charge. Watching from the deck, McKeever felt a tingle through her spine. Something strange was happening. Where was Davis (a talented IMer who would end up finishing 13th in this very event at NCAAs the following month)? And what in the world was Ng doing so close to the lead?

In her role as captain, Ng, a popular junior, had sometimes butted heads with McKeever, and there had been a measure of tension in their relationship. Right now, however, McKeever was aglow over what she was witnessing in the water. During the breaststroke laps, as Griffith pulled into the lead, Ng, as if tethered to the senior, charged right along with her. McKeever clapped her hands together nervously—the versatile swimmer from San Ramon was swimming the race of her life!

Now it was freestyle time, and Griffith was only getting stronger. Suddenly, she was the hotshot teeanger from Virginia once again, swimming a variety of strokes with authority while spectators marveled at her skills. Ng wasn't backing off, either—the Bears, somehow, were going to finish 1–2. Yet over in Lane 1, as the final laps played out, someone was moving even faster. Tiedeman, known for her even-paced distance swims, was knifing through the water like an accomplished sprinter, making a run at Davis for fifth. Griffith had already touched the wall and was heading over to embrace Ng when they heard the roar—Tiedeman had gotten the essential fifth-place point and had nearly caught Cameron for fourth.

Throughout the stadium, graduates and students of two of the nation's most prestigious universities were doing some quick math in their heads: Stanford's lead was now just 145–138. If Cal could win the relay (11 points) and take third with its B team (2 points), the Bears would win the meet; anything less would mean a Stanford victory.

Everyone in the Cal section stood up and yelled, as did the fired-up swimmers; this was their time, and they knew it. Momentarily stunned into silence, the Stanford fans and swimmers soon followed suit. It was a gorgeous, sunny afternoon that featured college athletics at its finest, and it would all come down to one thrilling race.

Coughlin had waited too long for this opportunity to allow even a shred of hope to her opponents. She burst off the blocks and immediately seized control, swimming her 100 meters in an NCAA record 52.97 seconds—just 0.05 second slower than Jenny Thompson's American record. As long as no one left early, the Bears had first place locked up, especially with Medina anchoring.

Meanwhile, the pivotal battle for third was playing out, with Cal's Chandler and Reilly each securing a slight lead over the Cardinal's Ashley Daly and Sarah Jones, respectively. But in the third leg, Stanford freshman Lisa Falzone caught and passed the Bears' Palsson, and anchor Morgan Hentzen entered the water with a ½-second edge on Keiko Amano.

For a few seconds, every Cal fan's heart sank. It was as if this one relay leg symbolized the vast differences between the two programs. On paper, it was no contest: Hentzen, a decorated, powerful swimmer with extensive international experience (she had won the 800 free and finished second in the 400 free at the 2003 Pan American Games) against Amano, the throwaway recruit whom the Bears had left temporarily stranded in San Francisco. Visually, it was even more of a mismatch: Hentzen was 6 inches taller than the 5-foot-2 Amano and looked to be adding to the Stanford lead with every stroke.

The Cal swimmers, however, knew better. They'd learned about Amano's heart and poise during her meet-clinching swim against Arizona 3 weeks earlier; now, even as she trailed coming out of the first turn at 25 meters, they knew she had a shot. "Come on, Keiko—run her down!" Coughlin screamed. *Stay with your technique,* McKeever thought, holding her breath. Hentzen, a distance swimmer, was unlikely to run out of gas, but if Amano could resist the temptation to thrash, her exceptional form could allow her to prevail.

On the second lap, Amano made her run. She pulled nearly even coming into the turn, and as the two swimmers pushed off the wall in unison, somehow the short one catapulted to the front. Now the rest of the Bears were screaming, clutching each other like blankets on a freezing night. Hentzen tried to charge, but Amano kept building momentum, and now she was drawing out. One last turn, and her lead remained intact. Hentzen made a final push in the last 25 meters, but Amano stayed a full second ahead. When she touched the wall, a deafening roar echoed across the stadium. There wasn't a single dry eye among the jubilant Cal contingent.

After the victory became official, most of the Bears jumped into the pool to mob Amano, though McKeever resisted being thrown in herself. The swimmers celebrated instead by singing an encore rendition of "Big C," chanting "Un-de-*feat*-ed," and savoring what surely was the greatest dual-meet victory in school history. Cal had done the near impossible, fighting back to win the meet by a 151–149 score.

There would be a party in Berkeley that night, and the Bears and their friends on the men's swim team would toast McKeever for helping to inspire it.

That night, at halftime of Cal's sold-out basketball game against Stanford at Haas—alas, those Bears would fall short in their bid to upset the second-ranked Cardinal—McKeever and Hite stood in a corridor and recounted the wild events of the afternoon. "I was devastated when Lauren lost the 200," McKeever admitted, "but it's not like she tanked. She swam a 1:58.7, which is the fifth-fastest time in the country. I mean, Whitney: *Lauren Medina* has the fifth-fastest time in the country. Think about that."

A few miles away in Emeryville, the heartsick Coughlin was still out of sorts. After the meet, she and teammates Burden, Palsson, and Miller had gone shopping in San Francisco—and Coughlin purchased a $400 powder-blue Coach purse in an attempt to cheer herself up. It wasn't really working. But as she went to bed that night and closed her eyes, one of the last things she saw before drifting off was the Avery Aquatic Center scoreboard and the immaculate 151 on the Cal side.

If that didn't make her smile, nothing could have.

CHAPTER THIRTEEN

ONE FOR THE TEAM

Whitney Hite saw the familiar 706 area code flash on his caller ID and picked up the phone immediately. Sure enough, the call was from his old friends in Athens, Georgia— the Lady Bulldogs' coaching office, to be exact. "Hey," Georgia assistant Jerry Champer said, "we're all here in the office. Looks like that 800 free relay you guys swam at Pac-10s was pretty fast." Hite smiled. The Bears had closed out the first night of an otherwise disappointing Pac-10 Championships by winning the 800-yard freestyle relay in a meet-record time of 7:08.13, and he knew his old colleagues were curious as to how formidable a challenge Cal might present in the event at NCAAs.

"Yeah," Hite said. "It was okay."

"Which leg did Natalie swim?"

Hite paused for dramatic effect. "She didn't."

Indeed, with Erin Reilly, Micha Burden, Ashley Chandler, and Lauren Medina each recording personal bests for the 200-yard distance, the Bears had been able to cruise to a conference title in the relay without requiring the services of their best swimmer. Now, with Coughlin poised to replace Burden at NCAAs, Cal would have a legitimate shot at breaking the 3-year Georgia/Auburn stronghold over the relay events. The increased workload might jeopardize Coughlin's chances of defending her titles in the third of her individual events, the 200 backstroke, but at this point she didn't care. She was so sick of her collegiate winning streak and the accompanying pressure that she just wanted to get that part of her career over with and start preparing for the Olympic Trials. Winning a relay sounded so much better than anything she might accomplish on her own, because, for a change, it wouldn't be about *her.*

Finally, after all the dissension of the past 8 months, and before embarking upon the pursuit of individual Olympic glory, this would be Coughlin's chance to be one of the girls.

As the NCAA Championships approached in mid-March of 2004, the Bears were a team in need of a boost. For the first time all season, they had failed to achieve one of their team goals—to "win the swimming" at Pac-10s. Scoring the most points at that meet, McKeever knew, would be virtually impossible because of Cal's inferiority in the three diving events. (To put the disparity in perspective, the Golden Bears would score 33 diving points at Pac-10s; the next-lowest total of any team was 180, and the next-lowest after that 290.) So the Bears hoped they could outshine their Pac-10 rivals in the rest of the competition, even if they would be the only ones keeping track of that score.

Though there were some impressive Cal swims at the Belmont Plaza Pool in Long Beach, California, the Bears' overall performance was somewhat flat. For one thing, the meet was somewhat anticlimactic after the undefeated dual-meet season, and particularly the dramatic victory over Stanford—with the far more important NCAA meet still to come. And with so many Cal swimmers having already made their cuts for NCAAs, there was less of a sense of urgency than normal.

The Pac-10s also served as a sobering reminder that dual-meet success does not necessarily equate to similar prosperity under a different

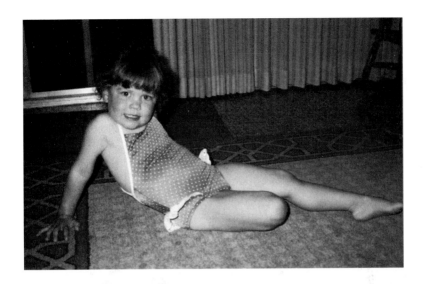

Natalie enjoys her early swimming days.

Butterfly anyone?

Young blue and gold.

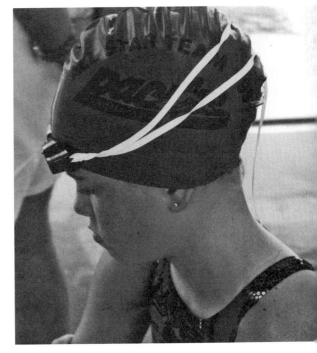

Nat on her first travel team.

Terrapin teen.

The trophy is as big as Natalie.

Decorating shirts at training camp.

Natalie and Teri buying diamonds in Athens.

Natalie and boyfriend Ethan Hall.

Teri and Nat on a gold-medal night in Athens.

The Today *crew giving Natalie a birthday cake.*

Ann Curry and Natalie on the Today *show.*

scoring format. Whereas dual meets reward depth and emotionally charged efforts, competitions like Pac-10s and NCAAs winnow out less accomplished swimmers with preliminary rounds and penalize inconsistency. Not only does a swimmer have to be one of the fastest in her event to score a lot of points, but she must prove it twice in the same day: Fail to finish in the top eight in the prelims, and that night the best a swimmer can do is to place ninth, even if her time in the consolation final was faster than that of the winner's in the championship heat.

Coughlin, of course, was well familiar with that setup. What she wasn't as accustomed to was—well, virtually everything else going on in her life at the time. She and Ethan Hall were still dealing with relationship issues, and she was also experiencing some sleep deprivation, thanks largely to a faulty fire-alarm system in her condo complex. Several false alarms on one particularly brutal night forced her to make repeated trips down to the lobby. Delirious come morning, she promptly took a psych midterm in the one upper-division class she cared about—and, in her words, "bombed." (It was a relative term; Coughlin, it turned out, got a B.) Then, on the Friday night before Pac-10s, Coughlin cooked herself some jambalaya and, an hour after dinner, contracted food poisoning, probably courtesy of some spoiled sausage. She spent the next 24 hours, in her words, "vomiting my guts out."

Other than that, it was a great week.

During those moments when neither her condo's security system nor her stomach was sounding alarms, Coughlin managed to make some progress on the agent front. She and McKeever, along with their friends at CSI Management, Leland Faust and Steven Clark, interviewed three finalists separately in San Francisco: Octagon's Peter Carlisle and his posse of associates; Evan Morganstein of Premier Sports Management; and Janey Miller. As McKeever had predicted weeks earlier, Coughlin was taken by Miller's down-to-earth personality and unpretentious, stripped-down approach. Having repped such prominent Olympians as Michael Johnson, Apollo Anton Ohno, and Amy Van Dyken before she'd left IMG, Miller offered big-league experience with personal service. "I'd be her first client, which is sort of cool, if you think about it," Coughlin said. "I'd know that whatever she's doing at a given time, she'd be out there working for me."

Miller, said McKeever, was "the only one who said she wouldn't have a problem with Natalie having different agents for Australia and Asia, which are places she could theoretically cash in. It would be sort of exciting to go with Janey, to blaze a trail."

Coughlin was initially skeptical of Morganstein, who had carved out a niche as a "swimmers' agent"—he had 20 of the world's best in the sport and also did some work for coaches, such as McKeever. Coughlin didn't want to be treated as one of a large group or packaged with others as part of a marketing strategy. But after their meeting, she said, "Evan really surprised me. He had really thought it through. He told me he'd use a specific publicist out of LA, for one thing." McKeever agreed that "Evan was really impressive. He had a plan for everything, and he told Nat how she was special, how he'd treat her differently, and how she'd be in charge of the big decisions, which is perfect for her personality." The Octagon crew, by comparison, had seemed stiff and slick. "They had five people there," McKeever said. "If she were the big-firm type of person, I don't think she'd have come here to swim in the first place."

That Coughlin was still an amateur at the 2004 Pac-10s was somewhat of an upset, given the mentality she'd carried into Pac-10s a year earlier. Even McKeever was surprised when Coughlin, during a team meeting the night of the Bears' arrival in Long Beach, got up to address her team-mates—as did each of the seniors—and said, "A year ago at this time I was sitting there listening to the seniors talk and I was sure it was my last Pac-10s. But it worked out that I was able to come back, and I'm really glad I did." *Whoa*, McKeever thought.

Though she would be swimming her usual trio of individual events at NCAAs (the 100 and 200 back and 100 fly), Coughlin had chosen a different schedule for Pac-10s. She was intrigued by the notion of going head-up against USC's Kaitlin Sandeno in the 200-yard individual medley, the event in which Coughlin had shined back in December during the Princeton Invitational. (And yes, the Pac-10 meet, unlike each of the season's dual meets and NCAAs, would be conducted in yards, rather than meters, if only to further confound those who were trying to derive meaning from the times.) Back in her previous incarnation as a teen phenom, Coughlin had been especially potent in the IM events, but she had largely abandoned them during most of her collegiate career. This, however, was for a good cause: Not only was Coughlin no fan of the Trojans, but she also relished the idea of beating the formidable Sandeno. The showdown took place on the meet's second day, and it was no contest. Coughlin cruised to victory in 1:54.95—the second-fastest 200-yard IM ever, well ahead of Summer Sanders's Pac-10 record—while Sandeno was second, in 1:57.53.

"How did you get her to swim the 200 IM?" USC coach Mark Schubert asked McKeever.

"I just asked," she replied, shrugging.

Coughlin also won the 100 back and 100 free and led off Cal's meet-closing victory in the 400 free relay. Dramatic swims by breaststrokers Marcelle Miller (in the 200) and Erin Calder (in the 100) pushed the Bears' total of NCAA qualifiers to 15, an all-time high. Yet Cal fell well short of being the highest-scoring team in the swimming events and finished fourth behind Stanford, UCLA, and Arizona in the overall tally.

For Coughlin, at least there was improvement on one important front: Upon her return to Berkeley, she and Hall had worked through their problems, and their relationship had become stronger than ever.

∾

Erin Reilly knocked on McKeever's office door a few minutes after one of the team's final practices before the NCAA Championships and slipped her slender frame inside. Check that—for a swimmer, Reilly wasn't slender; she was toothpick thin. Whereas some of the fleshier competitors benefited from Fastskin suits because the tight material constricted their fat and reduced buoyancy, Reilly need not have bothered. The bodysuits actually appeared slightly baggy on her. The pretty strawberry blonde would probably be the skinniest swimmer at NCAAs, not to mention the fairest skinned. She was also one of the more durable, a workhorse willing to literally go the extra mile.

"You wanted to see me?" Reilly asked, thereby doubling the total number of words her coach had heard her utter in the past week.

"Yeah, sit down," McKeever said, motioning toward the small couch near the door. "Let's talk about what you're swimming at NCs."

Specifically, McKeever wanted to address the second day of the 3-day meet, when Reilly planned to swim the 200-meter freestyle prelims in the morning and then, if she produced one of the 16 fastest times, come back and do it again that night. The catch was, that was also the night of the 800 free relay, meaning she wouldn't be at her freshest with a national title at stake.

Reilly was set on swimming the 400 free the first day of the meet and the 1,500 free the third day; that left either the 200 free or the 200 fly, and both she and Hite were sold on the former. On the final night of Pac-10s, Reilly had competed in the 1,650 (yard) freestyle, finishing sixth, and the 200 fly back-to-back. It was a vicious double that Reilly had vowed not to repeat at NCAAs, which had a similar schedule on the third and last night of competition. While acknowledging that Reilly, who had the nation's 17th-fastest seed time in the 200 free going in, was more of a natural fit for that event than she was the 200 fly (for which she was seeded 13th), McKeever asked her to consider making a sacrifice for the good of the team.

"Look, Erin, I really think we have a chance to win a national championship in the relay, and you'll be part of that," McKeever told Reilly. "Now, that may happen to you again before you're done here, and I hope it does, but there are no guarantees. I just want you to understand how incredibly special that could be, something you'll remember for the rest of your life. I want you to have that experience. We might be able to do it even if you're not fully rested, but if you're fresh, it gives us an even better chance."

Equally important was what McKeever didn't say: *This is what you're doing, period.* Though passionate and secure in her convictions, McKeever simply wasn't that kind of coach. Just as she would never dream of ordering Coughlin to swim the 200 back rather than the 100 free at Olympic Trials, she wasn't going to mandate this switch to Reilly. It was going to have to come from her, and in this case, Reilly saw the logic in her coach's presentation and quickly agreed.

Later that day, McKeever sat in her office, staring up at the scores of mementos on the walls, most of them snapshots of current and former team members during retreats or other group activities. There were also framed magazine covers featuring Coughlin, Haley Cope, Staciana Stitts, and other former Cal stars, and a tray on her desk with paperwork piled up taller than Keiko Amano. "In a way it will be liberating when Natalie finishes," McKeever confessed, "so I can start *really* coaching some of these other swimmers, like Erin Reilly. Right now I just tell her how great she is because I think she needs to understand that most of all. But there are so many technical things I'd really like to try with her, because she could end up doing some really amazing things."

At the same time, McKeever was wistful about the impending end of Coughlin's collegiate career. "What most of these girls don't get is that this is the best it will ever be," the coach said. "Sure, they have classes to go to and papers to write, but they don't have to work. They get to swim, and they get to be part of a team. Someday, Danielle Becks will have kids, and at some point they'll start swimming, and they'll know who Natalie Coughlin is and what she accomplished. And Danielle will tell them, 'I swam with her for 4 years, and we were on a relay that set an American record, and we beat Stanford together for the first time in 28 years.' Some of them might sit there now and complain about Natalie—how she always gets to swim in the same lane at practice or how I give her special treatment—but they don't get what she's meant to this program or this university. Someday they probably will, and I'll bet they'll see things differently."

For a team intent on finishing in the top five nationally, the Bears seemed oddly vulnerable. "Keiko Amano was in here earlier today," McKeever said, "and she started crying as she was complaining about her shoulder pain. I said, 'Keiko, think about where you are. When you came to Cal, did you honestly think you'd make NCAAs?' She said, 'I didn't have any goals.' I said, 'You're 5 foot 2, and you've been a huge part of our success. You've clocked the fastest time on all those relays—faster than Danielle and Emma, faster than everyone except Natalie. You need to enjoy the moment and get through this last stretch.' She's stressed about missing school, which I understand, but I want her to realize what an opportunity this is."

McKeever, too, was emotional as NCAAs neared. She was jarred by the recent departures of two of her friends in the small community of female swim coaches: Longtime Minnesota mentor Jean Freeman had retired; and Iowa coach Garland O'Keeffe, according to McKeever, had been pushed out after having recently had her first child. "I was a mess last week," McKeever said. "I got frustrated with someone every single day, to the point where I realized I had to get away. It's so great having Whitney, because I knew that even at this point of the season, I could leave and he'd have it totally under control. So on Saturday I flew down to LA for the day and saw my brother Mac and his kids, and my sister and her new husband drove up. It was a nice reminder that there's more to life than swimming, which was exactly what I needed."

The Bears' workouts had been especially light since they'd returned from Pac-10s—not that McKeever was using the "T" word. Though her swimmers reduced yardage before big meets, it was erroneous, she felt, to infer that her swimmers tapered before big meets. "I don't like using the word *tapering*," agreed Dave Salo of Irvine Novaquatics, McKeever's old coaching colleague, "but I've succumbed to my athletes' desire to have it defined that way. It's probably more psychological than anything. Traditionally, tapering is a methodical approach to cutting back on yardage before major competitions. I think 'fine-tuning' is actually a far more accurate term."

McKeever was not averse to her swimmers engaging in another traditional pre-NCAA ritual: shaving their bodies. Some swimmers in other programs, in an effort to achieve more dramatic results come competition time, accumulated as much body hair as possible until "shaving" time arrived. Coughlin viewed the process far more casually. "I have the hairiest legs in the world, but I only shave once a week," she said. "I'm so lazy. So, yeah, I'll shave for this meet, but with the Fastskin suits, it's really not as big an issue as it used to be."

Then there was teammate Helen Silver, who, while hanging out with teammates after Pac-10s, impulsively picked up a pair of blunt scissors and sheared off roughly two-thirds of her blond locks. "Hey," she later explained, "sometimes you just have to feel the moment."

Four of her teammates were about to, in a big way.

≈

Lauren Medina could feel another panic attack coming on, this one at the least opportune time imaginable. The night session of day 2 at NCAAs in College Station, Texas, was nearing its conclusion, and Medina and fellow swimmers Coughlin, Reilly, and Chandler were getting ready for the 800 free relay, an event they fully expected to win. Yet they were worried, because Medina, their tough-as-dorm-food relay anchor, hadn't been herself for more than a week, and now she looked shakier than she should have as the start time neared.

Back in December, when Medina had had her anxiety attack at the Princeton Invitational and had to be pulled from the pool by a lifeguard, she figured it was a onetime freak-out and tried to block it from her mind. But while anchoring Cal's winning 800 free relay at Pac-10s, she'd started to feel the same strain in her breathing, and ever since then at practice, she'd been subject to similar symptoms. A week before NCAAs, Medina had started thinking about the relay during a workout set and become panicked again, eventually clinging to the wall as she hyperventilated. McKeever helped her to the deck, and Medina began bawling. "Teri, I'm terrified," she finally said. "I'm scared we'll win. I'm scared I'll let us down and we'll lose."

For the next 7 days, McKeever, Hite, and the other Cal swimmers had attempted to keep Medina loose and calm, but now—well, this was crunch time, and the ebullient junior literally had to sink or swim.

"Lauren, look at me," McKeever implored a few minutes before the race. "It's going to be okay. No matter what happens, I'm here for you. If you need me to walk behind the blocks with you and hold your hand until it's time to jump in, that's what I'll do."

Medina began to relax. It had been an inspired meet so far for the Bears, who were on pace to reach their goal of a top-five finish. On day 1, Chandler had finished fourth in the 400 free, officially shedding her previous year's label as a freshman bust. Natalie Griffith had placed 13th in the 200 IM, an event won by Sandeno. Earlier in day 2, Coughlin had defended her titles in the 100 fly and 100 back, while freshman Annie Babicz had placed 15th in the 100 breast, and Chandler (fourth) and Medina (11th) had scored in the 200 free. Medina had gotten through her individual race without incident, but now, with the relay approaching, she looked like a swimmer who wanted to be anywhere other than where she was.

Cal was seeded fifth in the relay based on season-best times, behind Auburn, Michigan, Georgia, and Florida, but everyone knew the Bears would have a lead after the first leg. That was because Coughlin, despite having already swum four races that day (prelims and finals for the 100 fly and 100 back), was primed to lead off with a bang. The question was whether Reilly, swimming second, would be able to hold that lead. Georgia was a particular threat, with star sprinter Kara Lynn Joyce set to swim the second leg. Reilly did not relish her role as the hunted, and she, too, had a serious case of nerves before the race. As she later recalled, "I was warming up in the diving pool, and Nat was standing there in her parka. I was really nervous. Nat looked down and put her hands on my shoulders and said, 'We can do it. You know we're gonna win. You know you've worked so hard for this.' It really calmed me down. She's so good at making me—at making a lot of people—feel comfortable in a situation like that."

Then Coughlin went out and swam a sizzling 1:55.82 first leg, which really made the Bears feel comfortable. Coughlin's time was faster than Auburn's Margaret Hoelzer's had been in winning the 200 free earlier that night, and it put Cal more than 2½ seconds ahead of Auburn and nearly 3½ ahead of Georgia. Reilly, mindful of Hite's last-minute instruction not to "blow it in the first 100," dove in and tried to maintain an even pace, fully expecting Georgia's Joyce to make her run. "I remember every wall going into my turn and expecting to see Kara Lynn," Reilly recalled.

She never did—Reilly held her ground against Joyce, swimming a split of 1:57.97 to Joyce's 1:57.44. It was the equivalent of a freshman basketball player hitting a game-winning three to send his or her team to the Final Four. By race's end, Reilly had recorded a faster split than two of the women who would join Coughlin on the US 800 free relay at the Olympics—USC's Sandeno (1:58.15) and Wisconsin's Carly Piper (2:00.00). When Ashley Chandler came through with an impressive 1:58.60, just 0.61 second slower than the 200 she'd just swum in the individual final, it was pretty much over—provided Medina was able to manage her anxiety.

During Reilly's leg, Medina had looked into the stands and spotted her brothers and other family members, which sent her heart racing. "Natalie," she said, turning to Coughlin, "tell me I can do this."

"Lauren," Coughlin said forcefully, "you can do this."

She did, easily. "It was almost like as soon as Lauren jumped in, we were home," Reilly recalled. One assistant coach from a Pac-10 rival actually walked up to Hite and congratulated him during Medina's first lap. When Hite reminded him there were seven additional laps remaining, his colleague scoffed and said, "That's Lauren Medina in the water—you guys have got it." Sure enough, after cruising home in 1:58.55, Medina joined her teammates in a gleeful and borderline hysterical celebration. The Bears had won in 7:50.94, shattering Arizona's NCAA record by nearly 5 seconds and beating second-place Georgia by nearly 2½. For the first time since 2000, a team other than Georgia or Auburn had won a relay, and the Cal contingent danced around like it had won a team championship.

At that moment it was all worth it for Coughlin: the decision to come back for her senior season; the sniping she'd endured from grumpy teammates; the 13 swims over 3 days (nine to this point) that would sap her of precious energy by meet's end. Because each of her fellow relay swimmers' journeys resonated with her, and because she recognized them as products of the uncanny McKeever/Hite coaching partnership, Coughlin was overcome by tears as she reveled in their unmitigated joy. "Natalie is a very private, subdued person most of the time, and sometimes we have a hard time seeing her humanity come out," teammate Helen Silver said. "But the way she was after that relay, you could totally see how much she genuinely cared."

So, too, did the other relay swimmers, none of whom had ever appreciated Coughlin quite so much as they did at that moment. "Thank you for believing in me!" Medina screamed as she wrapped Coughlin in a Golden Bear hug. Reilly was especially animated; her gesticulating victory dance during Medina's final lap was captured by ESPN's cameras on its tape-delayed telecast, allowing swimming fans to watch her, as she described, "looking like such a dork." Coughlin, too, made fun of her teammate when, a few minutes after the race, Reilly asked, "Do they give us our rings on the award stand?"

"Erin," Coughlin answered, laughing, "they have to measure us for them first. We get them in like a month or two."

❧

When Jim Coughlin saw the flameout, he jumped from his seat and instinctively moved toward the pool. His little girl was in distress, and he was ready to jump into the water and save her, right there during the 200-meter backstroke final. "Natalie was born with a heart murmur," he would later explain. "When I saw her just *stop* all of a sudden, I didn't know what had happened, but I feared the worst."

Later, upon learning of her father's recollection, Natalie rolled her eyes. "Oh, come on," she said, laughing. "My heart murmur is not a big deal. Lots of people have them. It's nothing."

To her worrywart dad's great relief, Coughlin was in no physical danger—she was merely dead in the water. After charging to the lead on a pace that would have earned her a seventh world record, Coughlin, with two laps remaining, felt her legs abruptly desert her. Flummoxed by the physical breakdown, Coughlin's technique went to pieces, and an audible gasp could be heard in the natatorium. This remarkable swimmer, who had never lost a meaningful race in college, who was an unprecedented 11-for-11 in previous NCAA individual finals, was finally going to be beaten. As Coughlin slogged through the final two laps, a pair of Auburn swimmers, Kirsty Coventry and Margaret Hoelzer, swept past her, setting off a rowdy celebration among the eventual team champion's contingent. McKeever and her swimmers, meanwhile, looked like wax-museum figures. As Swedish swimmer Emma Palsson later told a teammate, "I think I had some sort of a heart attack."

Drained physically and emotionally after the previous night's drama, Coughlin had not been in the best space before the race, an event she happened to detest in the first place. Largely because of Helen Silver's proficiency in the event, Coughlin had swum the 200 back just once all season, in December at the Princeton Invitational, and seemed confused as to how to pace herself once it began. She swam as though she merely wanted to get the race over with—which, in fact, she did. Even as Coughlin was humming, at 75 meters Hite, watching from the stands, had winced: He knew it was over. Sure enough, coming out of the turn at 150, Coughlin suddenly appeared as though she'd been zapped by a Taser gun.

At race's end, Coughlin pulled off her goggles and gasped for air, draping herself over the lane line like an exhausted preschooler at the end of a swimming lesson. Her legs were throbbing; her heart was pounding; her head was spinning. This was the moment, in theory, that she'd been dreading, yet defeat, that most unfamiliar of concepts, washed over her with a surprisingly gentle touch. The first thing she thought was *Thank God it's over.* She braced herself for the next emotion—misery, searing anger, panic—but relief was all she felt.

She walked gingerly to the warm-down pool and began swimming slowly. Her legs felt like wet stacks of all her newspaper clippings, and no one, not even McKeever, felt compelled to bother her. Coughlin had one last race to swim as an amateur, the leadoff leg of the 400 free relay, which would take place in less than an hour. Satisfied that she had rid her exhausted body of enough excess lactic acid to ward off additional pain, Coughlin did an ESPN interview, smiling gracefully throughout the conversation, then got out of the water and entered an adjacent hot tub. "Are you ever going to get out of there?" the coach of an opposing team asked, and Coughlin smiled faintly and shook her head no.

Finally, tentatively, McKeever approached the tub, discerning correctly that she was the last person Coughlin wanted to see. The two women possessed a mother/daughter closeness that, in the wake of this shocking defeat, triggered the first traces of anger in Coughlin, irrational though they may have been. *Why did Teri make me swim this event I hate, just because of some stupid streak I have? Why does she want me to swim it in the Olympics, when I'm so much more comfortable with the 100 free?*

Within seconds, Coughlin let it all go. By the time McKeever asked, "Are you okay?" the swimmer had regained her swagger. "I'm fine," she said, slapping the water with her left hand. "Maybe it hasn't hit me yet, but I'm okay with this." McKeever, who already knew the answer, asked if she'd be able to go in the relay; Coughlin glared back and said, "Yeah, I'm *fine*." She rose from the hot tub and joined her teammates on the pool deck, channeling what was left of her emotional energy.

In terms of reaching their goal of a top-five finish, the Bears were now in a tough spot. Notorious in previous years for disappointing efforts at NCAAs—at least among the Cal men's swimmers, who often teased them about it—the Bears had altered that pattern during the meet's first few days and seemed destined to finish no worse than fifth, behind Auburn, Georgia, a surprisingly potent Arizona (a team Cal had defeated in a dual meet), and Florida. Stanford, however, was lurking, and on the third night the Cardinal was closing fast. "I have to give Stanford and Richard (Quick) a lot of respect," McKeever had said shortly before leaving for the meet. "Every time they have to come up with big swims— at least, until this past dual meet—they've done it at key times, for years and years."

The Bears' best chance to put away their rivals had been in the night's first event, the 1,500 free. Chandler, having already produced a pair of individual fourth-place finishes to go with the 800 free relay triumph, was the 13th-seeded swimmer coming in, and another stellar effort would allow Cal to breathe easier. But Chandler, never a fan of the grueling event, simply wasn't into it; she was overheard telling teammate Kate Tiedeman that "by the end of this race, they'll never ask me to swim the mile again." She finished 36th.

Reilly, meanwhile, gave the Bears some solace: Seeded 24th, she shaved several seconds off her best time, to finish 14th. Amazingly, she then turned around and finished 12th in the rigorous 200 fly, capping a freshman season that defied anyone's reasonable projections, save those of her coaches.

One event earlier, Georgia's Kara Lynn Joyce had won the 100 free in 53.15 seconds, officially an NCAA record. As the 400 free relay neared, Coughlin flashed back to the previous 2 years. Twice, former Bulldogs star Maritza Correia had set NCAA records in winning the 100 free. On each occasion, just before the start of the relay, Coughlin had stood on the blocks and listened to her grandfather, Chuck Bohn, yell, "Take it back!" Both times she had dutifully complied, meaning that Correia's collective total of NCAA-record ownership had spanned an hour and 40 minutes.

Taking back this record from Joyce seemed far-fetched, given the way Coughlin's body had just collapsed in the 200 back. *But this was a travesty*, she thought. *I don't need to take back this record, because I already own it*. Indeed, at the Stanford dual meet, Coughlin's opening split in the meet-closing 400 free relay had been 52.97 seconds, just off Jenny Thompson's American record and well below the existing NCAA mark. Yet, she later learned, Stanford officials had neglected to measure the pool, a requirement in order to submit the record for certification. It was another reason to dislike Stanford and, more important, another source of motivation before the final race of her collegiate career.

Standing on the blocks, Coughlin looked to a nearby lane and saw Joyce, whom she liked, getting into her crouch. *I'll kick her ass*, Coughlin thought. As the starting gun sounded, she darted into the water like a torpedo, summoning perhaps the best start of her entire season. Four laps later, when she touched the wall, Coughlin was still seething. She looked at the scoreboard and saw her time: 52.81 seconds, a new American record. So much for her demise. "She set that record on guts and anger,"

Whitney Hite said the day after the race. "Physically, she clearly wasn't in a good place. But she's tough when she's angry. Anyone who believes she's vulnerable now and who questions her dominance will be in for a rude awakening. She'll use this as fuel to get better, and she'll channel the anger and go to another level."

The Bears hung tough during the relay, and Medina, in another display of heart, managed to hold off Arizona's fast-closing Marshi Smith to take third place by 0.03 second. It was an utterly impressive effort, but when the final scores were posted, Cal had lost out to Stanford for fifth place by a mere point and a half.

Disappointed at first, McKeever was nonetheless heartened by the way Coughlin responded to her stunning defeat—and by the message it sent to the other swimmers. "Everyone has to deal with disappointment," McKeever said in her postmeet address to the team. "It's how you choose to bounce back from it that's important. And Natalie's way of dealing with her disappointment told you everything you need to know about her. As far as our team goals, we fell just short, and now I hope you'll give Whitney and me the license to push you even harder."

Different emotions swirled through McKeever's head in the hours after the meet. She was angry that Stanford's Tara Kirk, winner of both breaststroke events, had been voted by a panel of coaches in College Station as the NCAA Swimmer of the Year—the first time Coughlin had failed to win the award. She felt guilty that she'd contributed to Coughlin's defeat in the 200 back, having introduced some new Pilates principles and tinkered with the swimmer's technique—including the addition of a sideways component to her backstroke kick—so close to NCAAs. Hite, too, questioned his own culpability, having pushed her to do the 800 free relay.

Coughlin, however, was already over it. After having set the American record to start the relay, she said to McKeever, "See, this is a sign—I'm a 100 free swimmer, not a 200 back swimmer"—a reference to the looming decision about which event she'd swim at the Olympic Trials. When she walked past the Georgia swimmers, one of them, in reference to

Coughlin's having broken Joyce's 100 free record, said, laughing, "You've got to stop doing this to us."

"I didn't do anything this time," the smiling Coughlin said, explaining that she'd produced a faster time than Joyce's during the Stanford meet.

With that, Coughlin left the natatorium and, along with Palsson, walked to a bar called the Salty Dog. It was teeming with agents and sponsors, all of whom were eager to curry the favor of the star swimmer who was celebrating the end of one of the greatest careers any college athlete had ever enjoyed. Palsson later joked to McKeever that she had "saved Coughlin from signing an exclusive apparel deal with Dolfin swimwear—for $2."

As she soaked up the festive atmosphere, Coughlin noticed that failing to win the 200 back wasn't bothering her in the least.

Losing was something she didn't plan on experiencing again for a long while.

CHAPTER FOURTEEN
FREE AT LAST

She is a full-fledged professional now, and something about the college senior in the faded jeans and gray scoop neck seems different. She looks more mature, more chic, more… *brunette?*

"I dyed my hair brown," Coughlin says, laughing, as she reaches for a succulent samosa in the middle of a bustling Indian restaurant shortly after returning from the NCAAs in late March. "I'm so mad, because Marcelle (Miller) and Emma (Palsson) beat me to it and dyed theirs first!"

It seems that at least on a literal level, the Golden Girl is no longer golden. But in parting with her blond persona, Coughlin has also performed a symbolic cleansing of her cluttered psyche. This is one case in which, at least in the pool, she can claim that brunettes have more fun. "It's hard to explain," she says, "but I just feel so much lighter now. In practice this morning I was just so crisp and dialed in. I'm really, really excited about getting into my long-course training and making some adjustments in Pilates and with my technique. Honestly, this is the best I've felt in a long time."

In fairness, the samosas may have something to do with it. Having finally found the clandestine lunch haven in West Berkeley for which we've been searching for several weeks, Coughlin and I have, as usual, erred on the side of gluttony. This is the second time we have come searching for Vik's, an order-at-the-counter eatery inconveniently located in the middle of an industrial neighborhood, and only because we were persistent in questioning passersby did we actually find it. "Vik's? It's in there," a pleasant woman finally informed us, gesturing with her thumb.

There? But it's a warehouse.

"Yeah, in there."

We walked tentatively toward the massive steel door at the side of the structure and pulled on the oversize handle. It opened, leading into a corridor that, a few yards away, spilled into a cool, high-ceilinged room containing more than 100 diners chowing down on marsala and curry and other delectable dishes.

Less than 96 hours earlier, Coughlin had suffered the defeat that reverberated throughout the swimming world, finishing third in the 200 back in the final individual race of her amateur career. Even allowing for the fact that she'd previously avowed her acting aspirations, her unfazed demeanor was utterly convincing. She seemed about as rattled as Meryl Streep after failing to win an Oscar—*like I needed* that *to validate my eminence.*

"Everyone expects me to freak out over this, but honestly, I really don't care that much," she said. "For one thing, I just really don't like that event. The only reason I swam it was because it was the best thing for the team back when I was a freshman, and then, once I won it my first 2 years, people wanted me to keep winning those same three events. I was doing it for them, not me. I could've won the 100 free or 200 free and enjoyed myself much more. It wasn't like I lost the 100 back or something I cared about. Basically, I just went out too fast, and I died going into the seventh lap. When I die, I just lose it in my legs—and I rely on my legs for power more than most people. When it was over, it was almost like a relief. It was my last college race, and now I could stop thinking about the Streak. It basically cast a shadow over my last 2 years of swimming, and now that I actually had to face losing, it wasn't so bad."

Her words carried plenty of ramifications, including a bias against the 200 back that could affect her decision whether to swim that or the 100 free—or both—at Olympic Trials. They also spoke to an uncharacteristic strain of tension between her and McKeever. When Coughlin spoke of the "people" who wanted her to swim the 200 back at NCAAs, it was her coach to whom she was referring. So strong was the connection between them, so deep the trust, that both women were able to live with their rare philosophical divides and remain focused on the larger picture. In this case, that meant moving full speed ahead toward Athens.

Besides, it wasn't as if McKeever had neglected to beat herself up over what had happened in Texas. "In retrospect, I probably shouldn't have introduced the new stuff we're doing in Pilates so close to NCAAs," the coach had said 2 days earlier. "It probably tired her out. Because if Natalie says she'd going to do the exercises, she's not going to half-ass it. I can't wait until she sees the tape, because her technique, until it broke down, was awesome, the best it's ever been. We're trying some new things, and it can get better and better. The more I think about it, the more I realize that in the grand scheme of things it's not that big a deal. For someone who's going to swim as long as she is, you're going to have races where things don't go the way you like. It happened to Jenny Thompson, to Summer Sanders, and to Tracy Caulkins, and it'll happen to Michael Phelps. At some point, it happens to everyone."

It wasn't difficult for McKeever to spin it forward. "From now on she'll be swimming only for herself," the coach said of Coughlin. "There are some negatives that go along with that, but also a lot of positives. At Trials, she won't have to care how her Cal teammates are swimming. Emotionally, it'll be about preparing herself to do really well for specific races, and that's it. Even on an Olympic team, it's all about you. You might like the other girls—Jenny or Amanda (Beard) or whomever—but it's not like they're your college teammates. You want them to do well, but it's really not that big of a deal if they don't."

McKeever's sights were firmly on the Olympic Trials, with Coughlin scheduled to compete in just three long-course meets, all in California, before heading to Long Beach for the biggest competition of her life. In fact, with the US staging its post-Trials training camp at Stanford and with her magazine interviews and photo shoots (*Time, Glamour,* the *New Yorker, Vogue, Vanity Fair*), as well as other media commitments (mostly to NBC) set for LA and the Bay Area, Coughlin would have to leave the Golden State only once before heading across the Atlantic—to attend a 3-day training session at the US Olympic training facility in Colorado Springs.

McKeever, too, would make that trip—not that her Cal coaching responsibilities had ebbed much. Still heavily involved in recruiting with the approach of the spring signing period, McKeever also had her share of housekeeping with which to contend: That morning, for example, she'd screamed at one swimmer whose commitment, she felt, was in question; later, she'd received a phone call from a hysterical Keiko Amano, whose dog had died. It was easy to see why McKeever viewed the push toward Greece as a welcome respite from the daily grind.

The coach's next challenge was to make sure she and Coughlin were propelling themselves in the same direction. "Sometimes I'm afraid to push her because of the relationship we have," McKeever conceded. "That's why I was hesitant to approach her after she lost that race—I know that she trusts me not to make her uncomfortable. Whereas with Whitney, he'll just confront her with things without feeling restricted. One thing I want to do when I see her tomorrow is convince her that with 105 days to go before Trials, I have a specific plan, and here's what it is…to show her that it's going to be okay. I don't think she'll doubt herself, but the fact that she's talking about not wanting to do the 200 back scares me a bit."

∾

Soon there was comforting news: A third member of the team had been welcomed aboard. Going with her initial gut instinct, Coughlin had chosen Janey Miller as her agent, with the first and most important order of business being the consummation of a lucrative apparel deal. Miller, from Boulder, Colorado, was appealing for several reasons—she was a woman; she came highly recommended from sources such as former swimming star Janet Evans; and she had branched out to run her own shop, making her the closest thing to an antiestablishment candidate. Said Coughlin: "I'm not someone who is impressed by how big and established you are. It's the same reason I didn't go to Stanford."

Similarly, Nike's top-dog status in the sports world wasn't helping the shoe giant, though in some ways it was the company's lack of an established presence in the swim world that made the notion of signing there such a tough sell. It was true that Nike, with only a handful of swimmers in its stable (including Haley Cope), would have gained instant legitimacy with Coughlin. Michael Phelps had signed with Speedo, and Nike was seeking a face for its Athens campaign—not just within the swimming world but for the Games in general. With the BALCO scandal having cast track and field in a negative light, Coughlin was a logical candidate to become that face, should she choose the swoosh. Clearly, from a marketing standpoint, track's loss stood to become swimming's gain. In June, a *Sports Business Daily* survey of sports and advertising executives ranked Coughlin as the third-most-marketable prospective Olympian, behind Phelps and US softball pitcher Jennie Finch.

Yet Nike's chief competitor for Coughlin's services had a distinct advantage: proven technology. You can't spell Speedo without *speed*, and the company's Fastskin suit was widely regarded as state of the art in terms of increasing buoyancy and decreasing water resistance. If Coughlin was going to wear suits that were considered slower (or at least less proven in that department) than those worn by most of her peers, Nike would have to convince her of the benefits of taking that risk.

Ultimately, there were other factors that would sway Coughlin toward Speedo. For one thing, the company had a flair for the dramatic gesture: Upon learning that Coughlin had her eye on a new Acura TL, Speedo amended its offer to increase her signing bonus by the exact purchase price of the car.

It was more than a mere matter of money, though. Coughlin felt that

Speedo employed a far more communal approach in its dealings with the swimming world. "They'll be at a big meet, giving out suits that cost $200 to $300 to any swimmer who's interested," she said. "It's like, 'If we come up with better technology, everyone benefits.' Nike has a reputation for being more secretive and proprietary. It's like, 'That's *ours*. Why would we share it with someone else?'"

(Some in the swimming community wondered, Why wear the suits at all? Not only did the Fastskins take some of the sex appeal out of the sport, but they also struck some swimming insiders as antithetical to its spirit. Because the suits cut down on what Speedo called friction drag— essentially, water resistance—some argued that they were basically doing the body's work, as a pair of fins might. According to Speedo, friction drag was responsible for up to 29 percent of a swimmer's total drag underwater. The original Fastskin, worn by most swimmers at the Sydney Olympics in 2000, had been modeled after the skin of a shark. The Fastskin II was an upgraded model that included different fabrics in various parts of the suit, came in stroke-specific versions, and increased buoyancy by contracting the body, creating another physical advantage for a swimmer—the bigger, the better. Thus, bodysuits were something of an equalizer, providing far less of an edge for a relatively lithe swimmer like Coughlin than it did for her fleshier rivals. "If Natalie is, say, 4 seconds better than anyone with no Fastskins involved, she's probably only a second and a half better with everyone wearing them," Whitney Hite speculated. "By being water-resistant, I think they take away from the essence of swimming, which is finding a way to move quickly through the water.")

For now, with the Nike-Speedo decision still unresolved, Coughlin was wearing a cute Puma jacket as she finished a postpractice breakfast at the Kensington Inn in early April. "I'm thinking about blowing off class," she said in a tone that indicated she'd already decided not to attend. "It's the only one I've got left, but I'm just not in the mood."

That's what being on the verge of signing a seven-figure sponsorship deal can do for a college kid. In reality, though, Coughlin already had cash stashed away, thanks to NCAA and USA Swimming rules that allowed her to pocket medal money for her finishes at certain elite national and international competitions. Such an arrangement might have come as a surprise to, say, Leon Powe, the star freshman forward on Cal's basketball team, who many believed had NBA potential. Powe, an Oakland native, had lived on the streets during part of his destitute childhood and needed every cent of his full athletic scholarship to survive. Yet even while he helped to bring in hundreds of thousands of dollars for the athletic department Powe, to remain eligible, could take nothing above that scholarship limit. He couldn't even share in the proceeds from the jerseys bearing his name being sold at the student store. In that sense, Coughlin knew, she was comparatively fortunate.

On the other hand, how many swimmers actually made money, period?

Yet as she awaited the spoils of her many, many hours of labor, Coughlin certainly wasn't tensing up or behaving in an overly conservative manner. "We played Ultimate (Frisbee) the other day in the middle of the track, and Teri told us whichever team won would get a special surprise," Coughlin said. "So I said, 'Okay, we're *winning*.' I had Lauren (Medina) and Erin Calder on my team—they can't catch to save their lives. I was like, *Catch the disc!* It was windy, so I was telling people to keep it low. And I was making diving catches like crazy." Sure enough, Coughlin's team won, though she received a "special surprise" beyond that which had been offered by McKeever, which was getting out of practice early. "I got this awful rash from the pesticide on the grass," she said. "I was scratching so hard you could see the blood vessels under my skin."

Then there was Coughlin's recent trip to Orchard Supply Hardware to purchase patio furniture for her condo. When she got home, she remembered two things: There was no elevator up to her condo, with four flights of stairs leading up to the master bedroom; and she had not thought to enlist any friends. "So I put on athletic clothes and did it all myself," she said. "I hauled a 60-pound wine barrel up to the fourth floor—I'd pick it up, sprint up a flight of stairs, and then stop to rest."

Coughlin's time in the pool since she'd returned from NCAAs had been far more fruitful. "I've had more good workouts this past week than I did the entire college season," Coughlin said. "People have told me, 'You look so much happier'—that's because I am happier. It's just felt so much lighter lately. Plus, Teri's workouts have really been tailored to me, which is nice."

Five days later, Coughlin was officially part of the Speedo family. She and McKeever had flown to Phoenix, where the newly signed swimmer posed in fashionable one- and two-piece swimsuits with Jenny Thompson for a series of promotional photos. As part of the Speedo deal, Coughlin negotiated a clause that gave 5 percent of all the bonus money she earned—including incentives for Olympic medals and world records—to Cal's women's swimming program. "That," McKeever told the swimmers at the team's annual banquet in late April, "tells you how much she cares about this university and this team."

"I'm so happy to have signed with Speedo," Coughlin said. "It just feels right."

She had but one remaining major decision hanging over her head, and it stood to affect the fortunes of swimmers across the globe.

For 8 months now, Coughlin and McKeever had been involved in a psychic tug-of-war over what she would swim in Athens. Scheduling conflicts had all but ruled out the 100 fly and 200 free, meaning that besides the 100 back and the three relays, Coughlin could swim only one more individual event. It would be either the 200 back or the 100 free, two events in which Coughlin held the American record. It was very clear which one McKeever thought she should choose.

Often, their push-and-pull played out in subtle fashion. McKeever would remind Coughlin how dominant she was in the 200 back and how capable she was of setting a world record in the event. Coughlin, meanwhile, would grouse about how much she hated that race and draw attention to her potential as a freestyler. That Coughlin had suffered her first significant defeat as a collegiate swimmer in the 200 back at NCAAs hadn't helped the coach's cause, especially after the seemingly shot senior rebounded 50 minutes later to set an American (short-course) record in the 100 free on the leadoff leg of the 400 free relay. Following the 200 back, Coughlin had done an interview with ESPN for its tape-delayed telecast, and she couldn't resist smiling into the camera and saying, "Maybe this is a sign."

"As soon as the Olympic schedule came out, we started talking about the 200 back versus the 100 free," McKeever had said a few days later. "In the 100 free, there's less margin for error, and if anyone is going to come out of nowhere and medal, it will probably be in that race. She and Inge (de Bruijn) are the only women who have gone under 54, but this 15-year-old Italian girl no one's ever heard of just swam 54.4, and a girl from Finland emerged at Worlds and won it with a fast time. Plus, Jenny Thompson will try to swim it.

"Ultimately, it comes down to Natalie being comfortable with what she's doing. I still think she should swim the 200 back, but if she ultimately decides the 100 free is her comfort zone, then so be it."

Nine days later, McKeever was still pressing her case. "What I'd like is for her to give me 3 weeks to work with her on the 200 back, to get her feeling comfortable with the event again," the coach said. "I think the world record is there for the taking. Of course, it doesn't matter if I think that; she's the one who has to convince herself of that, ultimately. If, as Trials approach, she's still feeling like the 100 free is where she's most comfortable, she'll probably just end up swimming it."

Yet as McKeever spoke, some startling developments were taking place Down Under at the Australian Olympic Trials. Nineteen-year-old Libby Lenton had clocked a 53.66 in the semifinals of the 100 free, breaking the 4-year-old world record set by de Bruijn, the 2000 Olympic champion from the Netherlands. And another young Aussie, Jodie Henry, had gone 53.77 in her semifinal heat, matching de Bruijn's prior record. Suddenly, instead of being one of only two women to have gone under 54 seconds in the 100 free, Coughlin was one of four.

"Yeah, but I know I can go faster, too," Coughlin said. "When I set my American record, I had a horrible finish, and my dive off the start is way better now than it was then."

Still, in an interview with the *Oakland Tribune* in late April, Coughlin, when asked what events she planned to swim in Athens, answered, "Basically it's the 100 back and 200 back, unless something changes."

On May 1, 2004, on an inhumanely hot day in LA, something did change. Competing in the USC/Speedo Grand Challenge, the first of three walk-up meets to Trials, Coughlin swam her first long-course 200 back since the previous summer and plodded to a prelim time of 2:19.24, nearly 11 seconds slower than the American record she'd set in the summer of 2002. The Speedo meet had an unorthodox format in which only the top four finishers made the final, and Coughlin ranked fifth, behind former Olympic gold medalist Beth Botsford; Auburn star Margaret Hoelzer (one of the two swimmers who'd beaten Coughlin at NCAAs); another former Olympic gold medalist, Misty Hyman; and Haley Cope. Coughlin improved to 2:17.53 in winning the consolation final, but even before she completed her last lap, she had soured on the 200 back even more. *Why is it always such a struggle to swim this event?* she wondered. Sure, it was early, with more than 2 months left before Trials. But she'd had no trouble winning the 100 free in 54.87. This, she concluded, was another sign.

Another of Coughlin's swims in LA had been revealing: her victory in the 200 free. McKeever was in constant communication with Mark Schubert, the USC coach in charge of the US women's team, regarding Coughlin's potential for winning a spot on the 800 free relay without having to swim the 200 free at Trials. Though Schubert couldn't officially guarantee anything, he indicated that were Coughlin to record the fastest 200 free time of any US swimmer headed into Trials, he'd almost certainly be satisfied that she'd be a very viable option. Otherwise, she might have to swim the event at least once at Trials—a problem, since its preliminaries and semifinals would be on the same day as the 100 back final. Obviously, the better option was plan A, and Coughlin was anxious to see how she'd swim the 200 free in the Speedo meet. Her time of 2:00.24 was impressive, but something else was even more encouraging. Coughlin had recorded a "negative split"—meaning the second half of her 200 (59.87 seconds) was faster than her first (1:00.37). This is a rarity for most swimmers, who typically become winded toward the end of the 200 free; Coughlin, however, often employed a strategy designed to allow for a finishing kick. Her negative split in LA was seen as a sign that she had plenty of room for improvement, once she reacquainted herself with the race's rhythms.

Just for fun, Coughlin swam a pair of other races in LA: the 400 free, in which she finished fourth with a career-best time of 4:15.35, erasing a PR she'd recorded when she was 14; and the 50 free, in which she scratched after qualifying fifth with a time of 26.60, just behind fourth-place Cope.

With Trials a little more than 2 months away, both Coughlin and McKeever were concerned about the potential discomfort of having Cope in such close quarters. Not only had the relationship been strained since Cope's decision to leave Cal the previous October, but she also had a knack for saying the most maddening things at the least optimal times. McKeever's memory of Coughlin's landmark, American-record-settting 100 free swim in Yokohama, Japan, in 2002, in which she became only the second woman to go under 54 seconds, includes Cope's untimely scream of "Oh my God—she's gonna *die*!" after seeing Coughlin's 50-meter split of 25.98.

The weekend before the Speedo meet, McKeever, Coughlin, and Cope had traveled to Colorado Springs to be part of a US national team camp. The trip had been notable for two reasons: Coughlin's workouts at high altitude, McKeever said, were "exceptional"; and it was the first time McKeever and Cope had seen each other since their breakup. On the flight back to the Bay Area, McKeever asked Coughlin, "How do you want to handle it if Haley tries to come sit with us at these meets or at Trials?" The two agreed that they'd prefer that Cope stay away. "If she does try to approach us," McKeever later explained, "I'm going to have to tell her, 'Haley, this is what you gave up when you left. You can't sit with us anymore.'"

Of course, 2 weeks before that, Cope had reentered the Cal universe in style. At a birthday party for former teammates Ashley Chandler and Danielle Becks, she arrived wearing a Cleopatra outfit complete with chain-link bra and spent much of her time drinking beer out of a Viking horn.

~

The skinny 14-year-old girl emerged from the pool and bounded across the deck, waving and smiling and soaking up cheers. Katie Hoff, a heretofore little-known swimmer from Baltimore, had just stunned the crowd at the Santa Clara Invitational in late May, annihilating the competition in the 400-meter individual medley. Her time of 4:39.82 was the world's second best of the year to that point and was less than 2 seconds shy of Summer Sanders's American record. In less than 5 minutes' time, Hoff had thus announced herself as a bona fide Olympic hopeful. Her future appeared to be unlimited.

Up in the stands, many of the other swimmers competing in the meet were dubious. "Let's see what happens when she gets hips," one said. "Yeah," added another, "wait till she gets her period."

Had Coughlin heard the comments, she would have empathized with Hoff. Back in the day, she, too, had been a 14-year-old phenom, obliviously blowing away more established swimmers and seemingly getting more dangerous by the day. That she was here at all now—let alone here as a wiser, more accomplished competitor—was somewhat of a miracle. In a sport notorious for eating its young, Coughlin had survived and thrived.

In that sense, Coughlin felt instinctively protective of a sudden star like Hoff, whose career could be slowed or destroyed by so many potential pitfalls. Some swimmers burned out or branched out into other interests. They got beat up physically, mentally, and emotionally, or they simply grew tired of being slower than they used to be. Eating disorders, depression, drug abuse—Coughlin could name dozens of once-prominent swimmers who'd succumbed to those and other perils.

Any adult swimmer—even one who loved the bare essence of the sport as much as Coughlin—who claimed to have never thought about quitting was lying. So brutal was the training regimen that the "Q" word was on everyone's mind at some point. "It's funny how I quit swimming at least once every practice," one of Coughlin's teammates told me a couple of weeks before the Santa Clara meet. "I get all mad that we're doing something really hard and I'm like, *I don't have to do this; I can quit anytime I want. In fact, that's what I'm going to do. I'm quitting.* But then by the time we warm down, I've forgotten about it. I think everybody does that, which is kind of disturbing and certainly weird."

Sometimes it was over in a flash. Seven months earlier, Coughlin and her teammates had been pining for the services of high school senior Diana MacManus, reasoning that the former national champion in the 100 and 200 back would be the plum of their recruiting class. MacManus had chosen Texas over Cal, but now, 6 weeks before Trials, she was nowhere to be seen. She had stopped swimming, at least for the moment, and would not even show up in Long Beach. Four years earlier, as a 14-year-old, she had been the Katie Hoff of her era, finishing fourth in the 100 back at Trials. And now—poof, she was gone.

Whether or not MacManus had been a victim of excessive yardage wasn't certain. But in general Coughlin believed that most of her peers were susceptible to burnout, as she had been as a teenager. "There's too much overtraining," she said, "and some programs are just downright abusive. As some people begin to understand that and change the way they train, you'll see less people walking away. And I think that's why a lot of people are swimming longer and longer. Jenny (Thompson)'s training half of what she used to, and she's still fast. My attitude is, focus on yourself. I look at someone like (former Cal sprinting star) Anthony Ervin— people called him a slacker. But what I saw was that when he swam, he was focused, and it obviously worked for him."

"Swimming is such a wholesome activity, and it breeds so many driven, successful people," McKeever had noted in March. "But instead of selling that, USA Swimming touts Michael Phelps for not having missed a workout for 3 straight years—and that we're all up at 5 in the morning. It's like they make the sport intentionally boring and wear it as a badge of honor."

Stroke consultant Milt Nelms had convinced McKeever that training approaches would be radically different—if not in their lifetimes, then in Coughlin's. "If not missing a practice for 3 years is what it takes to be a prospective Olympic champion," Nelms told her, "then we shouldn't be doing it."

Coughlin was so convinced that technique-driven, lower-volume workouts were the most effective that as the Games approached, she deviated further and further from the traditional training model. She delved deeper into Pilates, each week making the 1½-hour round-trip drive to Mountain View, a Silicon Valley town just south of Stanford, to see Tom McCook, a former bodybuilder with a soothing voice, whom Nelms described as a "physiological genius." Before one morning session in early June at McCook's Center of Balance studio, Coughlin lauded the instructor as being someone who "thinks outside the box, which more people need to do." McKeever, who was also present, added, "I think, for a lot of us, this is the missing piece—to be able to concentrate, to listen to an instructor's cues, and then to apply that to what goes on in the water."

McCook had previously worked with a number of standout swimmers, including Jenny Thompson, Gabrielle Rose, and Misty Hyman, and had traveled to Sydney for the 2000 Games as part of Richard Quick's entourage. He was impressed by his latest client's ability to assimilate his teachings. "She's digested it all," McCook said. "Plus, she's a great mover. It's good to work with someone who gets it. My goal is to make her the authority, which should be the ideal. Your workout has to be related to improved functioning, and not just conditioning. It's really changing your view of what 'strength' really means. It's more about your body's intelligence and how to access it."

During their 90-minute session, Coughlin did a series of rigorous stretching and strength-building exercises, some on machines with amusing nicknames: Elvis, a rocking device designed to stretch one's pelvis; the Pegasus, a new contraption designed in Florence, Italy, that especially works the pectoral muscles; and the Reformer, in which the legs go into ankle straps on opposite sides of a sliding base—"my favorite,"

Coughlin said sarcastically of the latter machine. "The first time I did this, I had a profound fear that I was gonna fall and my legs would split."

"Yes," McCook said, "she thought she'd become a Siamese twin."

At various points throughout the workout, McCook and McKeever were able to reference Coughlin's performance in the water in relation to the stretches. After Coughlin placed a foam ball between her knees while lying flat on her back and doing breathing exercises, McCook said, "Now curl over and see if you get the sense that you're lengthening the muscles in your lower back…that you're elongating."

"I think that's what Milt was talking about with your backstroke start," McKeever chimed in.

"Right," Coughlin said. "I was tucking my tail too much."

Said McCook: "When you crunch your butt, you put a lot of tension in your sacrum. That's why you have to stay long. When the back is elongated, it lets go of a lot of tension, and that makes you a lot more functional. When your back is tight, it's really hard to hold your position when kicking—and then you'll overuse your quads."

～

Staying loose at Pilates was one thing; doing so everywhere else was another. Coughlin's pre-Olympics preparation was becoming more specific as she zeroed in on her schedule. By early May she had completely stopped swimming the butterfly, a development that made Coughlin's friend Jenny Thompson, the United States' other top threat in the 100 fly, utterly aghast. "What I love most about swimming is the competition," Thompson explained while standing above the warm-up pool of the Janet Evans Invitational, the final major event before Trials. "I kind of revel in it. When she told me she wasn't swimming the 100 fly, I was like, *Come on.*"

As Coughlin zeroed in on the biggest competition of her life and her media commitments intensified, McKeever did her best to keep things light. The coach was in a hopeful mood, having spent much of the spring house hunting amid the resplendent hills north of Berkeley. Unlike her modest apartment west of campus, McKeever felt, one of these houses would be a real *home*. Professionally, McKeever also had reason for optimism. Finally fed up with the Bears' diving futility, McKeever had met with Cal men's coach Nort Thornton and discussed the possibility of replacing longtime diving coach Phil Tonne. They then met with executive associate athletic director Teresa Kuehn and agreed to open up the job to any interested applicant. Tonne, at least in theory, would be free to reapply; however, McKeever believed several attractive candidates would emerge.

The atmosphere on the pool deck reflected McKeever's upbeat mood. One sweltering afternoon in late April, she had the swimmers doing a drill in which, one by one, they ran across the deck, dove into the pool without breaking stride, and then did various other novelty strokes, such as a two-handed backstroke, while shifting to the next lane at every other wall. As the drill played out, about a dozen members of Cal's women's water polo team, who were getting ready to begin practice, stood watching with bemused grins. The drill was designed to make the swimmers aware of body control and positioning; judging by some of their ungraceful gaits and awkward dives, this was not a bad thing. Coughlin, by contrast, could not have looked smoother as she pranced along the deck and vaulted herself into the water without making a splash.

A few days earlier, volunteer assistant/team manager Jen Strasburger had ended practice with a relay featuring two teams of seven swimmers apiece swimming a pair of broken-up 25-yard legs, all while wearing one of four devices: an AquaJogger, a pair of inner tubes that conjoined one's ankles, a water parachute, and a mono fin. The race was a reasonably competitive one, and the swimmers were laughing practically the entire time.

Coughlin, of course, tended to be far more serious during practice, as she was on a June afternoon while swimming freestyle laps with a snorkel and resistance boots. After finishing a protracted set, she took off her mask and, a second later, did a double take. Famed sprinter Gary Hall Jr., an Olympic gold medalist in 1996 and 2000, was walking by in a skimpy Speedo. There was nothing unusual about that—Hall was one of the many standout sprinters training under the renowned Mike Bottom, a former swimming great who was now an assistant to Nort Thornton.

What caused Coughlin first to stare openmouthed, then burst out laughing, was the sight of the tall, mop-haired Hall sporting a faux handlebar mustache the eccentric sprinter had apparently applied with a Sharpie marker.

At the Santa Clara meet, Coughlin had enjoyed a burlesque moment of her own when she was fiddling with the bubble-shaped outer cap that Speedo had provided in an effort to test its latest technical innovation. Already self-conscious about what she called her "enormous head," Coughlin sheepishly attempted to find the proper fit for the cap while sitting in the stands before the 100 free final, and in doing so she bore an uncanny resemblance to the character the Great Gazoo from the old *Flintstones* cartoons. "When she wears that cap," her father, Jim, said, "she looks like she's about to get shot out of a cannon." Some of her teammates joked that she had walked off the set of the movie *Spaceballs*. Laughing, Coughlin removed the black cap and then once again placed it over her silver Cal swim cap, and the resulting shift of air caused a funny noise. "It farted," Whitney Hite said, and everyone cracked up.

Then Coughlin left to get ready for the 100 free, walking to the blocks a few minutes later with the other finalists, each trailed by a young girl carrying the swimmer's belongings in a plastic bin while Verve's "Bittersweet Symphony" blared over the loudspeakers. Still, the mood was entirely casual as the race began—only because it was an Olympic year were those outside the swimming community even paying attention to meets such as these, with Michael Phelps's participation and Katie Hoff's emergence as the primary story lines. Coughlin won comfortably in 54.77 seconds, and her teammates in attendance seemed genuinely thrilled for her.

"Natalie's really enjoying being a professional," Marcelle Miller noted. "I think the team dynamic was hard for her this year. We expected certain things out of her, but I'm not sure we did enough to support her and the things she was going through. I can't even imagine the pressure she's under. It's definitely gotten more intense this year than in the past, and as we get closer to the Olympics—oh, man. I wouldn't want to be her, I'll tell you that."

Two nights later, while watching the 200 free consolation C final, Miller smiled as she caught a glimpse of Cal's future. "I love watching Erin (Reilly) swim," the breaststroker said. "At some point she's going to realize how good she is and put it all together, and it's going to be scary." In another lane, meanwhile, Lauren Medina was making a late push that would see her edge several higher-seeded swimmers at the finish to win in 2:03.60. The Cal contingent was visibly moved. "Medina just refuses to lose," Miller said, to which Hite replied: "Lauren just needs someone to run down. If she could get to the final heat of Trials, she would beat two people in that heat—the girl on her left and the girl on her right—even if she had to go 1:57 to do it." In that fantasy scenario, Medina, by finishing sixth, could represent the United States in the Olympics, as the top six finishers in the 100 and 200 typically made the team as a means of providing depth for the relays.

However, it turned out there was a more plausible scenario that could land Medina in Athens. At Cal's meet against USC in January, the director of Mexico's national swim team had seen her swim and had subsequently contacted her with an offer: Given her grandparents' ancestry (three of four were born south of the border) Medina would be eligible to represent Mexico in the Games and would almost certainly qualify to do so based on her times. She was still mulling it over. "I've never been to Mexico," Medina said sheepishly, "and my Spanish sucks. But yeah, I'm definitely thinking about it."

Meanwhile, a far more celebrated choice loomed: the Decision. What would Coughlin swim, and how would it impact the rest of the elite US and world swimmers? "There are definitely people that walk around going, 'Oh my God, what's Natalie going to do?'" said Maritza Correia, the former Georgia sprint star who was attempting to become the first black American woman swimmer to make an Olympic team, between races in Santa Clara. "I'm pretty good about just focusing on myself, but there are definitely others who get caught up in it." Rowdy Gaines, the former Olympic champion turned swimming commentator, understood Coughlin's dilemma when it came to choosing between the 100 free and 200 back. "Maybe she should swim the 200 back at Trials and then decide," he said, "but if you hate an event, it's really tough to swim it. In 1984 I had the world record in the 200 free, and I finished seventh at Trials. I just really hated swimming that event, and it played with me mentally—and when it came time to swim it at Trials, I choked. The thing with Natalie is, if she swims the 200 back in Athens, she'll either get first or 36th, because it's such a mental thing with her."

Given the mental machinations and Coughlin's physical breakdowns before the 2000 Trials and at the '03 Worlds, Gaines believed she could best serve her country by scaling down her ambitions. "The United States needs Natalie to be at her best, badly," he said. "Otherwise, we could lose all three relays. The more events, the worse it is for the relay, because she's the key to all of them."

McKeever, for one, hadn't given up on the possibility of Coughlin's swimming both events, at least at Trials: "She may swim all three in Long Beach and then choose," McKeever said. "They're now telling me that there are 37 minutes between the first 200 back semis and the 100 free final—that's doable. You'd like to have that order reversed, but in her case it's better to get the 200 back over with, because she'll be motivated for the 100 free regardless."

In Santa Clara, Coughlin competed only in the 200 back prelims, clocking 2:12.29—just off the meet record, yet far from where she'd like to have been at that point. And yet, with no other American even close to having emerged as a medal candidate, would USA Swimming officials pressure Coughlin, at least via McKeever, to go that way? "I don't think anyone will pressure her to swim anything, to their credit," McKeever said as Coughlin, toward the end of her warm-down swim, had her ear pricked by the officials present in Santa Clara to test her blood for lactic acid. "If they've been watching her and what kind of athlete she is, they know she's not going to let anyone tell her what to do. I'm certainly not going to start telling her what to do now."

McKeever continued: "After her 200 back prelim swim at USC (in

April), I told her, 'Nat, I think the 200 back is an incredibly weak event internationally—but I don't have to swim it. I want you to be comfortable with whatever you swim. If you want to swim the 100 free, that's what you'll swim, end of story. Either way, we might as well keep our options open right now. If nothing else, training for the 200 back will help your 100 back.'"

Three weeks later, at the Janet Evans Invitational, McKeever and Coughlin huddled in the stands of the temporary pool outside the Long Beach Convention Center—the same place Trials would be held in less than a month's time—and discussed race strategy for the upcoming 200 back prelim. The 100 free, as it seemed was always the case, would also be contested that morning, and as McKeever reminded Coughlin to "stay upright, and tuck your chin a little bit," she sensed that the swimmer wasn't all there. Finally, Coughlin blurted out, 'Can I not swim the 200 back tonight?"

McKeever froze. Not swimming the 200 back in the finals of the last meet before Trials meant Coughlin wouldn't be swimming it, period. Was it really over? Coughlin looked at McKeever as though the coach were a foreign visitor who understood no English. "This is going to be my last 200 back," Coughlin said. "After this, I just want to focus on the 100 free."

"What are you saying—that you've made your decision? This is it?"

"Yeah, this is it." Coughlin said. "I thought you already knew that. This is my last 200 back. Ever."

Ever? McKeever thought to herself. *I didn't sign off on that!*

But the coach let it go. "I've got to pick my battles," she said later.

~

"How many did you retire today?" Dave Salo asked McKeever only semi-sarcastically as they left the deck of the warm-down pool later that morning. He and his assistant Adam Crossen, who had joined Salo after leaving Cal, had stopped to schmooze with McKeever and Whitney Hite, a somewhat awkward convergence of related parties in an insular universe. "We retired one," Salo continued, "and we prolonged a couple of careers, too."

All four coaches agreed that the mood in Long Beach was tense. "Everyone's wigging out here because it's too close to Trials, and it's too late to change," Salo said. "They now realize they should've listened before: *He wasn't kidding when he said it's only 700 days to Trials.* I actually got mad at them one day recently and put up on the chalkboard, 'Only 1,400 days until the next Trials.' You better believe that pissed some of them off."

Everyone laughed and continued the lighthearted conversation as begoggled swimmers and concerned coaches scurried past. Before the madness of Trials and the locked-down intensity of Athens, this was the last actual swim meet that would take place for a while. The break between morning prelims and the evening's finals served as an extended social hour.

"Well," Salo said, finally breaking up the conversation, "I've gotta go find my Katie Hoff."

McKeever went over to find Coughlin, whose mood was bright in the wake of her decision to swim the 100 free. It was all systems go heading into Trials: Coughlin's winning time of 1:58.31 in the 200 free had all but assured her a spot on the 800 free relay in Athens. The coach's job between now and Trials would be to keep Coughlin as loose as possible while resisting the compelling urge to become a stress case herself. When McKeever reached the swimmer, Coughlin had a grin on her face the size of a gold medal. She was on her way to the official's table to withdraw from the 200 back final—the last time, she hoped, she'd ever be entered in that race she so hated—and when she signed her name to complete the task, it was as if an ecstatic current surged through her entire body.

"Should we frame it?" I asked.

"Yeah!" she practically screamed. That night, after winning the 100 free in 54.47, Coughlin found her buddy Jenny Thompson, who had flown in but was not competing, on the deck of the warm-up pool. They compared hats—Coughlin's beige Kangol lid, Thompson's pink zip-up cap—and gossiped and giggled, all the while mindful they were headed for a spirited 100 free showdown in Long Beach.

At this point, the specter of having to beat Thompson—or Inge de Bruijn, or Libby Lenton, or Jodie Henry—didn't faze Coughlin in the least. "The 200 back is a weak event internationally," she said, beaming, "but I don't care. I know Inge is there in the 100 free, and those two Australian girls went under (or tied) her world record—well, I can set world records, too. It's a tougher path, but I embrace it. And if I win that gold medal, it'll really mean something."

In the meantime, the selling of Coughlin as a Golden Girl was proceeding in earnest. During one marathon 10-hour session at Spieker Pool in late May, Coughlin completed a nonstop run of interviews and photo shoots. Shivering in the water as a *Time* magazine photographer coaxed her into various poses, Coughlin, her hand clutching the gutter bordering the pool, was stung by a bee.

Far more enjoyable was the movie-trailer skit she filmed for NBC as a means of hyping the network's Olympics coverage. The scenes Coughlin shot in Southern California, which were later juxtaposed with those featuring other Olympians to form the trailer, gave her a taste of the acting experience, an avenue she hoped to explore when her swimming career was done. She had unsuccessfully lobbied the producers to allow her to drive the 2005 Corvette—one of only five in existence at the time—that was featured in the mini-film. A stunt double did the honors instead. "They dropped a log on it like 20 times," Coughlin said, "but they didn't trust me to drive it 10 feet."

To be sure, Coughlin was getting far less attention than Michael Phelps, who would grace the cover of *Time* in a skimpy Speedo and was being cast as the surefire star of the Games. Coughlin wasn't jealous in the least. "I'm glad I'm not getting all that attention," she said. "We're different people. He thrives on it. If I got that much attention that much of the time, I'd go crazy."

As June wound down and Trials neared, Coughlin's mental state seemed as solid as possible. She had even responded favorably to an out-of-nowhere suggestion by McKeever: Why not swim the 50-meter freestyle at meet's end? At first, Coughlin balked: The 50 was, at best, her sixth-most-accomplished event. "My time in the 50 is the same as my first 50 in a 100," she had told me a few weeks earlier. "I tend not to swim it because, it's like, what's the point?" But McKeever pointed out that in swimming the 100 back and 100 free, Coughlin would finish her responsibilities at Trials with 2 days remaining in the 8-day meet. The prelims and semifinals for the 50 would be held on the 7th day, with the final the following night, mirroring the schedule for Athens. Though Coughlin hadn't trained for the event, and wasn't convinced she could even make the finals, she figured, why the hell not?

McKeever liked the idea for two reasons: First, it would keep Coughlin's head in the meet, rather than allowing her to let up and become distracted in the wake of making the Olympic team. "She was going to have to be there anyway because of media commitments," McKeever would later reason, "so this way, she couldn't completely check out." Also, McKeever believed that swimming the 50 would help Coughlin's preparation for the 100 free, particularly in terms of her start and potential explosiveness down the stretch.

This wasn't particularly good news for Haley Cope, whose best events were the 100 back and the 50 free. Now, suddenly, her old friend Coughlin was in position to deny Cope her Olympic dream—twice.

When Keiko Price called to give her the news—"Natalie's swimming the 50 at Trials!"—Cope was stunned. "Why?" she demanded.

"Why not?" Price answered.

On the other end, there was complete silence.

CHAPTER FIFTEEN

HALF CHLORINE, HALF TEARS

She had snapped at the massage therapist, glared at a US Swimming official, and slept only in fits and starts since arriving in Long Beach for the most meaningful meet of her career. In another week, Teri McKeever would be either a pioneer in her profession or a profoundly disappointed coach, and she was feeling the heat as much as anyone in Southern California as the Trials got under way in early July.

"I've been a bitch," McKeever conceded shortly before Coughlin's first swim, in the last preliminary heat of the 100-meter backstroke on the second morning of the 8-day meet. "Obviously, I'm nervous. It's such a tense atmosphere around here. I mean, look at the times—most people are going slower than you'd expect, and that's because this meet is so emotionally overwhelming."

Many in the American swimming community argued that the US Trials actually were a tougher and more pressure-filled meet than the

Olympics, and they had a point: Because of International Olympic Committee Rules limiting each nation to two entrants per individual race, top competitors from a swimming power such as the United States or Australia had precious little margin for error. Some of the third-place finishers at the US Trials might be good enough to win an Olympic medal, were they allowed to compete—but, of course, the world would never know, because only the top two in a particular event would have the opportunity to swim it in Athens.

One false move—literally—could derail an entire career's worth of training. Never had that point been underscored more than during the Australian Trials 4 months earlier, when Ian Thorpe, the most decorated and beloved male swimmer in that nation's history, fell off the starting block seconds before the start of his preliminary heat in the 400 meter freestyle, an event he hadn't lost in the previous 7 years. Because of the zero-tolerance false-start policy, Thorpe was automatically disqualified, even though he'd merely slipped off his mark, rather than mistimed the gun. Faced with the prospect of having the 400 free world record holder denied a chance to defend his 2000 Olympic title, many Australians immediately began lobbying the second-place finisher at the Trials, Craig Stevens, to surrender his spot—mindful that by rule the next-ranked swimmer in the event who had qualified for the Australian team would get the nod: in this case, Thorpe. Since Stevens had already qualified to swim the 1,500 free (his best event) and the 800 free relay in Athens and was hardly a medal threat in the 400, it seemed the patriotic thing to do. After several weeks of indecision, complete with rampant public lobbying and a reported $60,000 payment from a Sydney television station to tell his story, Stevens did indeed offer to step aside, and Thorpe accepted.

In Coughlin's case, a false start was not the sole worst-case disqualification scenario. There was also the matter of the 15-meter rule, which required swimmers to emerge from under water by a specific point marked on each lane line after starts and turns. The rule, which originally mandated a 10-meter limit (it was amended 8 years later), had been instituted back in 1988 after US swimmer David Berkoff set a world record in the 100-meter backstroke at the Seoul Olympics using a 35-meter underwater start—one that NBC commentator John Naber nicknamed the Berkoff Blastoff. Though it might not have seemed logical to those unfamiliar with competitive swimming, Berkoff and many other elite competitors could go faster beneath the water than they could swimming above it. Coughlin, because of her skill underwater, was the most blatant representation of this theory: Theoretically, she could have shattered her own world record by spending most or all of the 100 back below the surface, were such a maneuver allowed.

Instead, she was limited to spending no more than 30 of the 100 meters underwater—a rule she typically pushed as close to the allowable threshold as possible. Two months earlier in Santa Clara, Coughlin had come so close to surpassing the 15-meter mark off her start during the 100 back final that whistles filled the evening air—the result of numerous fans voicing their belief that she was cheating. "I wasn't," Coughlin said afterward, shrugging. "They don't even understand the rule. It's where your head is when it hits the surface that counts, even if your arm is beyond the line. And the only way you can judge it with the proper per-spective is to stand at the 15-meter mark."

At Trials, however, Coughlin was taking no chances. "I think I'm gonna go 11 instead of 12 off the start," Coughlin told McKeever about an hour before her 100 back prelim race, referring to the number of dol-phin kicks underwater. "I'm getting a little close."

There was a palpable closeness between Coughlin and her coach in Long Beach as 4 years of shared sacrifice waited to be validated. On the morning of Coughlin's first swim, McKeever, as was her custom before big meets, presented her with a gift card and a present, in this case a "blessing ring" she had purchased immediately after the NCAA meet 4 months earlier. "Should I read it before or after I race?" Coughlin asked.

"Your choice," McKeever said.

Coughlin opened the card and absorbed its message: "Life is a journey, not a destination." Life, McKeever continued, wasn't just one journey, either—it was a series of overlapping journeys. "This begins your Olympic journey," she wrote. "Thank you for letting me share your journey to this point. I'm sad that I have to start sharing you, but the good thing is that so many people will see what an amazing woman you are."

It turned out to be an emotional morning for McKeever, beginning with Coughlin's preliminary swim, a meet-record 1:00.71, easily the fastest among qualifiers. The fastest 16 would compete that night in a pair of semifinal heats, with the top 8 overall finishers advancing to the following evening's finals. Such a three-round format was largely unnecessary—"What do the semis do, really?" asked Adam Crossen, McKeever's former Cal understudy—but it mirrored the format that would be used in Athens. "The deal is that the people who run the Olympics want swimming to last a week," Crossen explained, "and US Swimming wants the experience here to be similar. Basically, they want to give Michael (Phelps, and other swimmers with multiple events) an idea of what it will be like to swim all those events in Athens. I mean, they could pick the same team in 4 days by just swimming prelims and finals, but this is the system we have." (The counterpoint to this argument, of course, is the notable exception: In the 2000 Trials, for example, Gabrielle Rose snuck into the semis of the 200-meter individual medley with a 16th-place finish. She went on to finish second in the event and placed seventh for the United States in Sydney.)

Haley Cope, with the fifth-fastest prelim time, was right there in the 100 back mix. And in the ultracompetitive 100-meter breaststroke, McKeever's former star Stacianna Stitts had made the morning's biggest statement with a scorching preliminary race to lead all qualifiers, even favorite Amanda Beard. Attempting to make her second consecutive Olympic team, Stitts produced a time (1:07.20) that was the third-fastest in the world in 2004, behind only the first- and second-place finishers at the Australian Olympic Trials.

"She'll just feed off that," McKeever said after Stitts's swim. "I really, really hope she makes it. Stace means so much to me. I remember sitting in her living room when I was recruiting her, and her saying, 'I want to set a world record and win an Olympic gold medal.' And I'm thinking, 'I so want to help her do that.' My dream is that she, Haley, and Natalie will make the team, and we'll all be there together, and everyone will bury the hatchet."

For all that was on the line, the prelims still lacked an energy from the stands commensurate with the gravity of the situation. Entire careers were being decided—childhood dreams alternatively dashed and cashed in—yet the scene played out in relatively muted fashion. When swimmers were introduced at the starting blocks, there were sporadic cheers, mostly from family members and close friends, as if the whole thing were one giant junior high school graduation ceremony. Coughlin, of course, was different. "Listen to the crowd when she's introduced," Crossen said. "With everyone else, it's their team and their parents cheering. With her, people go nuts. They love her."

To swimming loyalists, Coughlin represented the greatest chance for Olympic glory among American women—but it wasn't just that. After all she had been through, there was both an acknowledgment of her struggle and a sense among the fans in Long Beach that they could collectively will her to overcome her previous disappointments in major meets. With the Olympics only 5 weeks ago, Coughlin was theirs now, and they intended to send her off to Athens with as much support as possible.

McKeever's friend Susan Teeter, the Princeton coach, passed her on the pool deck and said, "Nice swim this morning." McKeever thanked her. McKeever, of course, hadn't set foot in the water. Coughlin's swims were *her* swims.

A cell phone rang, and McKeever pulled it out of her pocket and answered it. "Hey," she said. "Where are you? I'll come up there when it's all over. I love you." She hung up and swallowed hard. "Why does talking to your mom always make you feel like crying?" she asked.

The following evening, as the brilliant Southern California sun began to droop toward the Pacific Ocean, casting a glimmering reflection off the newly gentrified downtown shops and restaurants, the temporary stadium outside the Long Beach Convention Center was abuzz with anticipation. Phelps had been the story of Trials thus far, but this was to be Coughlin's coronation as America's Golden Girl in waiting. NBC would be broadcasting live, and 10,000 fans packed the bleachers to see whether she'd deliver.

In the previous night's 100 back semis, Coughlin had won her heat in a relatively leisurely 1:00.91, 0.2 slower than her effort in the morning. She remained the fastest qualifier, ahead of Cope (1:01.67), the only other swimmer to break 1:02 in either session. Now, as the prohibitive favorite, Coughlin planned to go out and seize the moment. As usual, she would use her underwater prowess to vault to a lead and build it into the turn, and she was, simultaneously, exceptionally confident and horribly nervous as she walked to the starting blocks.

Once in the water, Coughlin relaxed slightly. This was still, at its core, a race against seven other swimmers, and all she had to do was beat at least six of them. She could handle that. The gun sounded, and Coughlin disappeared under the surface and stayed down as the other competitors, one by one, began to pop up and extend their arms backward. Finally, comfortably before the 15-meter line, Coughlin emerged, well ahead of the competition. The crowd roared. She shot through the water like a buoy being pulled by a speedboat, utterly in command of the opening lap. Fans screamed her name, urging her to keep charging. Her turn was perfect, and as she came up from her second underwater session, less than 40 meters stood between her and an official berth on the Olympic team.

Then, for a few seconds, Coughlin began to drift toward the lane line, triggering a haunting flashback to those in the crowd who had witnessed her effort at the 2001 World Championships in Fukuoka, Japan. In that race, Coughlin had enjoyed a similarly dominant second-lap lead, when she veered to the lane line and straddled it for much of the race's final meters. She had managed to win nonetheless, but her navigational difficulties may have cost her a world record—her time of 1:00.37 was .21 off the standard then owned by China's Cihong He, a mark that would stand for nearly 8 years before Coughlin finally smashed it in the summer of 2002.

None of the other swimmers in Long Beach seemed to be gaining on Coughlin; only the lane line, it seemed, could keep her off the team. But Coughlin righted herself and backed into the wall for a winning time of 59.85 seconds, the third-fastest effort in history, surpassed only by a pair of her previous performances. Coughlin raised her left arm triumphantly and flashed an All-American smile that resonated all the way to Athens.

It seemed like an entire commercial break passed before the next swimmer finished, and when Coughlin saw who'd scored the other berth on the team, her grin grew even larger. Cope, with a time of 1:01.24, had beaten Hayley McGregory by 0.7 to fulfill her longtime Olympic dream— only Cope was one of the last people in the stadium to realize it.

Cope had smiled broadly during prerace introductions, but inside she was as scared as she'd ever been. In the 2000 Trials, she'd been in the perfect position to make the team in this event but had died in the final stages. This time, the race proceeded fantastically for Cope until the homestretch, when the sprinter's legs began to get heavy once again. She feared she'd be caught by McGregory, whom she could see approaching in the next lane. During the last 25 yards, Cope thought to herself, over and over, *Oh my God. This can't happen again. This isn't happening. I've worked too hard. No, no, no, no, no, no!*

When she touched the wall, Cope, fearing the worst, kept her head down and resisted looking at the scoreboard to see where she'd finished. By the time Cope finally pulled off her goggles and glanced upward, she already knew something good had happened. Coughlin, having moved into Cope's lane, was practically drowning her old friend with excitement. For all the tension that had plagued their relationship over the past 9 months, since Cope's abrupt decision to leave Cal and McKeever, this moment was so special that it suddenly made everyone whole.

Standing up and clutching a railing on the opposite end of the pool, McKeever was overcome by emotion. She was teary eyed as Cope, after gathering her gear, came walking by a couple of minutes later. McKeever called her over, and the two shared a sincere hug.

"I couldn't have done this without you," Cope said.

"Haley," McKeever replied, "that's all I ever wanted to hear."

Then McKeever and Coughlin had a similarly sweet embrace, and the celebration began in earnest. Following her warm-down session, Coughlin returned to the pool deck for the awards ceremony, first taking a victory lap that once again brought the fans to their feet. As a horrific techno-polka tune blared over the loudspeaker, Coughlin waved and soaked up the cheers. She looked overjoyed and unburdened, as if she had just shed a backpack full of bowling balls she'd been carrying the past 5½ years.

Familiar faces were spread throughout the stadium—her parents, Jim and Zennie; her younger sister, Megan; her grandparents and Aunt Yvonne, Zennie's sister, along with numerous other relatives; two groups of clamorous college teammates; several friends from high school; her boyfriend, Ethan Hall; her agent, Janey Miller; and, standing proudly on the pool deck, the choked-up McKeever—but even from those outside her inner circle, Coughlin felt the love. Most everyone in the swimming community, it seemed, was mindful of Coughlin's bumpy journey, and the hearty cheers washed over her like a warm shower.

It was the best day of her life, with the promise of more to come.

For every swimmer who, like Coughlin and Cope, realized a childhood goal, there were scores of others at Trials who were coming to terms with the failure to achieve theirs. The end came with such haunting sudden-ness that the often muted crowd reaction didn't do justice to the magni-tude of the moment. "You should see the warm-down pool," said Amanda Hall, a former UCLA swimmer who now worked for the school's ath-letic department. "It's half chlorine, half tears."

"This meet, if you look under the grandstand, it's about crying," said Milt Nelms. "There's so much emotion being released, you can almost feel it."

A particularly painful scene played out on the fifth morning of competition, when Georgia swimmer Andrea Georoff froze on the blocks as the gun sounded for the sixth heat of the 100 free. A legitimate threat to sneak into the semifinals as one of the top 16 finishers—and thus, with six 100 free swimmers likely to make the team (because of relays), someone who had at least an outside chance of going to Athens—Georoff stood motionless as seven other swimmers dove into the water. By the time she finally dove in, it was already hopeless. The scoreboard measured each swimmer's reaction time off the blocks, and Georoff's was at least 2 seconds slower than everyone else's. She ended up with a time of 59.18, placing her 49th out of 50 finishers.

Watching that race as she waited to swim in the seventh and final heat, Coughlin was furious. All meet long, she and others had felt, the starts had been inconsistent and tricky. Swimmers would stand on the blocks for uncomfortably long periods, and then the gun would sound abruptly, catching swimmers off guard. Lindsay Benko, a 2000 Olympian expected to make the team again, had nearly been undone in the 100 free because of such a circumstance. *No biggie,* Coughlin thought. *It's only the OLYMPIC TRIALS!* Whereas international meets invariably featured fast starts, with a minimal amount of waiting on the blocks, starters at US meets tended to be more deliberate. This, however, was bad even by US standards. After winning her preliminary heat in 55.23 seconds to lead all qualifiers, Coughlin went to US women's coach Mark Schubert and complained about the starts, urging him to lobby USA Swimming officials to fix the problem before that night's session—not that it would do Georoff any good.

One of Georoff's Georgia teammates, Sam Arsenault, had also competed in Coughlin's heat, finishing in a somewhat disappointing time of 57.09 to place 26th overall. Arsenault and Coughlin were good friends from their youth swimming days and had hoped to room together for the 2000 Olympics until Coughlin's injury derailed the plan. "We were at the Pan Pacs (Pan Pacific Games) in Sydney in 1999, and we were sitting on this bridge overlooking the pool," Arsenault recalled while standing in a hotel lobby in Long Beach. "We held hands and made a pact that we'd be right back there, in that spot, and would room together for the Olympics. Then she hurt her shoulder, and in 2002, I hurt mine and had surgery. We were talking about all of this at the Santa Clara meet 2 months ago, and it was like, 'Don't even go there.' We got really emotional. Last time, I went and she didn't; this time she's going and now I have to go out and make it happen again. That's pressure."

But Arsenault, it turned out, was facing an even more daunting form of pressure: Doctors had recently discovered a tumor in her body, and she was delaying treatment until after her run at the Olympics.

On a much less vital level, the pressure was also getting to most of Coughlin's former Cal teammates. After swimming her preliminary heat in the 100 breast on the meet's second day, shaken sophomore-to-be Annie Babicz told McKeever, "I couldn't feel my hands." Realistically, none of McKeever's other swimmers was a serious threat to make the team, but their performances, for the most part, had been underwhelming. That all changed on the meet's third day, when Lauren Medina uncorked what might have been the most unlikely preliminary swim of Trials.

Months earlier, after having been approached by the director of Mexico's Olympic team, Medina had mulled the possibility of swimming for that country in the Games. "You should go to Trials for us," the coach had told Medina, noting that her ancestry qualified her for that nation's Olympic team. "I think you're that good."

"No, I'm not," Medina had answered sheepishly. But as the weeks passed, Medina began to consider the prospect more seriously. Though she had never actually been to Mexico and was not close to being fluent in Spanish, she was enticed by the opportunity to swim in Athens and intended to accept the offer. Everyone, including McKeever, was all for it—everyone, that is, except Medina's proud mother, Sandra.

"No way," Sandra Medina told her daughter. "If you swim for Mexico, that's saying that you're not good enough to swim for the United States. If you do it, I'm not going to support you."

The problem was that Medina, based on her qualifying times, wasn't close to good enough to represent the United States as one of the top six finishers at Trials. But bizarre as her methodology may have been, Sandra Medina helped bring out something in her daughter, as did Whitney Hite, who told her just before her prelim swim, "You've worked your ass off for this. You get in that water and show 'em you're the toughest one here." Then Medina, to the astonishment of virtually everyone in Long Beach, powered to a preliminary time of 2:01.84—1.21 seconds faster than her previous lifetime best. When the dust settled, Medina, the 42nd-seeded swimmer coming in, was in 7th place.

The Cal contingent was abuzz. If she could improve just one more spot, they told themselves, Lauren Medina would go to the Olympics for the *United States*. "If she can get to the finals," Hite told them, "there's no way she's going to let two people beat her."

The experience turned out to be too overwhelming for Medina, who spent the hours between her prelim swim and that night's semifinals bouncing around her hotel room. "I didn't sleep the entire day," she said later, "which was a big mistake. I'd had too much coffee, and I went to the bathroom like 30 times. I was so nervous, and I got exhausted thinking about all that was at stake."

Medina flamed out in her semifinal heat, finishing in last place with a sluggish swim of 2:04.50. But her success in the prelims had changed her outlook regarding her own potential. Prior to Trials, Medina had planned on taking a month off before gearing up for her senior season at Cal. She now agreed to swim at US Nationals, which would take place at Stanford in early August, just before the start of the Olympics. "If you skip Nationals, you're crazy," Hite implored. "You could win."

∾

Milt Nelms smiled as Coughlin pushed off the wall and began the second lap of her 100 free semifinal, already confident she had accomplished her objective. "She's shutting it out down," he said, turning to high-five me as we watched from a lower-level corporate suite while the rest of the fans in the packed stadium sweated out the rest of the race. "See how easy it looks."

Sure enough, Coughlin cruised home in 54.30 seconds, the top time among the eight qualifiers for the finals, ahead of Georgia's dangerous Kara Lynn Joyce (54.75) and legendary sprinter Jenny Thompson (54.94). "She's gonna rip tomorrow night," Nelms predicted. "We could see an American record."

Minutes earlier, Nelms had been far more stressed-out. Gary Marshall, an Oklahoman who had swum on his Conoco/Phillips 66 team back in Nelms's earlier life as a prominent coach, was about to compete in a loaded 200 breast final that included former Olympian (and 2000 silver medalist in the 100 breast) Ed Moses and 2001 world champion Brendan Hansen. "Back when I had him, I thought he'd end up being a world record holder," Nelms said of Marshall, for whom he clearly still had great affection. "He went to college at Virginia and got beaten down. He needed a Teri McKeever in his life; unfortunately, there is no college coach like that on the men's side."

As the race proceeded, Marshall, who had since transferred to Stanford, seemed to be in prime position for a second-place finish. No one was going to beat Hansen; he finished in 2:09.04, breaking the world record previously held by Japan's Kosuke Kitajima, following up an earlier world record effort in the 100 breast. Marshall looked solid until the final lap, when Wyoming's Scott Usher ran him down and secured the other spot on the Olympic team. Marshall, after finishing third, pulled off his goggles, climbed out of the pool, and walked off alone, pondering what might have been.

The whole scene unnerved Nelms. To him, the sight of Marshall striking that solitary pose revealed everything that was wrong with the sport at this level. "How Gary Marshall navigated his way through a culture to get to this level and almost make the team is just incredible," Nelms said later. "If the obstacles set up by the culture weren't there, he'd be a world record holder. As it is, he's a survivor. And after that race was over, and he came within one spot of making the team, neither of his coaches—his club coach and his college coach, who were right there, poolside—even spoke to him. What kind of message does that send?"

Nelms also resented the way many prominent USA Swimming officials and coaches had left Coughlin hanging during times of disappointment. "The culture has used her to pull their wagon on three occasions," Nelms said. "In high school she was the second coming of Christ, but then she hurt her shoulder and people forgot about her. Then she came back and did all those wondrous things with Teri, and USA Swimming hitched their wagon to her again. But when she got sick in Barcelona, they dropped her like a hot potato. After it was initially announced that she was sick, they didn't even update her condition on the Web site.

"That second time through made her grow up. From that point on, I think, her mind-set was 'This is about me, and I'm going to do it the way that makes sense to me.' When she made her schedule of events, there was a lot of whining about her not swimming the 200 back. That profoundly offended me. If we don't have any other elite-level swimmers in the 200 back, that's not Natalie's problem. It's USA Swimming that needs to get it together. We win a medal for every 11 or 12 million people; Australia figures out how to win one for every million and a half. The bottom line is that Natalie will do what Natalie chooses to do, and that's as it should be."

Of course, for Coughlin's strategy to pay off, she had to at least qualify in the 100 free, a race in which hundredths of a second could mean the difference between affirmation and abject disappointment. The top six finishers would likely make the team, in order to provide relay depth, but only the first two would be allowed to swim it individually in Athens. And while the United States might have been sorely lacking when it came to 200 backstrokers, the 100 free final was loaded. The field included Jenny Thompson, who'd won more Olympic medals than any US swimmer; NCAA champion Kara Lynn Joyce and her dangerous University of Georgia teammate Amanda Weir; former Georgia standout Maritza Correia, Hite's old friend from Georgia, who was bidding to become the first black woman (she was of Puerto Rican descent) to make a US Olympic swimming team; Lindsay Benko, the American record holder in the 200 free; former Stanford swimmer and Olympian Gabrielle Rose, who now trained at Cal with assistant men's coach Mike Bottom; and Colleen Lanne, one of Salo's sprinting standouts at Irvine Novaquatics.

Third at the turn behind Joyce and Weir, Coughlin made a charge and appeared to be in position to pull out a tight victory. She had intentionally stayed underwater longer off the turn to avoid running into the pronounced wake caused by the other swimmers. Because the temporary pool was essentially built on stilts and was relatively shallow, the wake was more of a factor than in normal meets, and Coughlin, given her reliance on technique, didn't want to take any chances.

In the final strokes, Coughlin pulled ahead, but then she made a potentially ruinous error, slightly misjudging the finish. She reached out her arm, expecting to touch the wall, and instead drifted an extra length before finally hitting it. When she looked up at the scoreboard, she had finished a close second to Joyce, 54.42 seconds to 54.38. The time was slower than her semifinal effort of 54.30 (she'd gone 55.23 in the prelims), and she hated finishing behind anyone. But within a few seconds Coughlin forgot all of that and shifted into celebration mode: She had done what she had set out to do at Trials, period, and now had a month to refocus and make a charge at Inge DeBruijn and the two Aussies.

Coughlin, dancing around in her black sweats like a prizefighter, was all smiles as she, Joyce, and the other top-six finishers (Weir, Correia, Thompson, and Lanne) waited to ascend to the medal stand. The six swimmers then took a spirited victory lap around the pool to the strains of Kool and the Gang's "Celebration." Coughlin accepted floral bouquets from fans and high-fived others, then threw a T-shirt and swim cap into the stands.

At her postrace press conference, Coughlin was asked how disappointed she was not to have finished first. She looked incredulous. "I really don't understand the question," she said. "The objective of this meet is to make the team in your events, and I made the team in two of my favorite events. That's been my goal. Now the goal shifts to what I do in Athens."

Later, as she stood outside a temporary trailer, waiting to supply her postrace urine sample, Coughlin remained upbeat. For one thing, she felt her performance was easily explainable—a lack of speed off the start, the misjudged finish, the extra time underwater at the turn, some other technical breakdowns, and a feeling that she was too relaxed on the starting blocks. "I was almost too loose," she had told McKeever immediately after the race. "It was like I wasn't anxious enough."

Another problem was that, in Coughlin's words, she was "focusing on the wrong things." For instance, in the final moments on the starting blocks, she was still fiddling with the funky, high-tech swim cap Speedo had provided—the one that had provoked so many giggles at the Santa Clara meet weeks earlier. Coughlin was having so much trouble that Joyce, in the next lane, offered to help her position it correctly just before the gun was about to go off. Coughlin declined the assistance but was so touched by the gesture that she and Joyce forged an instant friendship.

The concept behind the cap was that it reduced underwater drag by eliminating the wrinkle that typically formed at the top of traditional caps. But McKeever noticed that the flotation in the new cap also caused a slight change in Coughlin's head position during the race, and the coach's attitude was, At this late hour, why mess with success?

"I think we need to lose that cap," McKeever said after the race. "She's sitting there, fiddling around with it, right before the start of the race, instead of getting focused. I'm gonna tell her, 'You don't need *that*. You're faster than everyone anyway. Just swim.'"

As for the second-place finish, McKeever said, "I don't think because we got second in the Olympic Trials, we need to be in panic mode. It's like she's doing what she needs to do but nothing more. She's operating emotionally at about 80 percent. She's here, but she's not really here all the way. It's something she needs to figure out as she goes along. It's what's going to keep her in swimming, ultimately."

Standing outside the trailer, Coughlin was as loose and carefree as I'd ever seen her. "Honestly, I really don't care that I didn't win that race," she said. "As soon as I made the team, I just wanted the meet to be over with. I mean, I still have to swim the 50, but I really don't think I have a chance to make it in that event."

McKeever, who had just walked over, heard the last part and said, "Let's not concede before we even race." But either Coughlin was a realist or she was creating a self-fulfilling prophecy, because on the meet's final night, Coughlin, having qualified for the final in the 50, finished sixth in 25.31, well behind winner Thompson (25.02) and second-place finisher Joyce (25.11). Cope, with a 25.22, finished fourth, while incoming Cal recruit Emily Silver was 15th in 26.22.

At race's end, Coughlin barely had a shred of disappointment. She had accomplished everything she'd set out to do, which made her one of the few people in Long Beach who could say that. Her friends Keiko Price and Sam Arsenault and so many others had come up well short of realizing their goals—a feeling Coughlin remembered all too well from her previous Trials experience. She was also buoyed by the certainty that she was by no means a finished product. The adjustments she'd been making in the water, along with the principles of Pilates she'd incorporated, had several more weeks to take hold.

"A lot of the greatest athletes, like Michael Jordan or Reggie Jackson, have that extra level they can go to when they absolutely have to," Nelms reasoned. "It's always there, but it drains them incredibly to access it, so they save it for the most important moments. So the way I look at that 100 free is that Natalie is like a cat. Cats only use as much energy as they need. She was very aware that there's a pretty big meet in 4 weeks, and I think she's going to need every ounce of energy for that.

"As far as the technique, I think it's a matter of when her nervous system kicks in. I told Teri, 'It's like a foreign language. She's now fluent in it, but she's not used to speaking it. Once she gets that, watch out.'"

In the meantime, there was still one more golden moment for Coughlin to appreciate. At meet's end, the two US Olympic coaches, Eddie Reese for the men and Mark Schubert for the women, stood on the pool deck and introduced their assistants to the crowd. This was the moment for which McKeever had been waiting—a chance to secure her trip to Athens and to make history. Hopefully, McKeever's selection could open the floodgates for female coaches in the future.

Certainly, Schubert and McKeever had a good personal relationship. Moreover, it behooved Schubert to keep his most important swimmer happy, and he was particularly inclined to take care of Coughlin right now. By restricting her schedule to a pair of individual events, Coughlin had ensured that she'd be fresh and available for all three relays. "I truly think she wants the team to be successful, and you've got to have a lot of respect for that," Schubert would say later. "It would be real easy for her to be selfish, because she is so incredibly versatile. But she's made relays a real priority, and I'm delighted about that. I think the smart people understand why she's chosen to do it this way. Natalie and Teri have made their decisions looking at the whole picture, including the relays. And I think it's really important that they alone make those kinds of decisions, because they're the ones who'll be living it day to day."

Given all of these considerations, it would have been an absolute shock had Schubert not selected McKeever. But when he made the actual announcement, it was nonetheless an emotional one. McKeever had been tipped off a couple of days earlier by Schubert in a private conversation on the pool deck—she had revealed the news only to Coughlin and to her mother. On the final day of the meet, her selection became official in an unspectacular and awkward manner: While standing near the warm-down pool with virtually everyone else in the elite-swimming universe, McKeever was approached by a young USA Swimming employee and handed a red Team USA T-shirt.

Instantly, McKeever felt sheepish. She had no idea which other coaches had been selected for the men's and women's staffs, and she certainly didn't want to express any emotion in front of a soon-to-be disappointed colleague. As she received her shirt, Jack Bauerle, the esteemed Georgia coach, was walking by; he, it turned out, would not be part of either Schubert's or Reese's staff.

The coaches who had received the shirts were instructed to place them over their clothing, and soon afterward they lined up on the deck and, one by one, were introduced to the cheering crowd. As McKeever stood there, soaking up the adulation with her fellow assistants—including Dave Salo on the men's side, and Stanford coach Richard Quick and Arizona coach Frank Bush on the women's side—she glanced up at her mother and choked up. Mostly, however, McKeever didn't allow herself to get too swept up by the moment. *This is just the first step*, she told herself. *We still have 6 weeks of work ahead of us.*

Still, as she lay in bed that night, reflecting on the final night of Trials, McKeever had to smile. Coughlin, finally, was an Olympian. So, too, was Cope. Stitts had narrowly missed, fading to fourth in the 100 breast final and eighth in the 200. Medina had provided an unexpected thrill, and Emily Silver, if all went well, would be a serious threat to make the 2008 team.

McKeever, meanwhile, had made history, and she had earned it. And when she stood there on that deck, wearing that T-shirt—*The only red shirt I'll ever keep*, the coach thought, laughing—no one in that stadium was cheering louder than Coughlin.

CHAPTER SIXTEEN

GREECED LIGHTNING

Lhe spat was inevitable, considering the amount of time they'd spent together and the tension circling through the hot Athens air. Coughlin and McKeever had been cooped up in close quarters since the Olympic Trials, through the pre-Olympic training camps at Stanford, and on the Spanish island of Mallorca, a period that spanned 5 weeks. They'd had hundreds of conversations, many about how to approach the upcoming competition. Now, as they set up shop in Athens and prepared for the most important meet of either of their lives, the anxious atmosphere momentarily overcame them.

On Saturday, August 14, 2004, the first day of the 8-day swimming competition, Coughlin and McKeever were at the warm-up pool at the Olympic venue, preparing for a light workout before that night's 400-meter freestyle relay final, when the coach offered to carry the swimmer's bag. "I'll carry my own bag," Coughlin snapped.

McKeever recoiled. She understood that she had been hovering over

Coughlin but was taken aback by the intensity of the swimmer's response. "I know you're trying to help me," Coughlin said. "It's just that everybody's on edge, and it's driving me crazy."

That was a clear signal to McKeever to back off, and the coach did, ultimately viewing Coughlin's mini-blowup as a positive thing. "She was right; everyone *was* on edge," McKeever said later. "Her saying that allowed us to clear the air, and we were both in a much better space after that."

As both Coughlin and McKeever would learn over the course of the 8-day swimming competition, people respond very differently to intense pressure. In this case, some turned insular, while others attempted to keep things light. Still others were instigators—and some individuals completely buckled under the strain.

The vibe of the US team, in general, was one of supportive solidarity. Beginning in July, at the start of the team's 6-week training camp at Stanford, Coughlin had enjoyed bonding, particularly with legendary teammate Jenny Thompson, fellow sprinter Colleen Lanne, and roommate Lindsay Benko. But there had been some internal sniping. At breakfast one morning at the team's Palo Alto hotel, several of the team's coaches noticed that their colleague Dave Salo was missing.

"He went for a run," one of them said.

"Really?" another coach piped in. "Is he out there doing really intense sprints, then resting, then sprinting, then resting...?"

Everyone at the table laughed at the dig on Salo's nontraditional training techniques—everyone except Coughlin. *I wonder if they realize that he actually* did *run a marathon based on that training philosophy.*

The Stanford camp, only 45 minutes from her condo in Emeryville, felt exceptionally long to Coughlin—and not just because she signed more than her share of Cardinal-colored swim caps during poolside autograph sessions, fighting back the urge to offer the taunting postscript "Go Bears." Though US women's coach Mark Schubert allowed her to go home for a weekend, she was mostly frustrated by being cooped up in the proximity of family, friends, and familiar restaurants. In an effort to quell the boredom, she guilted most of her Bay Area friends into making the trip down at some point.

In such an intensely focused and insular environment, there was bound to be some tension. One day fellow Baltimore-area natives Michael Phelps and Katie Hoff waged an animated argument over whose coach was better—the two swam for the same club but were coached by different men. Haley Cope actually swam in McKeever's group (along with Coughlin, Thompson, and Lanne) without incident; in fact, she and Coughlin slipped back into friendship mode, relying on the familiarity of their connection amid a pressure-filled environment. Cope, however, did develop some animosity for a fellow swimmer whose behavior would later make the former "Girls of the Pac-10" model with the penchant for blunt critiques seem remarkably tame.

There was also some choppiness within the pool as the swimmers adjusted to the coaching staff and to their respective roles on the team. When it came time to practice relay starts, Coughlin and Cope were surprised to find that they seemed far more advanced than most of their peers. They had always known that McKeever emphasized the finer points, and now they were truly grateful. They also worked to help bring their teammates up to speed—once viewed as the favorites in all three relays, the United States now had stiff competition in the 400 free and 400 medley relays, primarily from the Australians. A bad start or exchange could mean the difference between gold and silver.

As always, the decision of who to swim on which relays, and in which order, was an intensely political matter. In past Olympics there had been glaring controversies over coaches' selections, and Athens would be no exception.

The first test would come on the opening day of competition, less than 12 hours after the conclusion of the previous night's Opening Ceremonies, at which many of the swimmers had elected not to march. In the preliminaries, the US team rested Coughlin, Thompson, and Kara Lynn Joyce, going with a lineup of Amanda Weir, Lanne, Benko, and Maritza Correia. The Aussies, meanwhile, used their big guns in the morning, resting only Petria Thomas, yet the team of Alice Mills, Libby Lenton, Sarah Ryan, and Jodie Henry managed just a 3:38.26 to the

United States' 3:39.46. Were the Aussies sandbagging? In another 8 hours or so, the Americans would find out.

For the US coaches, the question was who to team with Coughlin, Thompson, and Joyce. Weir, with a 54.50, had produced the best morning split, ahead of Correia (54.74) and Benko (54.80). Schubert and his assistants, including McKeever, concluded that Weir had seized the moment and proven she was the team's best option. When McKeever broke the news to Correia, the former Georgia swimmer burst into tears.

As it turned out, it wouldn't have mattered. As the relay finals played out, it became clear that the Australians were highly formidable foes—and that Coughlin's biggest obstacle in the 100 free might not be Inge de Bruijn, the defending champion, or Lenton, the world record holder, but Henry, who was ripping through the water like a tsunami, obliterating everything in her path.

Coughlin had preferred to lead off the relay, which would allow her, among other things, to utilize her superior form before the water became too choppy. It might also set up the United States with a nice lead, given that neither Lenton nor Henry was leading off for the Aussies. But in the end, the coaches told Coughlin that Joyce *had* to lead off, because they lacked confidence in her ability to time her start to another swimmer's touch. Joyce, apparently, had always been allowed to lead off for Georgia and had not yet perfected her relay mechanics.

That meant Coughlin would swim second, opposite Lenton, while Thompson, who had been perhaps the most clutch relay performer in US history (eight for eight in previous Olympic relay efforts, dating back to the 1992 Games in Barcelona) would swim the anchor leg against Henry. Ideally, Thompson would have a lead when she entered the water. For that to happen, Coughlin would have to hold her own against Lenton, and Joyce and Weir would have to win their respective battles with Mills and Thomas.

For the United States, the first sign of trouble came in the leadoff leg: Expected to push the team to a decent advantage, Joyce finished in a disappointing 54.74, essentially the same as Mills's 54.75. Coughlin, after falling behind Lenton in the early going, rallied to close the gap in the second lap. Her split of 53.83 seconds was the best of her career, close enough to Lenton's 53.57 to keep the United States alive. Weir made things more interesting with a 54.05 to Thomas's 54.67, giving Thompson the lead for which the US team had hoped.

Still, Henry entered the water and began closing on her almost immediately. It would take another magical anchor leg by the venerated Thompson, in her fourth Olympics, to pull off the gold.

Thompson, predictably, rose to the occasion, finishing with a sizzling split of 53.77 seconds. But it didn't matter; she was chasing a barracuda. Henry, the cheery 20-year-old from Brisbane, merely produced the fastest relay split in history: 52.95 seconds. The Aussies ripped home in a time of 3:35.94, breaking the world record set by Germany in 2002 by .06, while the United States (3:36.39, an American record) edged the Netherlands (3:37.59, powered by de Bruijn's 53.37 anchor leg) for the silver.

For Coughlin, the disappointment didn't last long: After all the years of adversity and anticipation, she was an Olympic medalist. She'd performed admirably in her first test on the world's grandest stage, and she'd dispensed with the first-swim jitters before the all-important 100 back.

After warming down, Coughlin—noticeably smaller in stature than the 11 other swimmers around her—stood proudly on the medal stand as the Australian anthem blared. She was upbeat at her press conference and, afterward, kept staring at her shiny new silver medal. She gave it to McKeever, who popped her head over the fence separating the warm-up pool area from the walkway behind the stands, where Coughlin's family members lingered. McKeever called Jim and Zennie Coughlin over and handed the medal to them above the fence so that they could inspect their daughter's prize.

McKeever, too, seemed both elated and relieved. It had been a good month thus far, beginning 9 days earlier, when Lauren Medina and Erin Reilly had competed for a national title in the 200-meter freestyle at Stanford. Already in Europe, McKeever had set her alarm clock in the middle of the night and had called to wish both swimmers luck. In the final, 15-year-old Kate Dwelley of the Terrapins swim club—one of Ray

Mitchell's latest teenage studs—led coming off the last turn. Then Medina, who had once doubted whether she'd be good enough to swim at Cal, thought to herself, *No way I'm letting this kid beat me,* and promptly ran her down. Medina won the race in a time of 2:01.89, ahead of Dwelley's 2:02.05, with Reilly taking fourth in 2:02.45. When McKeever heard the news, it kept her smiling all day: "Lauren Medina, national champion" had a heck of a ring to it.

Now, on the first night of competition in Athens, McKeever had fallen just short of helping to put together an Olympic championship relay. Her and the other coaches' decision to use Weir on the relay—and to swim Thompson on the last leg—certainly had been validated. "You know what? I'm a pretty damn good coach," she said, smiling with uncharacteristic bravado as she peered over the fence. She meant that after weeks of interacting with Schubert, Richard Quick, and Frank Bush, men who represented the best in her business, she felt neither out of place nor superfluous. She laughed at her statement, certain it sounded cockier than she'd intended. "I mean, I'm with some great coaches here," she clarified. "But I feel like there's a reason I'm here, too."

A couple of minutes later and about 15 feet away, Coughlin, too, popped her head over the fence. Some loitering fans looked on obliviously—one of the world's best swimmers was right there in front of them, but she might as well have been a Swedish team manager. Even Coughlin's family members were unaware; only Ethan Hall, Coughlin's boyfriend, noticed the new medalist's appearance.

Separated by the mesh-covered chain-link fence, they shared a couple of tender moments before Coughlin disappeared. Finally noticing the scene, two American women looked up at Hall and cooed, "Oooh, *that's* what he looks like." Then Coughlin was gone: The 100 back preliminaries would be held the following morning, and she needed all the rest she could get. "This is where the animals come so that we can see them," Hall joked afterward. "You can pet them, but you can't feed them."

Coughlin would have appreciated the joke—her bouts with boredom had extended from the Stanford camp to the August camp in lovely

Mallorca (where the team was basically locked down, what with the Games approaching) to the first few days in Athens. Rest was imperative, which translated to a lot of time impersonating a kalamata olive. Coughlin, armed with a serious DVD stash, got hooked on shows like *24* and *Nip/Tuck* and laughed at the outrageous comedy of Dave Chappelle.

Though there wasn't much time for sightseeing, Coughlin managed to make one memorable trip to the Plaka district of Athens, with McKeever and Dave Salo, 2 days before Opening Ceremonies. A year earlier, while visiting with a small US delegation after the World Championships, Coughlin and McKeever had shopped at a jewelry store called Aphrodites. Coughlin bought a pendant, while McKeever scored a pair of diamond earrings. During their return to the city, the two women planned to go back and duplicate each other's previous purchase.

"Let's wait until the swimming competition is over and you're totally relaxed," McKeever suggested.

Coughlin didn't want to wait. "People were trying to stay off their legs, so you'd sit in their rooms in the Village, watching TV and worrying about your race," Coughlin said later. "So many people were so worried about the beginning of the biggest meet of their lives; I just had to get out of there." So she and McKeever dragged Salo onto the subway and into Aphrodites, where Coughlin picked out a pair of luxuriant diamond earrings. The jeweler, whose name was George, agreed to set them while the trio had lunch. They had a glorious meal in the shadow of the famed Acropolis on a hot, clear afternoon, munching on Greek salads and pasta and fresh anchovies as George, a man who seemed to be friends with everyone in town, graciously picked up the tab.

By the end of the afternoon, after another couple of hours shopping and strolling along the Plaka's narrow streets, Coughlin was reenergized. She felt as though she'd broken out of a hermetically sealed bubble and reentered the real world. It was a world in which no one stopped her to ask for an autograph. The anonymity was nice. But in a few more days, she hoped, that all would change.

~

Chuck Bohn sat in the sweltering stands at the Olympic Aquatic Center, preparing to watch the first individual race of his granddaughter's Olympic career, as loud, proud, and unbowed as ever. Bohn, 67, knew all about the terrorist threats and warnings to American visitors not to flash their patriotic colors around Athens, yet here was the former Marine, sporting a red, white and blue "Go USA" cap and a Speedo-issued "Natalie Is Greeced Lightning" T-shirt.

In this post-9/11 world, with US forces occupying Iraq and suicide bombs exploding in Jakarta and Jerusalem, an unprecedented security detail swarmed all over Athens. Bohn, a former infantry soldier and sergeant major whose 24 years in the Marine Corps included three separate tours of duty in Vietnam, had decided not to hide his considerable national pride.

Back at his home in northern California, Bohn had loaded his suitcase with nationalistic shirts and hats while his wife, Zennie (the same name as their daughter, Natalie's mother), looked on disapprovingly. "What are you doing that for?" she asked Chuck. "They're telling us not to attract attention to ourselves."

"You know," he responded, "I've never had to hide who I am, and I don't plan to start now."

Any hesitation had completely disappeared on the morning after his arrival in Athens, as Bohn left his hotel in Omonia Square just after dawn and strolled alone among the nearly deserted streets to Syntagma Square. There he encountered a man wearing a "USA" T-shirt and instantly said hello.

"The guy could barely say good morning back to me; he spoke no English," Bohn said. "Everyone had been warning me not to wear my USA gear, but I figured, 'If that guy's wearing it, I sure as heck will.'"

Then Bohn laughed and said, "It's only been a couple of days, but the reception we've gotten in Athens has been great. I had more hostility when I was stationed at (San Francisco's) Treasure Island after I got back from Vietnam in the late '60s."

When Coughlin heard the story about Bohn's Syntagma Square encounter, she smiled. No amount of international tension was going to keep her grandfather from showing his true colors. Besides, she was grateful that he and her other family members had been placed in such convenient accommodations by Speedo. Coughlin's roommate in Athens, Lindsay Benko, hadn't been so lucky. The Benkos and the family members of another US swimmer, Brendan Hansen, had booked their rooms through a travel agency and had quite a surprise awaiting them: As they quickly ascertained, they had been placed in a bordello—one whose room rates had been jacked up from $35 to $900 per night to boot. With help from Speedo, the families had been relocated as soon as possible.

The Keller family—whose daughter, Kalyn, and son, Klete, both had qualified for the US team—arrived at their Athens hotel and discovered that it lacked one small detail: a roof. They, too, had been relocated.

The swimmers, meanwhile, were isolated in the Olympic Village, and they were thankful that their competition was held during the first week of the Games. As athletes finished up their events, they began to celebrate, which made for a louder and more raucous atmosphere inside the Village, a potential distraction to those competitors whose big moments would come later in the 17-day festival.

Coughlin was especially thrilled that the 100 back was her first individual event. Get the gold that seemingly awaited her at the end of that race, and she could loosen up and enjoy the rest of her swims.

Her preliminary race went off smoothly, with Coughlin clocking a time of 1:00.45 to rank third among qualifiers. In that night's semifinals, the water was exceptionally choppy, thanks to a stiff northerly wind, which theoretically should have led to slower times. But Coughlin, who'd trained and competed outdoors for most of her life, was unfazed by the elements. Even during her world-record swim in Fort Lauderdale in August 2002, she'd contended with a pronounced wind. This time, despite not going all out, Coughlin won her semifinal heat in 1:00.17, breaking the Olympic record of 1:00.21 set by Romania's Diana Mocanu during her gold-medal swim in Sydney.

Cope, meanwhile, went 1:01.13 to make the final, giving the 100 back a decidedly Cal flavor. (Indeed, there was Golden Bear magic all over Athens during the Games, especially at the swimming venue.

Between Bohn's loud "Go Bears" cheers and the Cal script swim cap worn by Croatian sprinter and Cal senior-to-be Duje Draganja, the university seemed to comprise its own nation. The many spectators sporting Cal gear wondered if, had Draganja not been nipped by .01 in the 50-meter freestyle—by American Gary Hall Jr., one of his training partners at Spieker Pool—the world would have heard "Fight for California" as he stood atop the medal stand.)

The second-fastest qualifier in the 100 back had been France's Laure Manadou, with a time of 1:00.88. As Coughlin went to sleep that night, with the 100 back final slated for the following evening, she did so in the rare position of knowing that in all likelihood, merely replicating her semifinal time in the finals would be good enough for gold.

~

If Coughlin was overly nervous before the biggest race of her life, the one that in many ways would define her swimming career, she sure did a great job of hiding it. On the morning of Monday, August 16, Coughlin slept in until 9 o'clock, had breakfast, and went to the pool to loosen up with a light workout. She went back to the Olympic Village, ate again, and proceeded to take a 3-hour nap. "Until that day I hadn't been sleeping very well," she said later that night. "The beds are really narrow, which means I have to sleep with my arms tucked in, which makes them numb. Plus, in the Village, you hear every little thing. But for some reason, today sleep came really easily."

The people closest to Coughlin weren't quite as relaxed, though they did their best to keep one another laughing. On the 20-minute ride to the Olympic Sports Complex via Athens's sparkling new subway line, Jim and Zennie Coughlin told a story about Natalie's younger sister that spoke to the family's apparently genetic supply of grit. "When Megan was 3, we were in Hawaii, and she walked all the way to the top of Diamond Head," Zennie recalled. "We were willing to carry her, but she insisted. Talk about focus and determination at an early age."

While Megan and her Athens roommate—Hall, her sister's boyfriend—made conversation with some fellow subway riders, Jim Coughlin then talked about his older daughter. Noting that Natalie had been born with a heart murmur, Jim said he becomes tense before every one of her important races. (Natalie considers this to be somewhat irrational on his part; heart murmurs, in her words, are common and "not a big deal.") This race, of course, would be the most important of all. "When she faded at the end of her 200 back at the NCAAs, the ESPN cameras showed my reaction—they showed it again this afternoon when we were interviewed for the *Today* show—and on the (tape-delayed) telecast it looked like I was devastated that she'd lost," Jim said. "But that wasn't it at all. I was terrified. We have a history of people dying young in our family. I thought something might be seriously wrong."

With a lump in his throat, Coughlin, the grizzled Vallejo police detective, then talked about his daughter's quest for gold: "You know, I've run big, complex task forces. I can be at a grisly murder scene, and I'm completely calm and composed. But when it comes to my own children, it's totally different. I'm a mess right now. People are acting like she's got the race won already. They say, 'What can go wrong?' Well, the thing is, we've seen it go wrong. We were there in Barcelona and in Texas. We know she *should* win, but until she does, we take nothing for granted."

Jim's effervescent wife, Zennie, was determined to enjoy the moment. The woman who used to save the heat sheets from each of her daughters' races was snapping photos with a disposable camera and soaking up the Olympic atmosphere at every opportunity. After disembarking from the subway and entering the Athens Olympic Sports Complex, where the track and other venues were housed alongside the pool, Zennie spotted a pair of young Asian-American men holding a giant Cal script banner. Smiling broadly, Zennie sprinted toward them, yelling, "Hey, go Bears!" while proudly flashing her similarly decorated shoulder bag.

For all of their understandable nerves, the Coughlins were, even on this night, model swim parents: supportive and upbeat without being crass or overbearing. Months later, when listing the reasons for her former teammate's success, Haley Cope would say, "You've got to give props to her parents. They're almost the perfect mixture of staying out of it and letting you do your own thing, yet being totally supportive."

In the minutes before the night's swimming program began, Bruce Springsteen's "Born to Run" blared over the PA system: *Someday, girl, I don't know when, we're gonna get to that place that we really wanna go and we'll walk in the sun…*a good, all-American omen? The Coughlins hoped so. Warming up behind the blocks, Natalie was all business, until her name was introduced. Then, despite her nerves, she smiled and waved to each section of the crowd, casting a quick glance toward the area where her friends and family members sat, before putting on her game face once more.

She entered the water, gripped the metal bars above her and waited, heart thumping, adrenaline surging. A career's worth of practice sessions and crucial races and Pilates workouts and technique adjustments had prepared her for this moment, and she intended to seize it.

A clean start, then her usual underwater mastery, and Coughlin had the lead. She built on it into the turn, touching nearly 0.8 ahead of the field and charging off the wall with power and purpose. Watching at home in Australia, Milt Nelms became more emotional than he'd anticipated. For one thing, he certainly wasn't one of those *What can go wrong?* people to whom Jim Coughlin had alluded; though Coughlin was favored, he worried that she'd be overwhelmed by the weight of expectations. "Few people realized the level of unwarranted expectation on Natalie," he would say later. "People had been talking about her for years, but she was still a virtual rookie with very little international experience and almost no significant international experience, if you consider the '03 Worlds. My perception is that those kinds of expectations, with all their attendant baggage, can cause an athlete to compete with a sense of need, rather than want. When this is the case, peak performance is almost impossible."

Watching with friends in Skanor, Sweden, Coughlin's close friend and former Cal teammate Emma Palsson was appalled when many of the young women in her midst expressed skepticism about Coughlin's chances. As the race wore on and Coughlin began to tire down the stretch, some were screaming, "See, she's going to lose!"

"No way!" Palsson yelled defiantly. *They don't know Natalie*, she thought to herself. *No way she'll let anyone catch her.*

Ethan Hall, who once possessed enough promise to envision himself in such a circumstance, now looked on helplessly as his longtime girl-friend tried to gut out the gold. Zimbabwe's Kirsty Coventry, the same swimmer who'd caught Coughlin in the 200 back at the NCAA Championships 5 months earlier, was closing in from over in Lane 1, continuing a pattern of "outside smoke" that seemed endemic to the Athens pool, perhaps because lanes 1 and 8 offered the most shelter from the wind. As with the previous night, the wind was blowing wildly, making the water choppy and making the directional flags above the swimmers' heads whip back and forth.

"She went out so fast, I thought she'd break her world record," Hall said of Coughlin after the race. "Then, at around 60 meters, I could tell she got real tired. It was weird; she doesn't usually get tired in the 100. She reached her hand to touch the wall, and it stayed there for a while. The other girl (Coventry) went *whip*, and I thought, *Oh, no—maybe she got beat*. But then I looked at the scoreboard, and it was all okay."

It took Coughlin a few seconds longer than Hall to experience the same sensation, but then the scoreboard rearranged and her name was on top—with a time of 1:00.37 to Coventry's 1:00.50. France's Laure Manadou had claimed the bronze in 1:00.88, while Cope was eighth and last in 1:01.76.

Coughlin's expression was one of joyousness and relief—but a few seconds after she exited the water, it seemed muted, almost showing shreds of disappointment. Her time had been slower than that of her semifinal heat, and she felt she'd failed to produce her best effort in front of by far the largest audience that had ever seen her swim.

"I'm gonna start crying," McKeever said, greeting Coughlin under-neath the stands as she came out of the "mixed zone" and began walking toward the warm-up pool. "I'm just really proud of you."

Coughlin still seemed subdued. It wasn't until she reached the medal stand that she began to understand: So what if she hadn't set a world record? She'd done *that* before. The goal had been gold, and now she'd achieved it, and no one—not any of those people who'd doubted her—would ever be able to take that away. The joy wasn't hers alone, either.

She'd won the first gold medal in Athens by any US woman in any sport—indeed, the first gold by an American not named Phelps. She'd honored her country, her university, and her coach—and, in the process, validated their training approach for the world to see.

Now, lining the railing in the stands above were the people closest to her, and they were unabashedly, ebulliently going nuts. That made Coughlin smile more, which in turn encouraged her significant other. "World record holder, Olympic record holder, Olympic gold medalist," Hall said, smiling proudly. "Not bad." Chuck Bohn went to buy beers at the concession stand; when he returned, he and his wife unfurled a huge "Natalie Is Greeced Lightning" banner. The wind had died down considerably, and as "The Star-Spangled Banner" played, Coughlin, wearing the wreath of small branches extended to all gold medalists in homage to the ancient Greeks, was so overwhelmed that she forgot to remove it during the anthem. She also neglected to put her hand over her heart and blanked on some of the song's lyrics.

She didn't forget to smile, however. Up above, at the top of the stands, a man stood alone, holding a small American flag, staring down intently at Coughlin as it swayed gently in the breeze.

Coughlin was spirited away to the media center to meet the press. Her agent, Janey Miller, was on her cell phones—one from home, one rented while in Athens—virtually nonstop, cementing endorsement opportunities and lining up interviews. Coughlin would join Katie Couric and Matt Lauer on the *Today* show, which taped the following afternoon. There would be no immediate celebration for the Golden Girl, however—she still had three more races to swim.

In fact, she wouldn't even get a proper meal. Upstairs in the press center, after her media obligations had been satisfied, Coughlin, wearing a white nylon zip-up Team USA sweatsuit, grimaced as she reached the cafeteria, which had long since closed. "Man, I've got such a headache," she said to McKeever. Her hair was pulled back in a bun, and she looked shellshocked. She took out her new, Jackie O–influenced Dior sunglasses and put them on, and then removed them after a few seconds. "Let's party," Coughlin joked.

A few seconds later she turned semiserious: "I'm going on the *Today* show tomorrow?" she confirmed with Miller. "I'd really like to wear those earrings." Alas, the diamond studs she'd purchased at Aphrodites had been locked up in a safe-deposit box for the duration of the swimming competition, as per team policy. McKeever grinned and said, "You know, Nat, I think they might make an exception."

Aaron Peirsol ambled by, looking like a surfer dude dragging his feet through hot sand. Like Coughlin, Peirsol had just won gold in the 100 back, adding to a big night for the US team. The two swimmers said hello, and Coughlin laughed at Peirsol's gait as he walked away. It was nearly midnight. "My stomach really hurts," she said, and McKeever sent for a US swimming official, who a few minutes later showed up with a couple of McDonald's bags filled with lukewarm chicken nuggets and fries. "Ah," Coughlin said, smiling once more, "the dinner of champions." She ate a couple of nuggets as she walked across the press center and downed the rest of them on the car ride back to the Olympic Village.

As Coughlin lay in bed long after midnight, reflecting on her accomplishment, her parents were toasting it over a round of ouzo at the bar of their Omonia Square Hotel. In walked Michael Phelps's mother, Debbie, and his sisters, Whitney and Hillary. They sat down at the table, with Zennie and Debbie exchanging a long, heartfelt hug—an embrace born of years of shared ups and downs (and brutal early-morning wakeup alarms) on opposite coasts. Michael had suffered a rare disappointment early that night, having finished third in the 200 free behind Ian Thorpe and the Netherlands' Peter van den Hoogenband, but the Phelpses weren't dwelling on that. This was the Coughlins' moment, and they graciously shared in the celebration.

"I'm so happy for you," Debbie said softly to Zennie.

"I know," Zennie said. "I know."

∾

The Games weren't over, of course. Coughlin would be a Golden Girl no matter what else went down, but she had no intention of letting up. If anything, she could now *loosen* up. Being interviewed by Matt Lauer—

and yes, she was wearing those earrings—was a surreal thrill. *He's so down-to-earth, so nice,* Coughlin thought to herself. It was the start of a lovefest with Lauer, Katie Couric, and the *Today* crew that would culminate with an appearance 2 days after the swimming competition concluded, on Coughlin's 22nd birthday, complete with the on-air presentation of a candle-topped cake.

Coughlin was happy that she didn't have to compete that Tuesday— her lone day off of the competition—because Wednesday she would swim the grueling 200 free as the leadoff leg of the US 800 free relay team.

That Coughlin, despite not having competed in the event at Trials, would nonetheless be included on the relay was not particularly controversial: She was the team's best swimmer and had recorded "unshaved" times going into the Trials that rivaled those produced by the top six finishers in Long Beach. But because there is no specific system for making relay-related decisions, drama surrounding the coaches' choices was virtually inevitable. Such was the case in 2000: At Trials, a talented US swimmer named Cristina Teuscher had the fourth-fastest preliminary time in the 200-meter freestyle. That night she hoped to qualify in the 200 IM, but first she would have to swim the 200 free semifinal. With a similar schedule set for Sydney, Teuscher, who'd won a gold medal as part of the 800 free relay in Atlanta in 1996, planned to focus on the 200 IM. However, she hoped once again to be part of the 800 free relay.

In an article Teuscher wrote for *Swimming World* magazine months after the Games, she claimed that Richard Quick, the US women's coach for the 2000 team, had assured her coach, John Collins, that she would be on the 800 free relay in Sydney—prompting her to disqualify herself from the 200 free semis at Trials. Further, Teuscher wrote, after she won a bronze in the 200 IM in Sydney, Quick told her to get some rest because she would "definitely" be part of the 800 free relay the following night. "I was ready to go the next day," Teuscher, a cocaptain of the 2000 US team, said in the article. "As is customary on national team trips, there was a team meeting before we left for the finals session. At the door, going into the team meeting, Coach Quick stopped me and told me that he was sorry, but he had taken me off the relay. It was 2 hours before finals. There were no explanations....I felt devastated—not only by Coach Quick as a person but by USA Swimming as an organization."

Quick's decision to replace Teuscher with Jenny Thompson, whom he happened to have coached at Stanford, worked out fine for the United States: Thompson anchored an Olympic-record-setting, gold-medal-winning performance. Teuscher, who had also been left off the preliminary relay—ostensibly because she was being rested for the final—missed out on a medal entirely. At the time, at least within swimming circles, this had caused somewhat of a stir. What was about to go down in Athens would dwarf it by comparison.

In choosing the 800 free relay lineup, Schubert and his assistants, as with the 400 free relay, would look to the afternoon's preliminaries to help them decide who would swim that night's finals. Coughlin and Kaitlin Sandeno, her old USC rival, were the two strongest swimmers on paper and would thus be saved for the finals. The same would go for 16-year-old Dana Vollmer, a tall Texan who had a serious heart condition that caused her heart randomly to stop beating sometimes; her mother thus stood by with a defibrillator at all of her competitions. Surprisingly, Lindsay Benko, Coughlin's Athens roommate, was not being rested. Benko, the American record holder in the event, had been struggling in practice and felt she couldn't come close to matching her best efforts. After a subpar effort in the individual 200 free competition—she swam 2:00.22 in her semifinal heat, nearly 3 seconds off her American record, to finish 14th—Benko came to a selfless decision. She went to Schubert and told him she could best serve the team by swimming in the prelims and skipping the finals. "Give my spot in the evening to Kaitlin," she advised him. "I'm just not going fast enough."

That meant that one of the other three swimmers in the prelims would join Coughlin, Vollmer, and Sandeno in the finals. The fairest way to make the decision would be to take the swimmer whose split was fastest in the prelims, but this presented a problem: The last thing a coach wants is for a relay team's members to place their individual goals above those of the foursome. If one of the swimmers dove in too early, anxious to post a fast split for herself, the US team would be disqualified, depriving all seven competitors of a shot at a medal.

The solution, the coaches decided, was to take the fastest splits while allowing for the start. Because reaction times are measured by the timing system, they could also be subtracted from the splits to provide an adjusted time for each swimmer.

"Don't worry about your takeoffs," the coaches told the four swimmers. "We'd rather have you leave late than too early, so just be conservative. We want all your starts to be slow. We'll make our decision based on the fastest adjusted times, so you don't have to think about the takeoffs, because they won't matter."

The preliminary swim went off seemingly without a hitch: No one left early, and the US team led all qualifiers with a time of 8:00.81. Carly Piper, a tall University of Wisconsin swimmer, had the second-fastest split, but when reaction times were subtracted, her adjusted time was the fastest. Schubert, after consulting with his assistants, confirmed that she would join Coughlin, Sandeno, and Vollmer for that night's final.

After breaking the news to the swimmers in question, Schubert walked away. Suddenly, there was a loud noise coming from the area near the massage tables that lined the edge of the warm-up/warm-down pool. One of the swimmers who hadn't been chosen was now screaming into a cell phone, a spectacle that soon attracted the attention of coaches and officials from the United States and numerous other countries. The swimmer, apparently speaking to her boyfriend, launched a profanity-laced tirade against Schubert, his fellow coaches, USA Swimming, and humanity in general. She resisted various people's attempts to calm her down, physically repelled both a teammate and a USA Swimming official, and continued her protracted rant.

Coughlin, like most of her teammates, was appalled. She felt the swimmer should be disciplined for her tirade—though, at the moment, that wasn't her immediate concern. First, she had to focus on setting a blistering tone on the relay's leadoff leg and, given the relative youth and inexperience of Vollmer and Piper, on inspiring those who'd follow to keep up the intensity.

Denied the opportunity to swim the individual 200 free because of the schedule—she'd have had to complete that semifinal minutes before her 100 back final—Coughlin wanted to prove that she was the best in the world at that distance. She had a plan, too: She would start out slowly, give her competitors a false sense of security, and then whip past them before they knew what had hit them.

"Don't worry if I'm behind at the second turn," Coughlin told Schubert, "because I'm going to burn the last 100."

McKeever wanted her to wait even longer. "At 75 meters," she told Coughlin, "you're going to drop the hammer."

Seventh after 100 meters, Coughlin jumped the gun on that plan slightly. With 90 meters remaining, she began transitioning to a faster gear; with 80 meters left, she kicked into overdrive. Soon she was burning like Cleveland's Cuyahoga River in 1969. One by one, Coughlin picked off her competitors, loving every minute of it. She hit the wall in 1:57.74, a pure time (given that it led off a relay) faster than that produced by the gold medalist in the individual 200 free, Romania's Camelia Potec (1:58.03). Coughlin felt incredibly energized, believing she could have gone another 50 meters at that pace—a sensation that would later convince her that she'd had the potential to set a world record in the 200 free.

Schubert's heart jumped—with Sandeno swimming the way she'd been swimming in Athens, the United States looked good as gold. If Piper and Vollmer could come through, well, something *really* special might be happening. The world record in the event was the oldest swimming mark on the books.

It was also, from the US perspective, the most objectionable.

Back in 1987, four East German swimmers had combined to finish the event in 7:55.47. The race was contested in an era marked by suspicion over steroid use, particularly by Soviet-bloc nations, amid unsophisticated testing procedures. After the fall of the Berlin Wall in 1989, documents kept by the Stasi, East Germany, secret police were discovered that confirmed widespread use of performance-enhancing drugs by East German athletes.

Schubert, the former Mission Viejo Nadadores coach, had bristled in 1976 when one of his star swimmers, Shirley Babashoff, failed to win a single individual gold at the Montreal Games. Babashoff was one of the greatest US swimmers in history, yet four times she finished second to an East German swimmer before finally earning a relay gold. When she complained about the possibility of drug use by the East Germans who had beaten her, she was dubbed "Surly Shirley" and widely criticized. For Babashoff—and for all the clean athletes who'd been shortchanged over the years by others' steroid use—Schubert and his colleagues wanted this record to fall.

Now, with Piper clocking a 1:59.39 in the second leg, it was within reach. Vollmer, who had gone 1:58.98 and finished sixth in the individual 200 free, stepped it up in the relay, charging home at 1:58.12. As Sandeno, her longtime rival in youth and collegiate swimming, entered the water, Coughlin started to do the math. "We can do this," she told the other swimmers. "Come on, Kaitlin!"

As Sandeno jetted through the water, it became obvious that the United States would win the gold. Her last lap was a run at history—and Coughlin was bouncing up and down on the edge of the blocks, screaming for every stroke. When Sandeno hit the wall, completing her leg in 1:58.17, all eyes went to the scoreboard clock. The winning time read 7:53.42. The Americans hadn't just broken the record—they had shattered it. China (7:55.97) and Germany (7:57.35) took the silver and bronze, and Mark Schubert took more satisfaction than most people knew.

"It feels real good to get that record off the books," he told reporters afterward. "It was the (record) that burned people the most. And we all knew the reason why. We're very proud to have that record back."

Coughlin, too, was elated. "Watching her after that relay, it was just pure joy," McKeever would say later. "When she won the 100 back, it was more like, 'Thank God that's over.' But this was Natalie at her best—part of a team, reveling in the challenge, doing something no one saw coming."

There was a celebratory atmosphere among the US delegation—but one American swimmer didn't share her peers' enthusiasm. Back at the Olympic Village, the swimmer who'd earlier snapped after having been left off the relay took no joy in the news of the gold medal. She once again picked up her cell phone and loudly voiced her displeasure, this time while standing on the balcony of her apartment. Various American and Brazilian athletes and other passersby began to gawk, and a US team psychologist was summoned. That night the swimmer was deemed so volatile that a USA Swimming manager was assigned to sleep outside her door. Part of the fear was that the swimmer would take out her anger on another team member. Meanwhile, her roommate—whose first race was scheduled for the next morning—had to cope with the surreal disruption. Cope, who observed the situation from her own room across the hall, later said: "My attitude was, if someone is sleeping outside (her) door because they feel she's that much of a threat, she needs to be taken out of there."

≈

Coughlin, too, had a race the next day—the 100-meter freestyle final. Her medal prospects were looking good because of two developments. First, there was her promising time of 54.37, the third-fastest behind Jodie Henry and Inge de Bruijn, in the previous night's semifinal, a race in which Coughlin had consciously eased up at the finish. The same could not be said of Henry. In the same heat, the Aussie continued her remarkable Athens run by winning in 53.52—breaking the world record her teammate Libby Lenton had set at the Australian Olympic Trials 5 months earlier.

The second development concerned an even bigger setback, this time for Lenton: The 19-year-old had, shockingly, failed to qualify for the final. After hitting the 50-meter mark in 25.1—"I can't even go that fast when I'm swimming a 50," Coughlin later marveled—Lenton faded to fifth in her heat and ended up ninth with a time of 55.17, slower than even her prelim time of 54.89 (just behind Coughlin's 54.82). Sitting in the Ready Room and watching the other semifinal race play out, Coughlin watched Henry gasp in horror as she saw Lenton's placing.

Normally, Coughlin would have spent the hours leading up to a race as important as the 100 free final by focusing on the task at hand. Even without Lenton, the race still included the formidable Henry and de Bruijn, as well as other medal threats such as France's Malia Metella and the United States' Joyce. Yet on this bizarre day, Coughlin spent most of her waking hours stressing out about the previous day's drama and what ramifications might follow.

That morning, Schubert had called a team meeting to address the situation. Some swimmers talked about what a privilege it was to represent the United States and the obligation that came with it. Others told the offending swimmer that they loved her and hoped she'd get over her disappointment. Then one decorated veteran registered, in stronger terms, her displeasure with the behavior; the swimmer instantly became defensive, ultimately offering a halfhearted apology for her self-described temper tantrum. The meeting ended without resolution.

Coughlin and most of her teammates wanted the swimmer sent home, but they soon learned that such a penalty was not going to be levied. The coaches said it was out of their hands—that because a US Olympic Team official, the psychologist, had been involved, it was now a USOC issue, and that ruling body was not inclined to force the swimmer to leave Athens. Because of this, Cope, even after having captured a silver medal, would leave Athens with something of a sour taste in her mouth. "It totally ruins the moment for you," Cope said of the swimmer's behavior. "The fact that she was allowed to stay, that she wasn't even fined, was tough to stomach."

In the hours before the 100 free, Coughlin stewed about the situation. McKeever, who was more keyed in to Coughlin than anyone, started to worry. "Here it was, less than 2 hours before the race, and that was all she could think about," McKeever said later.

The coach told Coughlin, "Nat, if you feel this strongly, you need to go talk to Mark."

"Now?" Coughlin asked.

"Yeah, now."

"It's not gonna do any good."

"It's not about outcome," McKeever replied. "You need to do this for you, so you can let go and focus on your race. Also, you need to do this for the future. Jenny (Thompson) will be gone after these Games—and you're going to have to step up and lead. This is part of that process."

So Coughlin spent 10 minutes with Schubert, voicing all of her frustrations. She didn't hold back, and when the meeting ended, Schubert thanked her for airing her opinions. Upon returning to the deck, Coughlin told McKeever, "I didn't intend to be so strong, but I told him everything. I feel so much better."

Said McKeever afterward: "That was something she needed to do. It's about her growth, about learning to handle situations."

A little more than 90 minutes later, Coughlin went out and swam an unfettered 100 free. Rather than distracting her, the meeting with Schubert had actually put her at ease. *I've already won my gold*, Coughlin thought to herself as she stood behind the starting blocks. *I just want to swim this race the best I can, and if I get any kind of medal, no matter what happens, I'll be happy.* Mindful that the pressure of the Olympics had perhaps caused many elite swimmers, including herself in the 100 back, to swim somewhat subpar times, she vowed merely to enjoy racing against the world's best in an event she loved.

Coughlin was in contention all the way, but in the end she was simply overpowered by gold medalist Henry (53.84) and silver medalist de Bruijn (54.16). Like those two, Coughlin, who took the bronze in 54.40—ahead of Metella (54.50) and Joyce (54.54)—was disappointed in her time. She'd gone 0.03 faster in the semis. But in the end, she was as proud of this medal as she would be of any other. This was the race she had wanted to swim, and she had captured a medal despite having gone up against the event's past three world record holders, in their primes. Whatever she might have accomplished had she chosen the 200 back, she would now have a lifelong keepsake to remind her that doing it her way had paid off.

The bottom line was, she'd competed in four events and won four medals. Now, with 2 days of competition remaining, would begin the drive for five.

In swimming the backstroke leg to lead off the 400 medley relay, Coughlin had a chance for redemption. Having been dissatisfied with her performance in winning the 100 back, she could now show everyone—including French bronze medalist Laure Manadou, who had griped after the race, "I thought I could have gone faster than the American"—how potent in that event she really was.

More important, Coughlin had to get the United States a big lead in a relay in which they looked vulnerable on the back end, with Australia's Henry set to swim the anchor freestyle leg against Kara Lynn Joyce.

Before that could happen, though, the United States had to qualify. In theory, with the preliminary heats set for the morning of August 20 and the finals not until the following night, Schubert could have gone with his best lineup (Coughlin, breaststroker Amanda Beard, butterflier Thompson, and Joyce) in the prelims. But using other swimmers in the prelims was a way to get them medals—which is why Haley Cope, rather than Coughlin, would swim the backstroke leg. She and three other teammates got the job done, setting up Coughlin, Beard, Thompson, and Joyce for a shot at glory the following night.

For the US women to have a happy ending in their final event of the swimming competition, Coughlin knew she had to set a blistering tone. She figured to beat Australia's backstroker, Giann Rooney, rather easily, but every hundredth of a second would count.

Yet having already endured the pressure of swimming the event individually, Coughlin was strangely devoid of stress. "I just realized it wasn't about me," she later reflected. "I could swim my pace and not worry about being favored to win the gold. It was more about the team, and for some reason that's always easier for me."

Easy and breezy, Coughlin was at the full force of her powers. The starting signal sounded, and she darted underwater and took her customary lead. She powered into the turn and built on it, and this time there was no hint of a fade. She hit the wall in 59.68 seconds—just 0.10 off her world record, and the second-fastest time in history. Germany's

Antje Buschulte (1:00.72) was the next-closest swimmer, while Rooney was well back at 1:01.18.

Now the onus was on Beard, the gold medalist in the 200 breast who, 5 days earlier, had finished a disappointing fourth (in 1:07.44) in the individual 100 in Athens. Australia's Leisel Jones, the world record holder, had finished third (1:07.16) in the same race. This time, Beard came through, building slightly on Coughlin's lead by edging Jones, 1:06.32 to 1:06.50.

The United States had a lead of nearly 1.7 seconds, but would it be enough? Into the water jumped Thompson, going for her record 12th career Olympic medal. So many times in the past, she had come up huge in relay scenarios, and the first lap of her butterfly was so crisp, it appeared she about to produce another clutch effort. But she faded in the second 50 as Australia's Petria Thomas—the gold medalist in the individual 100 fly—came charging from behind, catching Thompson before the wall. Thomas had gone 56.67 to Thompson's 58.81, putting Joyce in the brutal position of having to chase Henry from the outset.

It wasn't even close. Henry swam her leg in 52.97 seconds—just 0.02 off her anchor split from the 400 free relay, which had been the fastest in recorded history—while Joyce came in at 54.31. The Aussies won another gold and, with a time of 3:57.32, set another world record. The United States (3:59.12) edged Germany (4:00.72) for second, making Coughlin's final medal tally two golds, two silvers, and a bronze.

McKeever was waiting for the swimmers after the race, and Thompson reached her just before Coughlin. Devastated, Thompson gripped McKeever in a hug and began sobbing on the coach's shoulder, clinging tightly for more than a minute. It was an awkward moment— McKeever wanted to comfort Thompson but was also eager to congratulate Coughlin, who was waiting off to the side, on what had been an inspiring swim.

When McKeever finally approached her, Coughlin said, "*That's* how I needed to swim that race. I'm really happy."

She had many reasons to be, including the fact that in 2 days she would turn 22. After showering back at the Village, Coughlin did an interview with Bob Costas for NBC's prime-time coverage; the host, noting Coughlin's done-up appearance (black lace tank, denim miniskirt), teased her about heading "out into the Saturday night of Athens, Greece, to who knows what adventures." She, Hall, and their friend Matt, in fact, headed to the Heineken House, where Miller worked her connections to gain the group admittance to a private party. Upon entering, they saw a slew of orange clothing and blond revelers. "It was a Netherlands-only party," Coughlin recalled later. "We were a little out of place."

Later, the group relocated to the rocking *Sports Illustrated* party at the gorgeous Akrotiri nightclub, its outdoor pool deck carved into the banks of the Mediterranean. It was packed with famous athletes and celebrities, and Coughlin was certifiably A-list, even without wearing her gold medal around her neck, as did the US softball players in a curious bit of firefly bravado. Even McKeever, the ultimate teetotaler, had a celebratory drink. Coughlin and her group stayed out well into the early-morning hours, with no impending alarm clock to wake her up. *You know,* Coughlin thought, *I could get used to this.*

On the night of her birthday, Coughlin, Hall, Miller, and some other friends had a celebratory dinner. The next night, the group stayed out all night at the Speedo Beach Party, and then Coughlin went straight to the airport for a flight to New York City. Upon landing, she went immediately to Bloomingdale's and bought an outfit for her appearance on that night's *Late Show with David Letterman,* checking into her midtown hotel with only enough time for a shower. Groggy but still glowing, she taped the *Letterman* interview and continued her whirlwind, still barely able to feel her achievements.

~

By the time Coughlin returned to earth—or, at least, to Berkeley, where the Cal marching band showed up to perform at her welcome-home press conference—she had come to view her performance in Athens as a largely triumphant one. Certainly, the competitor within was peeved that she hadn't set world records or won more golds. But everywhere she went, strangers came up and congratulated her on an awesome Olympics, and when she sat back and thought about what she'd done, after how far she'd come, it was hard not to feel gratified.

Not only had Coughlin emerged as the most decorated female swimmer of the Games, but she had also garnered the most medals of any woman in Athens, period. Her five-medal haul matched the most ever by a US woman at a single Olympics, tying swimmers Babashoff (1976) and Dara Torres (2000), gymnasts Mary Lou Retton (1984) and Shannon Miller (1992), and track star Marion Jones (2000).

With two gold medals, two silvers, and a bronze, Coughlin had achieved the best overall performance by an American woman swimmer in Olympic history—and with the Beijing Games 4 years away, she wanted more.

"Everyone says, 'Wow, you won five medals,'" Coughlin said on a late-August afternoon between bites of Thai food in Albany, just north of Berkeley. "I sit there thinking, *Wait—I* expected *five medals.* I could have done even better. And maybe in 4 years, if I keep working hard, I will."

EPILOGUE

The solitary swimmer emerged from the locker room, dashed across the empty pool deck, and, 15 yards later, launched herself into the chilly water to begin her morning workout. Natalie Coughlin had established this run-and-dive ritual early in her Cal career. Now, a little more than a month after returning home from Athens, she had no reason to mess with success.

This was to be one of her final practices before leaving for Indianapolis, where she'd compete in the FINA World Short Course Championships, a meet she and many of her fellow US Olympians regarded more as a post-Athens appreciation tour than as a compelling competition. Everyone was tired and drained, Coughlin more so than most. Her training had been sporadic as she traveled cities around the US, attempting to make the most of her Olympic notoriety. But because of her short-course prowess, she figured she could fake her way through the meet and do well enough to please the US audience before embarking upon a well-deserved break for the remainder of 2004.

It was a sound plan, given the intensity with which she'd trained over the past 4 years. Except now, as she embarked upon her first practice lap, something was strange. Her left foot began to tingle, and the sensation persisted for several minutes. As she launched off the wall during flipturns, she noticed a throbbing pain. Coughlin stopped, got out of the pool, and, to her amazement, was unable to put any weight on the foot. She had suffered a stress fracture—not exactly the kind of break she had in mind.

Her first reaction was one of shock. It quickly was replaced by mind-numbing relief. *Oh my God,* she thought to herself. *What if I'd done this before the Olympics?*

Bizarre as it might have sounded to those unfamiliar with her story, Coughlin, for once, had just experienced a case of *good* injury luck. "In a way it was perfect timing," she said. "During my time off, I'd planned to run and do Pilates, but with the broken foot, that wasn't an option. The only workouts I could've done would have been in the pool—and I was definitely staying away from the pool. So I basically decided to be lazy until January."

Of course, Coughlin's idea of lazy wasn't quite as sedentary as that of the average couch potato. Despite her walking boot and cane, Coughlin still managed to go to events like the Women's Sports Foundation's awards banquet at the Waldorf-Astoria in New York City, the bulky footwear serving as an awkward accessory to her white satin Ralph Lauren gown. At home in Emeryville, Coughlin continued to go up and down the four flights of stairs that led from the ground to the top level of her condo, a process intensified by her acquisition of a Border Terrier puppy, which she named She-Ra, a few days after she broke her foot. As Coughlin recalls, "Hobbling down the stairs of my condo eight times a day when she was potty training was quite an adventure."

She jetted off to New York and other cities on a fairly regular basis, making appearances for Speedo and other sponsors, and enjoyed sleeping late and eating well. She spent time with her boyfriend, Ethan Hall, who had taken a job coaching a pair of youth swim teams, and socialized with family and friends.

Just after New Year's 2005, Coughlin got back in the pool, slowly working her way into shape, though her training goal was limited: She wanted to swim well enough at US Nationals in March to qualify for the FINA World Championships, which would be held in Montreal in July. Coughlin did what she considered the minimal preparation to accomplish that objective. She got busier away from the pool as well, reenrolling at Cal for the spring semester and completing her bachelor's degree in psychology. Though Coughlin would skip her graduation ceremony to swim in a meet at Stanford that afternoon, she later hosted family and friends for a party at her parents' house and reveled in the achievement, having finished up a successful stretch at one of the nation's most prestigious universities.

As with her academic success, Coughlin needed some time to pass before she could truly appreciate all that she'd accomplished in the pool. If Teri McKeever's constant directive, *Concentrate not just on the outcome but the journey*, was still ringing in Coughlin's ears, she nonetheless required ample distance from the experience before a true appreciation for that journey could be attained.

McKeever, armed with the benefit of far more experience, had a much more immediate sense of what Athens had meant to her, both personally and professionally. She arrived back in Berkeley acting and speaking like a woman who had been instantly transformed—and liberated—by her first taste of Olympic glory.

"It's a life-changing experience," she told me in early September as we nibbled on salads at Julie's, the Bancroft Avenue café at which Mike Walker had talked over her to Jim Coughlin on Natalie's recruiting visit. "I'm so grateful that I was able to be part of it, and now I hope that the people around me can benefit. By watching Natalie stay true to what she wanted to do and handle everything so gracefully along the way, I learned that I, too, need to stay true to my ambitions. I don't have to build a program in someone else's image, and I don't have to be invincible. I just need to create a situation that I can manage.

"What I want to do now is to find kids who are open to change and open to the possibility of being a world-class athlete, without necessarily subscribing to a preconceived notion of how to get there."

Though McKeever understood that her team, without Coughlin, faced a major adjustment in 2004–05, she was also convinced that their former teammate's Olympic triumph would have residual benefits on the Bears. "This is an exciting time for Cal women's swimming," the coach said. "I'm glad everyone will get to see Natalie around the pool every day, still working hard and carrying herself like a champion, because it will serve as a constant reminder of what's out there. The first meeting we had after I got back, I told the team, 'There's a piece of all of you in Natalie.' And there really is—they were part of her journey, of pushing her and supporting her every single day. I hope they realize that."

Perhaps the most noticeable change in McKeever was how eager she was to talk about things *other* than the team and its fortunes. Harkening back to the speech US women's Olympic coach Mark Schubert made at the final team meeting, McKeever found inspiration in his message that extended beyond the competitive realm. Schubert, McKeever recalled, told the swimmers and staff in Athens, "You've all been Olympians. That's an awesome thing. Whether you go home with a medal or not, you got here because you dared to risk everything. You were willing to put everything on the line to be the best, and not everyone can say that."

Said McKeever, "I know in my life I've been afraid to risk things. Certainly in my personal life I have, and even professionally; I go for things I think I can get. Now, I feel like, *Wow, you just accomplished something great.* If I apply myself and really go for something, I can do anything. I mean, I'm *proud* of that house I bought this summer. If you had told me I was going to buy a house in the hills with a view of the Golden Gate Bridge, I'd have said, 'No way.' You hate to look at finding a relationship as an accomplishment, but that's one of my goals as well. And it should be. On that flight home from Athens, I told myself that first and foremost, I'm going to get a life."

≈

A few weeks later, as Cal's most successful football season in 46 years was beginning to trigger a wave of sustained euphoria in Strawberry Canyon, McKeever showed up for a game at Memorial Stadium and began making conversation with a man whose season tickets were in the same row as hers. They had met the previous October while watching another game in which Nort Thorton, the Bears' venerable men's swim coach, was being honored on the field at halftime. The man had turned to McKeever and asked, "Are *you* going to be here for 30 years?"

"Hell no," she responded. She was surprised that anyone in the stands knew who she was and even more stunned that this fellow fan came off as such a nice guy. They talked throughout the rest of the game, and McKeever's understanding of football seemed to pique his interest further. He sent her an e-mail a few weeks later, but McKeever, who was busy and stressed, read it without responding and quickly forgot about it.

Now, even as they chatted once again, it didn't dawn on McKeever that this was the same person who'd sent her the e-mail 10 months earlier. Over the next several games, as Cal made a run at its first Rose Bowl since 1959—the 10–1 Bears were kept out after a controversial voting scandal gave the nod to Texas, whose coach, Mack Brown, had lobbied fellow coaches and writers to move his team ahead in the polls—the two forged a connection. In January the man, a San Francisco city employee, sent McKeever a Christmas card. In it, he asked whether she'd consider going to dinner and a play. She called and said yes, and a month later—hey, she was as busy as ever—they had their first date.

The man had a natural way of putting McKeever at ease, and their relationship blossomed over the next several months. By spring she was calling him her boyfriend, and her swimmers noticed that she seemed to be smiling a lot more frequently than she had in the past. Inside, McKeever could scarcely believe the turn her life had taken: All of her dreams were coming true.

Her swimmers, both in and out of the pool, still consumed much of her time and energy. As McKeever and her assistant, Whitney Hite, had expected, the season was an adjustment for the Bears. No longer assured of Coughlin's three individual victories (and dominant relay leg) in each dual meet, Cal struggled against many of the nation's elite teams. The Bears did make a major statement at the Georgia Fall Invitational in early December, edging the host Bulldogs, the nation's top-ranked team and eventual national champion, in the 800 freestyle relay, the event in which the Bears had scored their surprise victory at the 2004 NCAAs. Most outsiders assumed Georgia, with Olympians Amanda Weir and Kara Lynn Joyce on the relay, would overtake the Bears now that Coughlin wasn't there to lead off, and the Bulldogs were certainly motivated. But star freshman Emily Silver stepped in to swim the second leg—joining returnees Ashley Chandler, Erin Reilly, and Lauren Medina—and Cal won by 0.63.

Coughlin joined the team on its January training trip to Hawaii's Big Island, where the Bears prepared for the meet of their season. Cal lost its first Pac-10 dual meet resoundingly, falling 144–99 to a talented Arizona team, then defeated Arizona State, USC, and UCLA in succession. The anticipated rematch with Stanford at Spieker Pool proved to be far less exciting than the previous year's thriller. The Bears had their requisite diving disadvantage—though new coach Ron Kontura had helped infuse Thornton's men's program with talent, he failed to have a similar impact on McKeever's squad—but that was no excuse this time. Stanford's 172–128 victory, in what would turn out to be Richard Quick's final season, was thorough and impressive.

An air of disappointment hung over Spieker Pool through much of February. For one thing, Reilly struggled mightily to recapture the brilliance of her freshman season—not an unusual phenomenon for an athlete in any sport, but one that frustrated her coaches to no end. The other major bummer was the collapse of the senior class. While Medina remained an elite-level performer in individual races and relays, she was the only senior to qualify for the NCAA Championships, as Marcelle Miller, cocaptains Emma Palsson and Amy Ng, Lisa Morelli, and Erin Calder all failed to make their cuts. As the NCAAs approached, McKeever drastically lowered her expectations from the previous year. "I just want to finish in the top 10," she said shortly before departing for West Lafayette, Indiana, in March.

There were encouraging signs, however. Of Cal's 12 NCAA qualifiers, seven were newcomers to the program—five freshmen and two sophomore transfers. In addition, sophomore Annie Babicz had stepped up considerably, rebounding from a so-so freshman season to become a force in breaststroke and butterfly events. Ranked 11th going into the NCAAs, the Bears delighted their coaches with an eighth-place finish that included a slew of inspiring swims, including Emily Silver's fourth-place finish in the 100 free and Medina's fifth-place effort in the 200 free.

That ended the season on a positive note, with the promise of bigger things to come. McKeever's monster recruiting class for 2005–06 included breaststroker Jessica Hardy, a Dave Salo–coached standout who had narrowly missed qualifying for the 2004 Olympics, and Lauren Rogers, a backstroker and sprint freestyler whose club coach was far less inclined to recommend Cal or McKeever. Rogers, oddly enough, was a star swimmer for the Terrapins of Concord. She was, in fact, Ray Mitchell's most accomplished athlete since a kid named Natalie Coughlin.

Ray Mitchell had once told McKeever, in the wake of Coughlin's decision not to swim for him the summer after her freshman year, that he would never again send one of his swimmers to Cal. How had she managed to persuade Rogers to come? "You know, I'm not really sure," she said. "But I'm definitely not going to question it, because I'm very happy to have her."

～

Coughlin whipped through the water, touched the wall, and looked up at the scoreboard, nervously checking the results. A couple of seconds later, she screamed joyously and emphatically pumped her fist—an odd reaction given that she owned five Olympic medals, and this 100 freestyle victory, in 54.76, had merely qualified her for the 2005 Worlds in Montreal.

Except, as only a few people at the pool in Indianapolis last April understood, Coughlin wasn't celebrating her own success at all. Rather, she had reacted to Emily Silver's surprising sixth-place finish, meaning the Cal freshman would be joining Coughlin in Canada as part of the 400 freestyle relay.

McKeever had done it again—Silver, for all her raw talent, had seemed worlds away from this type of achievement a few months earlier. The coach knew the swimmer had a chance to make this type of break-through at some point, but to have it happen this quickly, a couple of weeks after the close of her freshman season, was truly gratifying. Before Silver realized what she had done, Coughlin was in her lane, offering a hug and congratulations.

"A year ago there was no way Emily would have been able to make a team like this," Coughlin said later. "I really like her, and we have a great relationship in the pool. I'm willing to give opinions about all kinds of things concerning technique and strategy, and some people like them, and some people don't. Emily asks me what my thoughts are and I give them to her, and she's someone who's very receptive. I was just so happy for her. It's funny, because when I reacted that way, people thought I was cheering for myself. I mean, that was a good time under the circum-stances, but it wasn't *that* good."

If the 2004–05 college season had been a transitional one for McKeever's Bears, the 5 months that followed served both to validate the coach's many success stories of the past few years and to illustrate the exceptional promise that the future held. The stars of Cal's incoming freshman class, Hardy and Rogers, made an enormous splash at the World Championship Trials in Indianapolis, with Hardy qualifying for Worlds by finishing second to former Stanford star Tara Kirk in the 100 breast and Rogers just missing with a third-place effort, .06 behind second-place finisher Jeri Moss. Rogers joined Lauren Medina and Ashley Chandler on the US squad at the World University Games in Izmir, Turkey, a meet in which sophomore transfer Sherry Tsai competed for Hong Kong.

Considering her relative lack of preparation for the Indy meet, Coughlin was pleased with her own performance, which included a vic-tory in the 100 back—albeit in the relatively unimpressive time of

1:01.08—and a third-place effort in the 100 butterfly, an event she later said she had swum only because of a miscommunication with McKeever. "Because of the time off after the foot injury, she wasn't in the greatest shape," conceded McKeever, who was picked to serve on coach Jack Bauerle's staff for Worlds.

As the meet approached, and she and her teammates prepared to head to Baltimore for a weeklong training camp before flying to Montreal, Coughlin noticed something else. *Whoa*, she thought. *Suddenly, I'm old.* With Jenny Thompson retired, this time seemingly for good, and stalwarts like Amanda Beard, Lindsay Benko, and a very pregnant Haley Cope nowhere to be found, Coughlin was not only an integral part of the US team but also one of its obvious leaders. "Now Natalie's articulating things to people like Emily Silver and Mary DeScenza, and that's a big step for her," McKeever said in July. "That's what she can bring to the national team, the same leadership that Jenny Thompson brought for so long. And that's important, because it's the type of thing that can keep someone like her in the sport. She'll need to be emotionally and mentally challenged."

It also stands to reason that Coughlin's competitive fires will need to be stoked, a process that might have begun with her mildly disappointing effort at Worlds. Her medal take—a gold, two silvers, two bronzes—was impressive, but she stunningly slipped to a third-place finish in the 100 back, with Zimbabwe's Kirsty Coventry (1:00.24) and Germany's Antje Buschulte (1:00.84) overtaking the fading Coughlin (1:00.88) down the stretch. She and France's Malia Metella (54.74) tied for second in the 100 free behind Australia's Jodie Henry (54.18). Coughlin won a gold as part of the 800 free relay, a silver with the 400 medley relay, and a bronze as part of the 400 free relay; Silver, who swam in the preliminaries of the latter race, also collected a bronze.

Meanwhile, the 18-year-old Hardy stunned everyone by setting a world record in the 100 breast in the semifinals; her time of 1:06.20 bettered the 1:06.37 standard set by Australia's Leisel Jones. In the next night's finals Jones (1:06.25) defeated Hardy (1:06.62), who left Montreal with three silver medals and a scary amount of potential.

A few days later, Coughlin and Hardy competed for the United States against Australia in the "Duel in the Pool" exhibition in Irvine, California, while various current and former Bears prepared for the upcoming US National Championships in the same Southern California pool. There, concluding a monumental summer for McKeever's swimmers, the Bears won a pair of relays—Emily Silver, Reilly, Chandler, and Medina in the 800 free, and Medina, Reilly, Silver, and sophomore transfer Lauren Andrews in the 400 free—and took second in the 400 medley relay, with Babicz and Reilly joining the Silver sisters. With Coughlin sitting out the meet, Helen Silver stormed to a surprise title in the 100 back. It was an enormous step for her, who would be named a cocaptain of the 2005–06 team, along with Chandler. She considered the 200 back, in which she finished third, her best event, making her effort in the 100 back all the more impressive. Rather than shrinking in the face of her little sister's ascent, Helen clearly had been energized by Emily's successes.

Coughlin, meanwhile, was storing up her energy for the challenges ahead—a journey that she hopes will end in Beijing in 2008, where she aims to achieve even greater glories than she did in Athens. "I'm in a really good place right now," she said in July 2005. "I'm having fun and not worrying about the pressure so much. My main focus is on 2008, and I'm trying really hard not to get too serious too soon."

While still set on swimming the 100 back and 100 free, Coughlin has designs on branching out, especially in the 200 free. Because that event inevitably seems to overlap with the 100 back in major competitions, Coughlin has precious few chances to swim it outside of the 800 free relay. She is hopeful that USA Swimming might petition FINA and Olympic organizers to separate the 200 free and 100 back, or at least to reverse the order of the 200 free semis and 100 back final at the next Olympics.

"I really, really, really want to do the 200 free," Coughlin said. "I honestly feel it's my second-best event, behind the 100 back. It just never works out with the format they use."

In the fall, Coughlin began training much more intensely than she had at any point since before the 2004 Olympic Trials, sending a clear signal that she has no plans to coast on her Golden Girl glory. "I don't see her ever just sitting back and living off the past," says Emma Palsson, Coughlin's close friend and former Cal teammate. "She is so competitive, deep down inside, although she hides it very, very well. I think she has a whole lot more she wants to accomplish."

To her credit, Coughlin has a clear understanding of how to pace herself, mindful that she will be enjoying more downtime than ever before. "I don't have to worry about school," she says. "I don't really have the time constraints that I did before the last Olympics, and since I've already gotten that gold, I don't have that hanging over my head." The result is that Coughlin is more open to experimentation than ever before as she and McKeever continue to incorporate concepts that many of their peers scorn.

"A lot of what Teri has tried to teach us is to always be willing to switch it up, that there is no right way to train and no wrong way to train," Coughlin says. "The key is never to be closed-minded. Swimming is such a young sport, and there is so much out there that hasn't been looked at or proven. So we're going to continue to be open-minded."

McKeever was even more emphatic: "The challenge now, for Natalie, is to take these nontraditional concepts that we've incorporated and push them even further. I'll still be there to coach her, but in a lot of ways she has to drive the process, to see what works for her and to tap into ideas and techniques that haven't really been tested. One of the things I most admire about her is that she is willing to venture outside her comfort zone and throw herself out there. Doing that will keep her motivated and energized, and who knows where it might lead."

Ideally, Coughlin and McKeever hope their past and future successes might lead to change—not so much a desire that everyone would adopt their ideas but that other swimmers and coaches would at least become more open to considering them. This can only happen, of course, if Coughlin continues to share her experiences and speak out about an approach that helped her rise from the teenage swimming scrap heap to the top of her sport.

"There is so much inertia preventing change, and it's tough to get enough momentum to alter something that entrenched," stroke guru Milt Nelms says. "What's needed is leverage, and when all is said and done, Natalie will have it. If she's willing to use it, that could mark a huge step in the development of the sport."

～

In October of 2005 Coughlin decided to tag along with Ethan Hall on a Saturday in which he was leading his rec team, Crow Canyon Country Club, in a dual meet against another local squad. Hall, who also coached a recently formed club team, the Crow Canyon Sharks, in San Ramon, California, hoped his rec swimmers, whose ages ranged from 4 to 17, would have a successful meet. He didn't need to do much in the way of motivational speeches. Many of the swimmers had decorated their parents' cars for the occasion, rolling up to the pool with slogans like "Eat My Bubbles" painted onto the sides of the vehicles.

The excitement in the kids' faces as they began their warm-up laps resonated with Coughlin. It reminded her of the days when she had lived for youth meets, wearing her swim cap in the house for hours before it was time to leave for the pool. Watching Hall's ebullient swimmers, Coughlin remembered how much she truly loved the sport and why she'd been willing to toil through lap after lap in the hopes of chasing what had begun as a much smaller dream. Long ago, back before that horrible senior year of high school and the nightmarish clash with her club coach, Coughlin had been one of those giddy, fresh-faced kids, and it had taken 4 enlightening years with Cal and McKeever and five Olympic medals to make her feel free once more.

As she watched the youngest swimmers at the meet, in the 6-and-under classification, stand nervously atop the starting blocks before the start of their 25-yard freestyle, Coughlin had another realization: This wasn't a flashback to her earliest memories of competitive swimming; rather, it was something better. This was a dual meet, complete with team spirit chants and pivotal relays and down-to-the-wire drama, and the kids absolutely loved it. It was quite possible none of them would ever grow up to be Olympians, but that wasn't the point. They were happy and fit and learning precious lessons about working together and healthy competition, and almost all of them were smiling in the process.

The starting gun sounded, and the tiny swimmers dove into the water and began thrashing toward the opposite wall. Parents and teammates and coaches yelled encouragement, and the lanky Hall practically sprinted across the deck with excitement. At that wonderful moment, with the California sun shining brilliantly and the familiar whiff of chlorine in the air, the Golden Girl had the broadest grin of all.